The EARL SCRUGGS BANJO SONGBOOK

In memory of Gary Scruggs (1949-2021),
whose guidance and dedication were invaluable
during the making of this publication.

Transcribed by Adonai Booth, Pete Billmann,
Jeff Jacobson, Ron Piccione, and David Stocker.

Edited by Jim Schustedt

Editorial consultant – Bob Piekiel
Additional editorial assistance by
Tony Trishka and Tom Adams

Photo by Tom Hill/Getty Images

ISBN 978-1-4768-1455-1

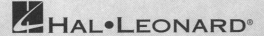

Visit Hal Leonard Online at
www.halleonard.com

Contact us:
Hal Leonard
7777 West Bluemound Road
Milwaukee, WI 53213
Email: info@halleonard.com

In Europe, contact:
Hal Leonard Europe Limited
42 Wigmore Street
Marylebone, London, W1U 2RN
Email: info@halleonardeurope.com

In Australia, contact:
Hal Leonard Australia Pty. Ltd.
4 Lentara Court
Cheltenham, Victoria, 3192 Australia
Email: info@halleonard.com.au

CONTENTS

4 Earl's Tunings – Keys –
Capo Positions – Scruggs Tuners

6 Foreword

8 Before I Met You

10 Big Black Train

12 Bugle Call Rag

18 Can the Circle Be Unbroken
(Will the Circle Be Unbroken)

20 Come Back Darling

22 The Crawdad Song

24 Daisy May

26 Dig a Hole in the Meadow

28 Doin' My Time

25 Don't Get Above Your Raising

30 Don't Let Your Deal Go Down

31 Down the Road

34 Duelin' Banjos

43 Farewell Blues

38 Fireball

40 Fireball Mail

53 Flop Eared Mule

58 Foggy Mountain Breakdown

48 Foggy Mountain Rock

50 Foggy Mountain Special

64 Get in Line Brother

66 Gotta Travel On

68 Hand Me Down My Walking Cane

63 Have You Come to Say Goodbye

70 Hear the Whistle Blow,
One Hundred Miles

72 Heavy Traffic Ahead

74 I Ain't Goin' to Work Tomorrow

76 I Saw the Light

78 I Want to Be Loved (But Only by You)

80 I Wonder Where You Are Tonight

82 I'd Rather Be Alone

79 I'll Go Stepping Too

84 I'll Just Pretend

86 I'll Never Shed Another Tear

85 I'll Stay Around

88 I'm Goin' Back to Old Kentucky

90 I'm Head Over Heels in Love

89 If I Should Wander Back Tonight

95 It's Mighty Dark to Travel

96 Jazzing

92 Jingle Bells

98 John Hardy Was a Desperate Little Man

100 Just Joshin'

101 Lonesome Road Blues

104 Love and Wealth

105 Love Is Just a Four Letter Word

110 Mama Blues

114 Molly and Tenbrooks

116 Mountain Dew

118 My Cabin in Caroline

117 My Home's Across the Blue Ridge Mountain

120 My Little Girl in Tennessee

122 My Long Journey Home

124 My Saro Jane

126 Nashville Skyline Rag

130 Nine Pound Hammer

132 Nobody's Business

141 Nothing to It

134 On the Rock Where Moses Stood

136 Pain in My Heart

138 Petticoat Junction

142 Pike County Breakdown

147 Polka on a Banjo

151 Roll in My Sweet Baby's Arms

154 Ruby, Don't Take Your Love to Town

156 Salty Dog Blues

158 Shortenin' Bread

150 Six White Horses

162 Soldier's Joy

166 Some of Shelly's Blues

161 Some Old Day

168 Somebody Touched Me

169 Somehow Tonight

170 Standin' in the Need of Prayer

171 Steel Guitar Rag

174 Till the End of the World Rolls Around

175 'Tis Sweet to Be Remembered

176 Toy Heart

184 We'll Meet Again Sweetheart

177 When I Left East Virginia

180 When the Angels Carry Me Home

182 Why Don't You Tell Me So

185 Will You Be Loving Another Man

186 You Can't Stop Me from Dreaming

188 Banjo Notation Legend

EARL'S TUNINGS – KEYS – CAPO POSITIONS – SCRUGGS TUNERS

G tuning:
(5th – 1st) g-D-G-B-D
Key of G

 12 Bugle Call Rag
 20 Come Back Darling
 25 Don't Get Above Your Raising
 34 Duelin' Banjos
 38 Fireball
 40 Fireball Mail
 53 Flop Eared Mule
 66 Gotta Travel On
 68 Hand Me Down My Walking Cane
 70 Hear the Whistle Blow,
      One Hundred Miles
 90 I'm Head Over Heels in Love
 95 It's Mighty Dark to Travel
 96 Jazzing
 92 Jingle Bells
 98 John Hardy Was a Desperate Little Man
100 Just Joshin'
101 Lonesome Road Blues
105 Love Is Just a Four Letter Word
124 My Saro Jane
130 Nine Pound Hammer
132 Nobody's Business
136 Pain in My Heart
138 Petticoat Junction
158 Shortenin' Bread
168 Somebody Touched Me
169 Somehow Tonight
177 When I Left East Virginia

G tuning:
(5th – 1st) g-D-G-B-D
Key of C

 24 Daisy May
 48 Foggy Mountain Rock
117 My Home's Across the
      Blue Ridge Mountains
126 Nashville Skyline Rag
154 Ruby, Don't Take Your Love to Town

Tuning:
(5th – 1st) g#-D-G-B-D
Key of E

 22 The Crawdad Song
 80 I Wonder Where You Are Tonight

G tuning:
(5th – 1st) g-D-G-B-D
Key of F

161 Some Old Day

G tuning (hook 5th string at the 7th fret):
(5th – 1st) g-D-G-B-D
Key of A

 72 Heavy Traffic Ahead

G tuning, capo at the 2nd fret:
(5th – 1st) g-D-G-B-D
Key of A

 18 Can the Circle Be Unbroken
      (Will the Circle Be Unbroken)
 28 Doin' My Time
 63 Have You Come to Say Goodbye
 76 I Saw the Light
 78 I Want to Be Loved (But Only by You)
 88 I'm Goin' Back to Old Kentucky
104 Love and Wealth
116 Mountain Dew
122 My Long Journey Home
134 On the Rock Where Moses Stood
142 Pike County Breakdown
170 Standin' in the Need of Prayer
185 Will You Be Loving Another Man

**G tuning, capo at the 2nd fret
(hook 5th string at the 9th fret):**
(5th – 1st) g-D-G-B-D
Key of E

166 Some of Shelly's Blues

G tuning, capo at the 4th fret:
(5th – 1st) g-D-G-B-D
Key of B

31 Down the Road
114 Molly and Tenbrooks
184 We'll Meet Again Sweetheart

G♯ tuning:
(5th – 1st) g♯-D♯-G♯-B♯-D♯
Key of G♯/A♭

8 Before I Met You
10 Big Black Train
58 Foggy Mountain Breakdown
50 Foggy Mountain Special
86 I'll Never Shed Another Tear
85 I'll Stay Around
89 If I Should Wander Back Tonight
118 My Cabin in Caroline
120 My Little Girl in Tennessee
156 Salty Dog Blues
150 Six White Horses

G♯ tuning:
(5th – 1st) g♯-D♯-G♯-B♯-D♯
Key of F♯/G♭

30 Don't Let Your Deal Go Down
82 I'd Rather Be Alone
175 'Tis Sweet to Be Remembered

G♯ tuning:
(5th – 1st) g♯-D♯-G♯-B♯-D♯
Key of C♯/D♭

84 I'll Just Pretend

G♯ tuning:
(5th – 1st) g♯-D♯-G♯-B♯-D♯
Key of D♯/E♭

171 Steel Guitar Rag

G♯ tuning, capo at the 2nd fret:
(5th – 1st) g♯-D♯-G♯-B♯-D♯
Key of A♯/B♭

64 Get in Line Brother
79 I'll Go Stepping Too
151 Roll in My Sweet Baby's Arms
180 When the Angels Carry Me Home

G♯ tuning (hook 5th string at the 7th fret):
(5th – 1st) g♯-D♯-G♯-B♯-D♯
Key of F♯/G♭

182 Why Don't You Tell Me So

C tuning:
(5th – 1st) g-C-G-B-D
Key of C

26 Dig a Hole in the Meadow
74 I Ain't Goin' to Work Tomorrow
141 Nothing to It
162 Soldier's Joy
176 Toy Heart
186 You Can't Stop Me from Dreaming

C tuning:
(5th – 1st) g-C-G-B-D
Keys of C and F

147 Polka on a Banjo

C♯ tuning:
(5th – 1st) g♯-C♯-G♯-B♯-D♯
Key of C♯/D♭

43 Farewell Blues
174 Till the End of the World Rolls Around

D tuning:
(5th – 1st) f♯-D-F♯-A-D
Key of D

110 Mama Blues

Scruggs Tuners

34 Duelin' Banjos
66 Gotta Travel On
174 Till the End of the World Rolls Around

Note: All of the above sharp (♯) tunings were utilized early in Earl's career when he and Lester Flatt tuned up a half step to accommodate Lester's vocal range. Rather than tuning up a half step, you can accomplish the same pitches by capoing at the first fret, or one fret higher than the capo positions listed above.

FOREWORD
By Jim Mills

First of all, I'd like to say being asked to write this Foreword is an honor in itself, as few people on earth, if any, have more respect for Mr. Earl Scruggs and the 5-string banjo style that he developed, than me.

Earl Scruggs was—and still is—my all-time hero on this planet, Earth. I was in my 20s and already making a living picking the banjo when I first met Earl in person. He was just as nice as I had ever imagined him to be, even more so. He was friendly and, to my surprise and delight, very complimentary—a true gentleman. We became friends, and I feel fortunate to say that some of the biggest highlights in my life were getting to share the stage with Earl from time to time.

I was born in 1966 and began trying to learn to play the banjo seriously at around 10 or 11 years old after hearing my older brother's vinyl copy of the 1949 Flatt & Scruggs recording of Earl's "Foggy Mountain Breakdown." By that early age, I had figured out that Earl Scruggs and his style of banjo playing was all I wanted to do.

Unfortunately, there were very few books on the subject and there were even fewer mediums of musical recordings to listen to or learn from. We had vinyl-playing record players (a/k/a "turntables") and 33⅓ rpm long-play record albums, 45 rpm "single" records and then of course a little later, we had the newest analog mediums of musical recordings—the *(gasp)* eight-track tape and cassette tape formats—there were no CDs, no DVDs, no digital streaming video or audio, and no YouTube. This must all sound absolutely archaic to most young people today, but that was *it…*

That said, us aspiring banjo players had few options with those vinyl recordings. Most of us would put them on the turntable, and then slow down the speed of the record player to try and listen as closely as we could to figure out just what Earl was doing. But before we could figure it out—*man!*—that banjo solo had gone by so *fast*, even with the speed slowed down! And then we'd have to raise the record player's stylus arm back up again and then set the needle back down on the vinyl record as close to the spot where we knew the banjo solo was patiently waiting to be played again and again and again.

My goodness, this sounds almost cavemanesque today! But that's the way it was, and that's what we had to do—over and over and over—to try and glean anything we could from Earl Scruggs' fabulous playing on those recordings.

A few years later after I was already playing pretty well, I went into a local music store to purchase some strings or picks or something, and saw a book titled, *Earl Scruggs and the 5-String Banjo*— and of course I had to buy it.

I didn't realize it had been in print for a good while before my finding it there. Thumbing through it, I noticed some pages of music notation and I realized I already knew many of the songs pretty well. There were also right-hand roll patterns written there with a "T," "I" and "M," signifying the "Thumb, Index, and Middle" fingers of the right hand—and markers where the left-hand fingers would go between the frets—they called it *Tablature*, a way to learn music "note for note." There were several songs I didn't have down completely at the time, so I figured out how to read this tablature and quickly learned the proper way to play the parts I was having a problem with— simple as *that*.

That little story brings us up to the present day and the tablature-filled book we are introducing here, *The Earl Scruggs Banjo Songbook*. This new and insightful book is a wonderful opportunity for countless folks trying to learn to play "Scruggs Style Banjo" today, only in a much easier and informative way to learn than I and many others endured way back when. And it's also a more reliable way of learning, with accurate tablature to many songs never before featured anywhere else to my knowledge.

This book includes tablature to many Flatt & Scruggs songs that were not available on any of their regular commercial recordings, but only accessible through hearing them performing live.

Many of us today were not fortunate enough to get to see and hear this monumental band, "Lester Flatt & Earl Scruggs and the Foggy Mountain Boys," playing live. Fortunately for us, we have the *Best of the Flatt & Scruggs TV Shows* on DVD now, featuring so many great songs and instrumentals that they never recorded commercially—instrumentals like "Shortnin' Bread," "Flop Eared Mule," and other awesome singing songs like "Love and Wealth," "Nobody's Business," and many more.

This new book, *The Earl Scruggs Banjo Songbook*, features 13 songs with tablature from those live DVDs, which to my knowledge, have never before been tabbed out in print. Having this book along with the DVDs will give banjo players who want to read the tablature to these rare performances not only a chance to merely hear those performances, but to actually get to see Earl and this remarkable band in their prime playing those songs as well! It's almost magical to see how relaxed and interactive they were with one another—with hot studio lights shining and TV cameras rolling—all while knowing they were coming into so many households across America through their popular television show.

There are 84 song titles listed in this book—plus the sound source for each title, since there is more than one version recorded by Earl or Flatt & Scruggs for several of the songs—a remarkable opportunity for any student of Scruggs Style Banjo to learn from *The Master*, himself, Earl Scruggs.

Here again, I'm proud to introduce *The Earl Scruggs Banjo Songbook*...*ENJOY!*

Sincerely,
Jim Mills
December 2020

*Editor's note: Jim Mills is a highly-acclaimed 5-string banjo player, having won multiple Grammy Awards and being named the IBMA "Banjo Player of the Year" six times. He toured as a band member with Doyle Lawson & Quicksilver for five years, and with Ricky Skaggs & Kentucky Thunder for fourteen years, before retiring from full-time road work to establish his business, Jim Mills Banjo Inc. Jim specializes in buying and selling pre-war Gibson banjos and conducting banjo seminars. His website is: **prewargibsonbanjos.com***

BEFORE I MET YOU

Sound source—*Lester Flatt and Earl Scruggs Greatest Hits*

Words and Music by CHARLES SEITZ,
JOE CANNONBALL LEWIS and BILL DENNY

(G tuning)
Key of G (Recorded in G# tuning)

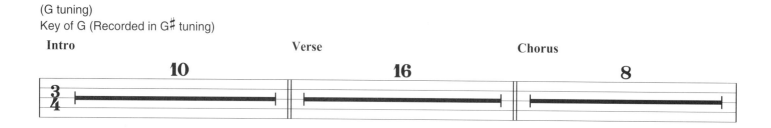

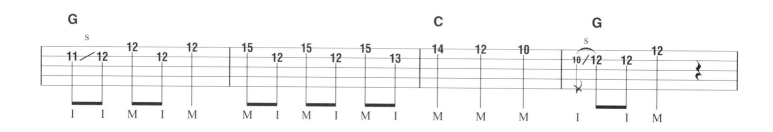

*1st break

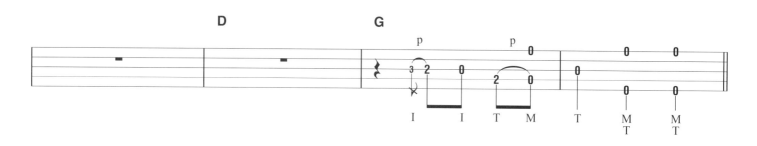

*The first 8 measures are backup for the fiddle.

(Banjo solo starts here)

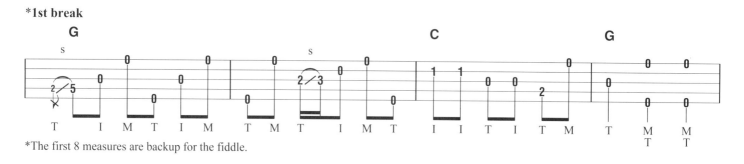

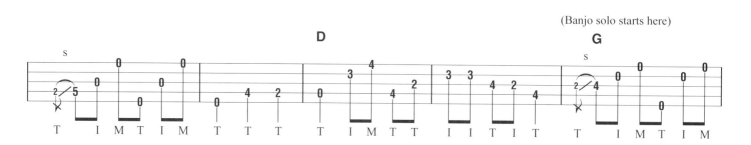

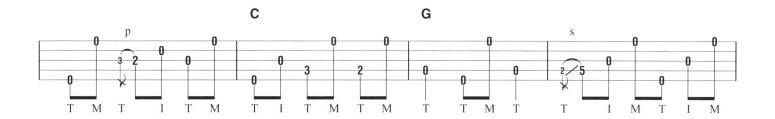

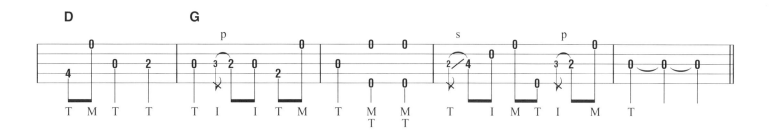

*2nd break

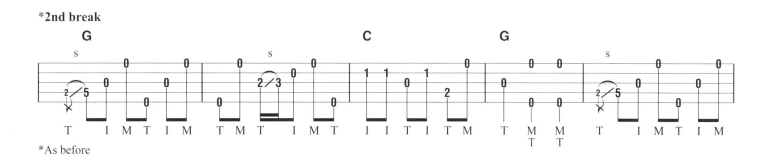

*As before

(Banjo solo starts here)

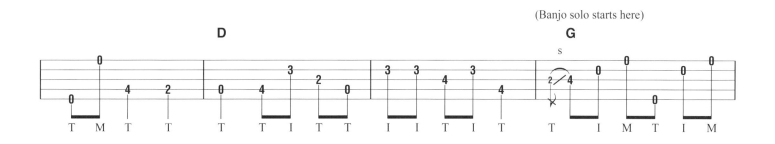

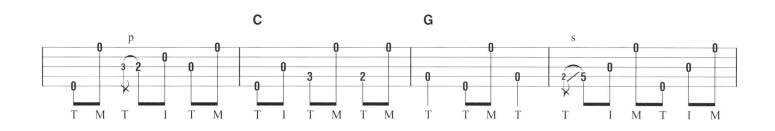

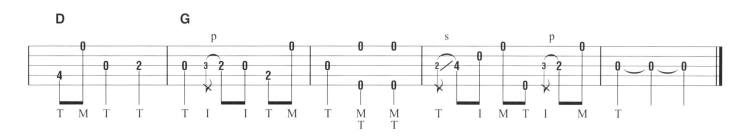

9

BIG BLACK TRAIN

Sound source—*The Essential Flatt & Scruggs - 'Tis Sweet to Be Remembered*

Words and Music by GEORGE SHERRY
and STANLEY EARL JOHNSON

(G tuning)
Key of G (Recorded in G♯ tuning)

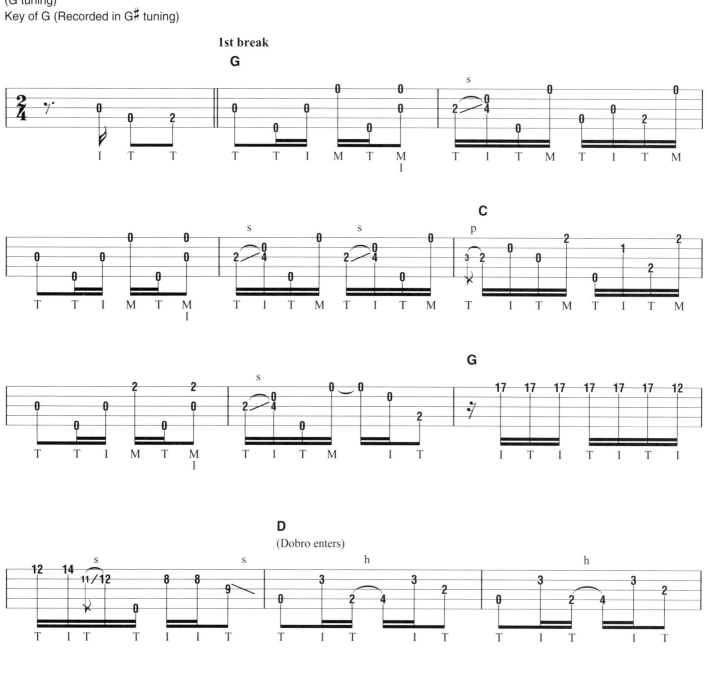

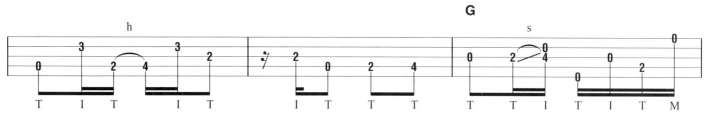

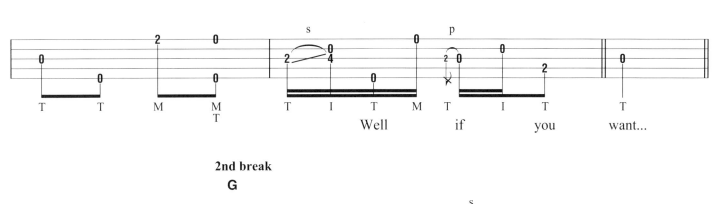

Well   if   you   want...

2nd break

G

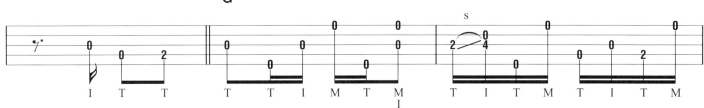

C

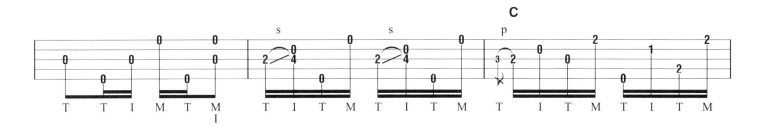

G

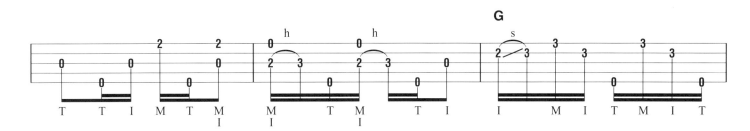

D

(Dobro enters)

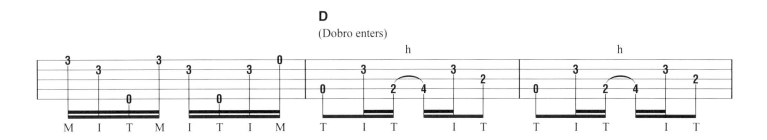

G

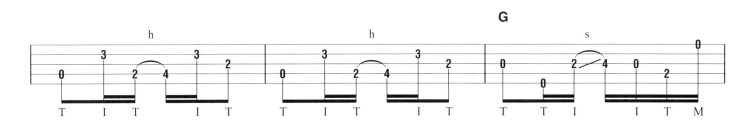

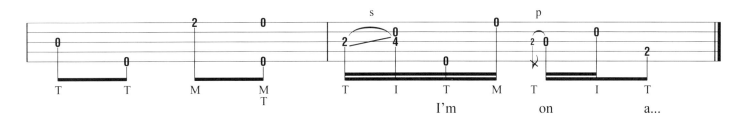

I'm   on   a...

BUGLE CALL RAG

Sound source—*Foggy Mountain Banjo - Flatt & Scruggs*

By HUBERT BLAKE and CAREY MORGAN

(G tuning)
Key of G

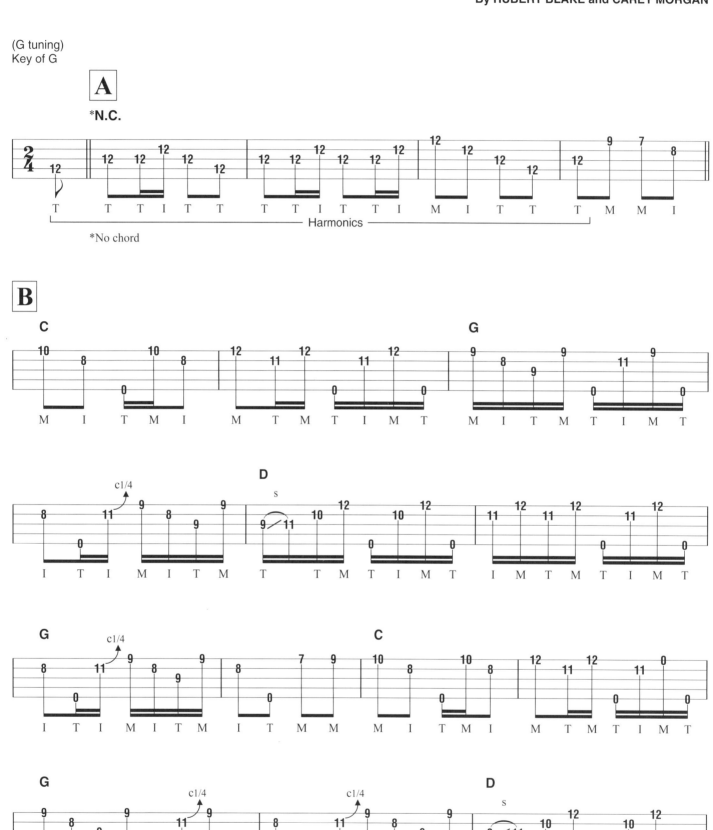

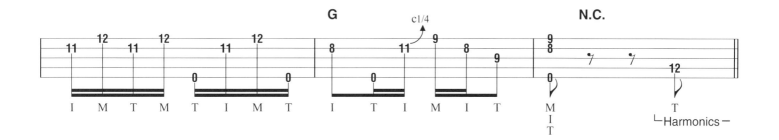

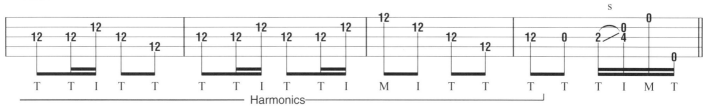

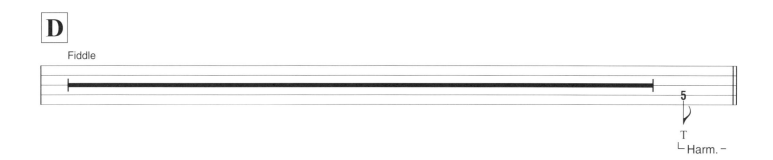

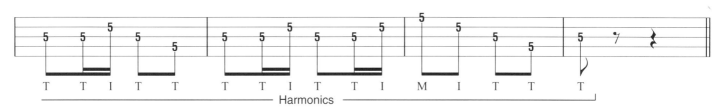

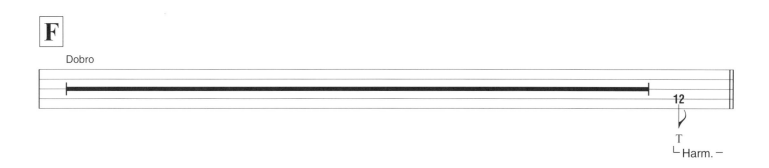

G

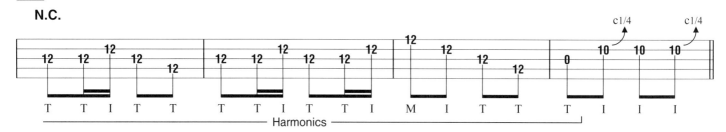

H

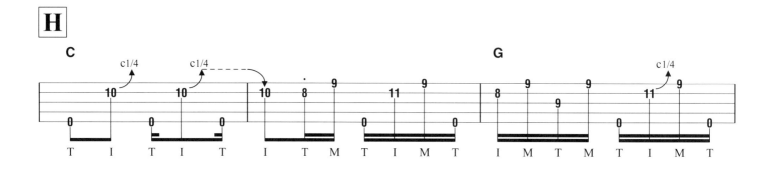

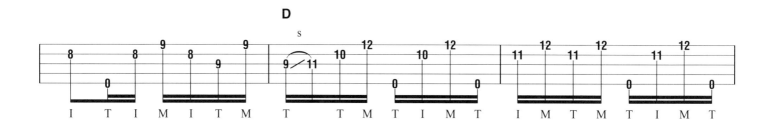

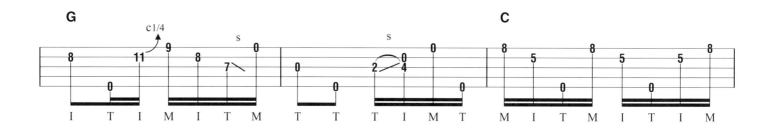

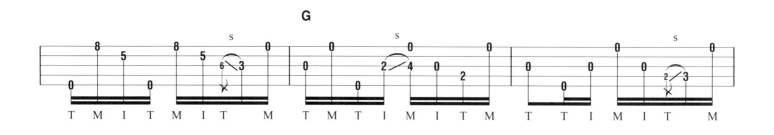

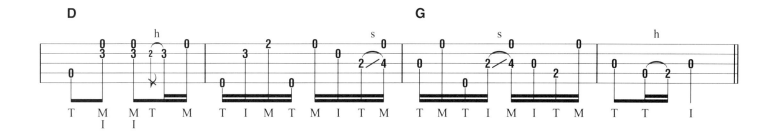

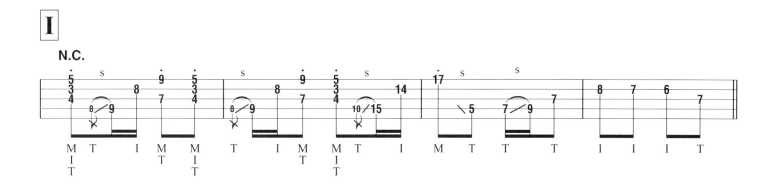

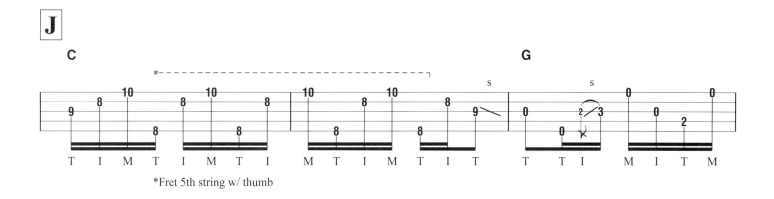

*Fret 5th string w/ thumb

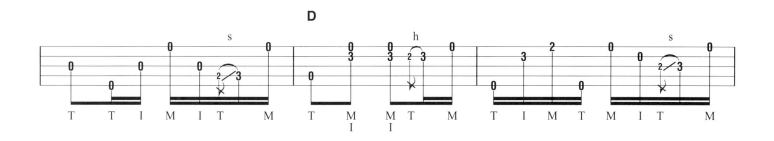

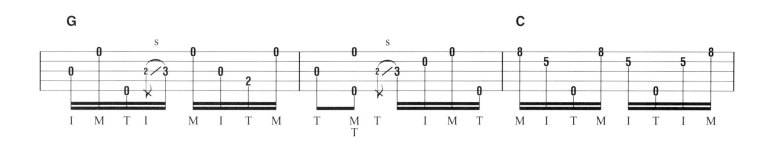

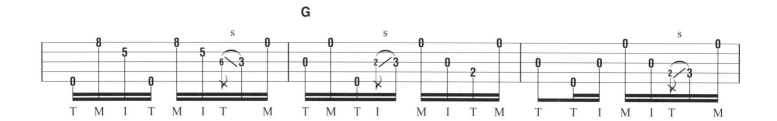

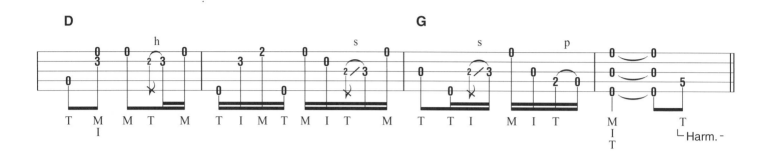

 K

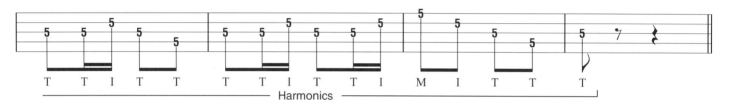

L

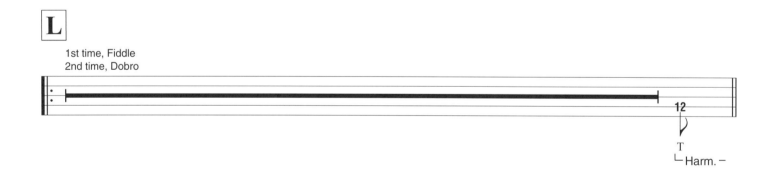

M

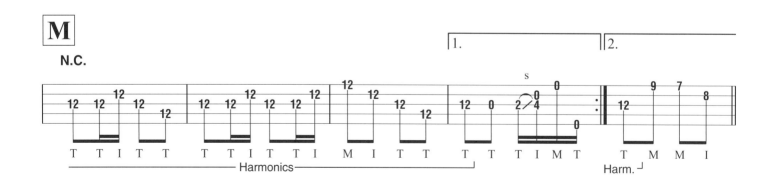

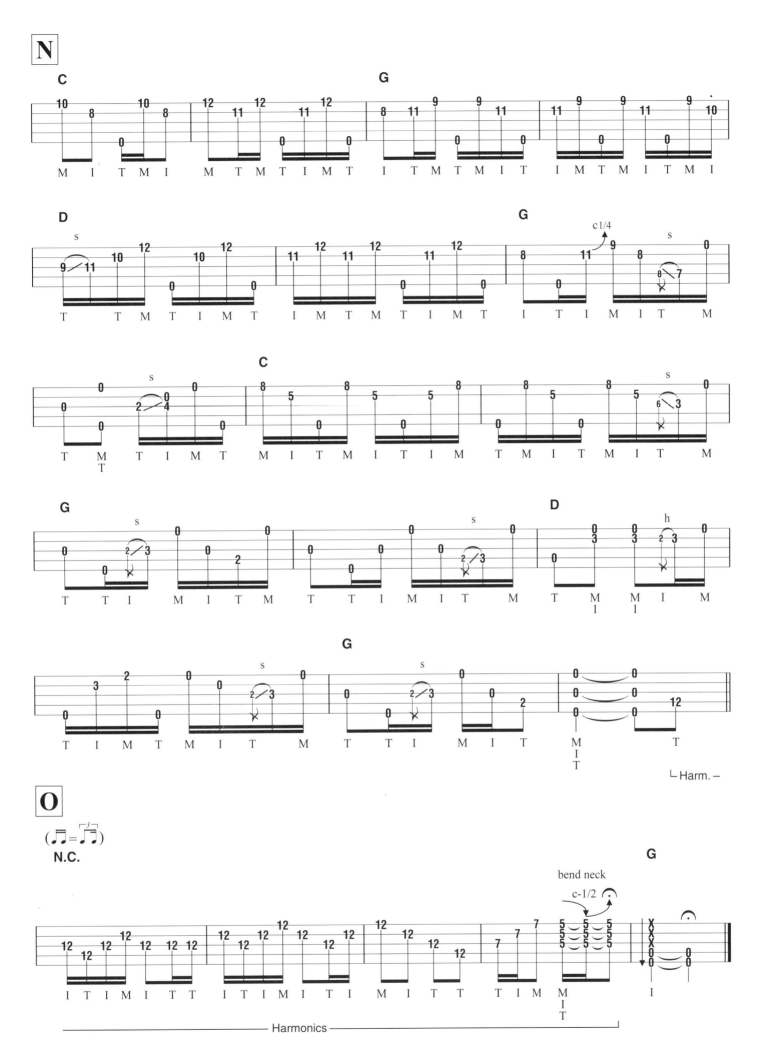

CAN THE CIRCLE BE UNBROKEN
(WILL THE CIRCLE BE UNBROKEN)

Sound source—Nitty Gritty Dirt Band - *Will The Circle Be Unbroken*

Words and Music by A.P. CARTER

(G tuning)
Key of A: Capo at 2nd fret and hook the 5th string

Intro

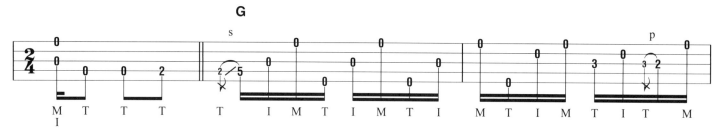

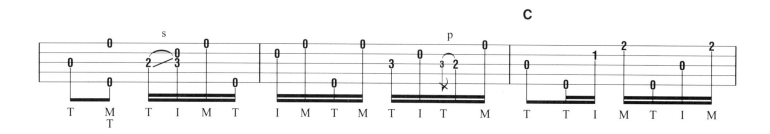

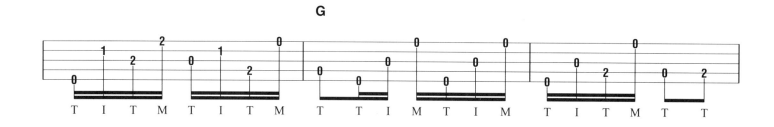

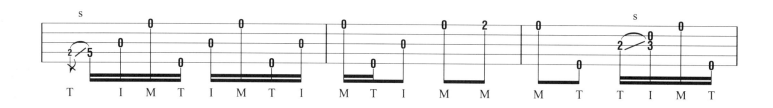

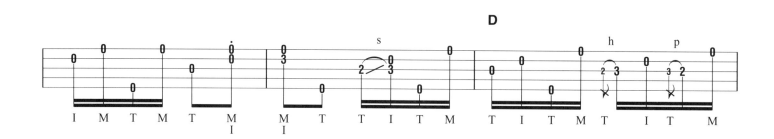

18

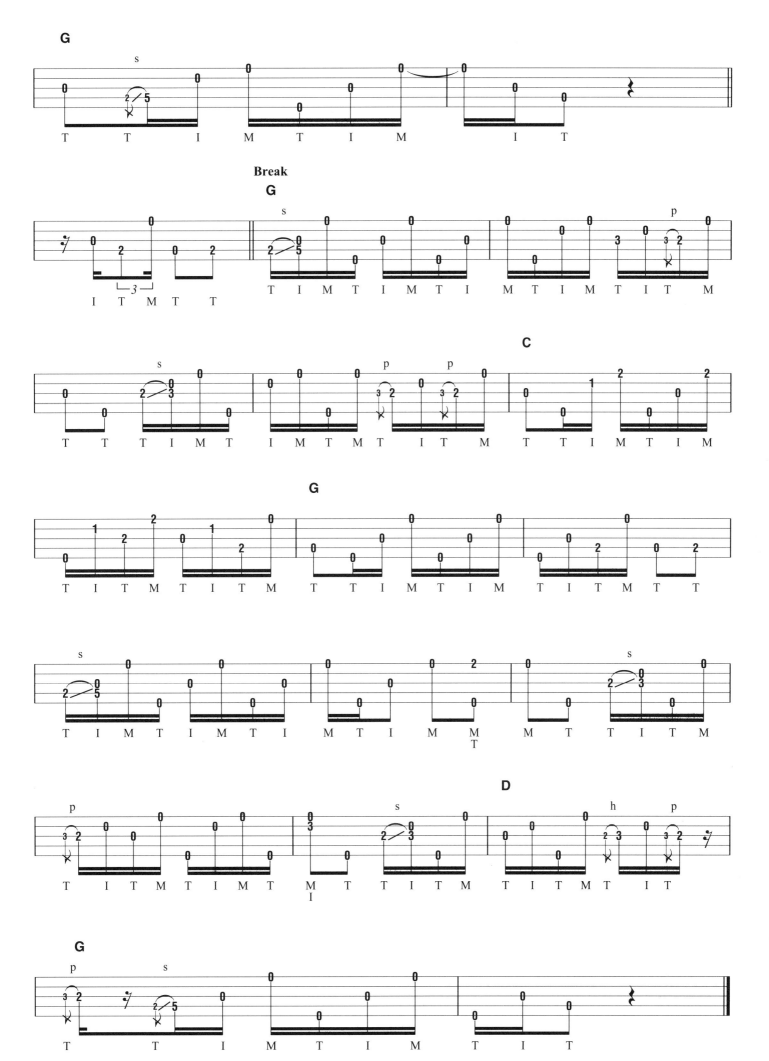

COME BACK DARLING

Sound source—*The Essential Earl Scruggs*

Words and Music by LESTER FLATT

(G tuning)
Key of G

Intro

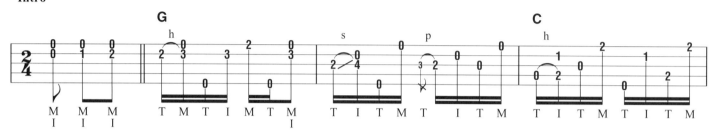

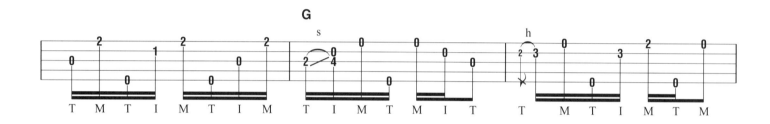

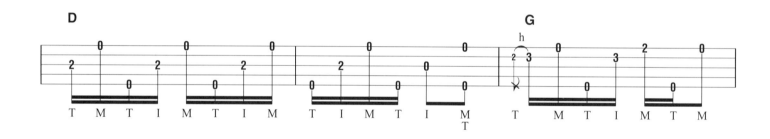

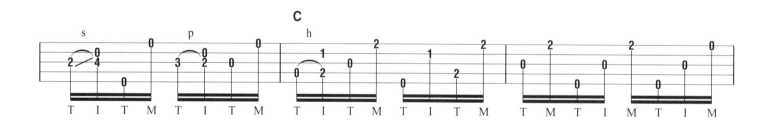

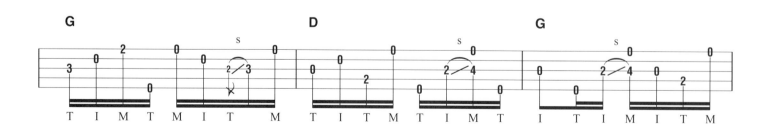

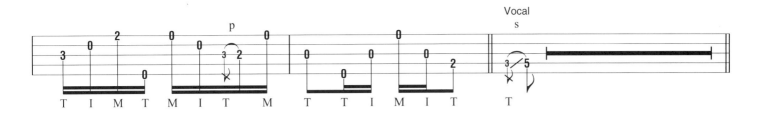

Break

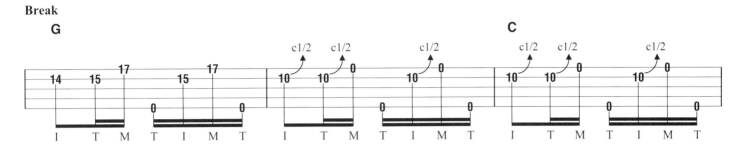

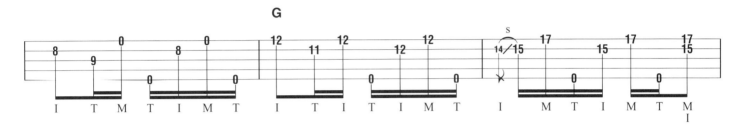

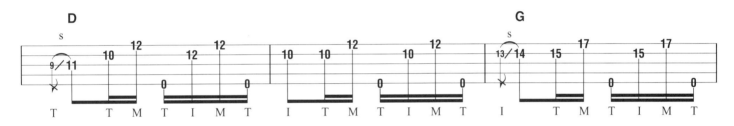

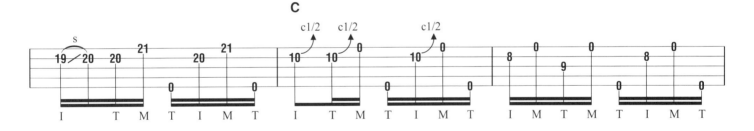

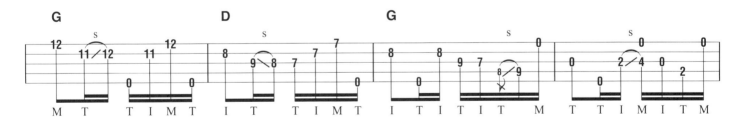

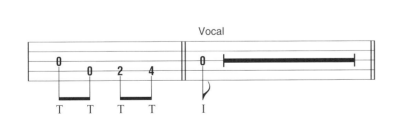

Tag

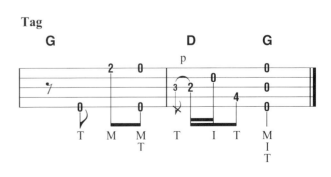

THE CRAWDAD SONG

Sound source—*Best of the Flatt & Scruggs TV Show Vol. 5*

TRADITIONAL

(G tuning)
Key of E: Hook the 5th string at the 6th fret
(Earl tuned the 5th string up to G#)

Intro

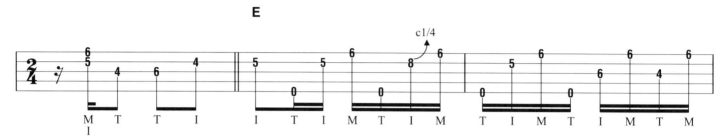

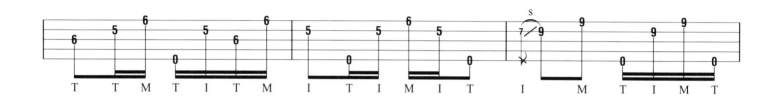

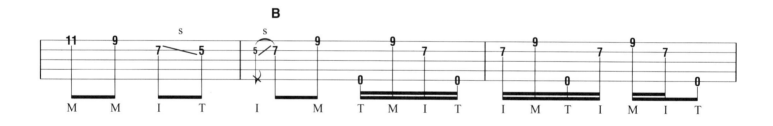

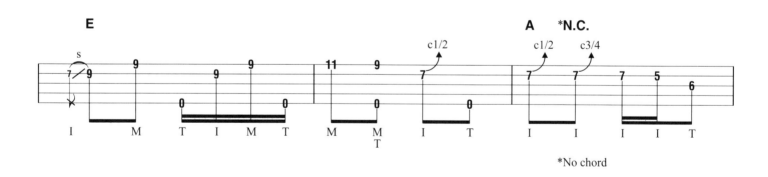

*No chord

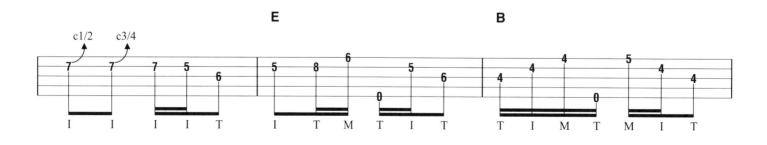

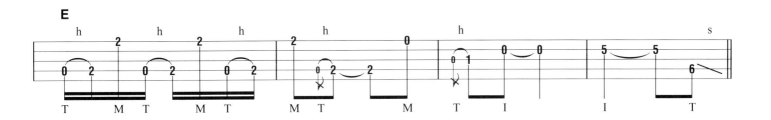

Break

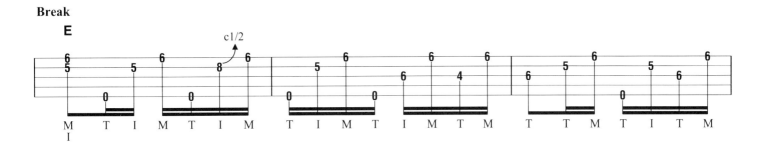

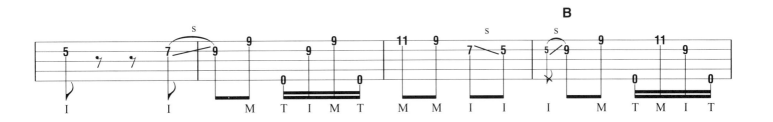

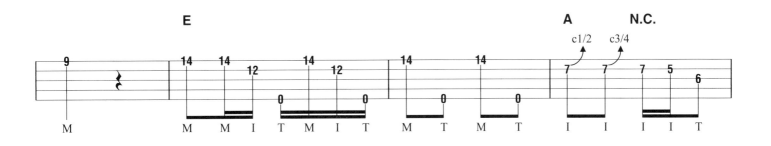

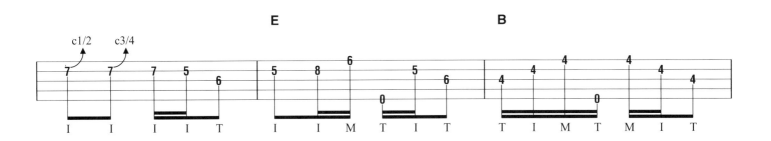

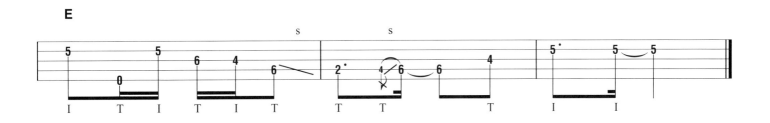

DAISY MAY

Sound source—*Best of the Flatt & Scruggs TV Show, Vol. 9*

Words and Music by FLOYD TILLMAN

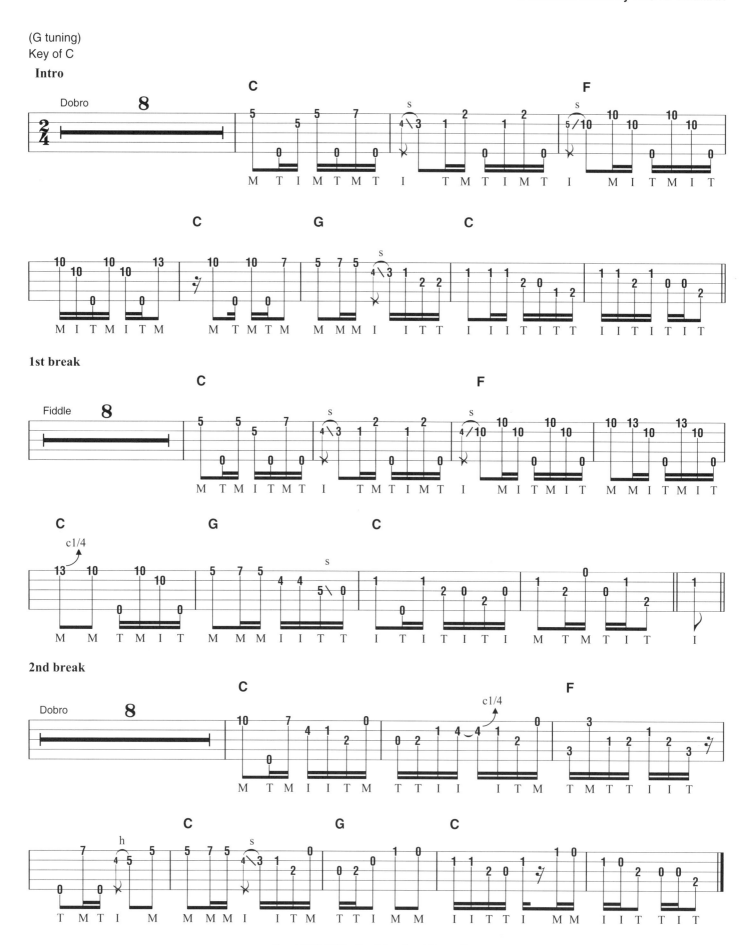

DON'T GET ABOVE YOUR RAISING

Sound source—*The Essential Earl Scruggs*

Words and Music by LESTER FLATT
and EARL SCRUGGS

(G tuning)
Key of G

Intro

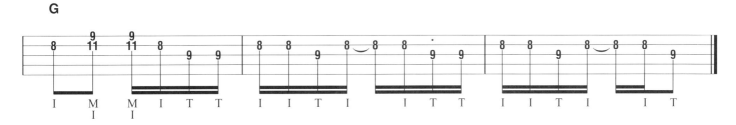

*No chord

25

DIG A HOLE IN THE MEADOW

Sound source—*Flatt & Scruggs at Carnegie Hall! The Complete Concert*

Words and Music by LESTER FLATT
and EARL SCRUGGS

(C tuning)
Key of C

Intro

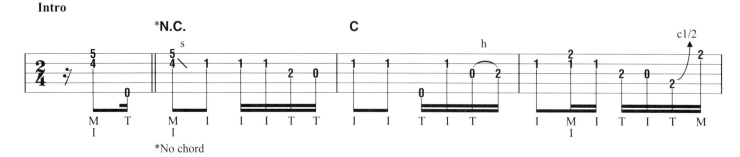

*No chord

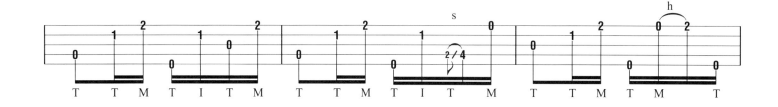

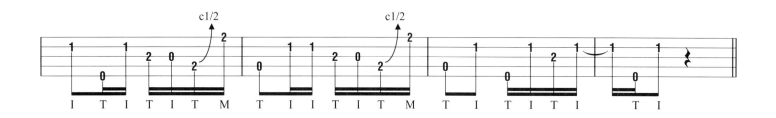

Chorus

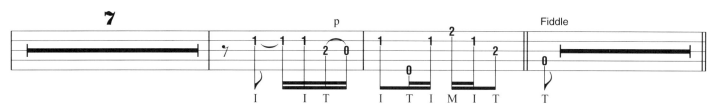

2nd Verse

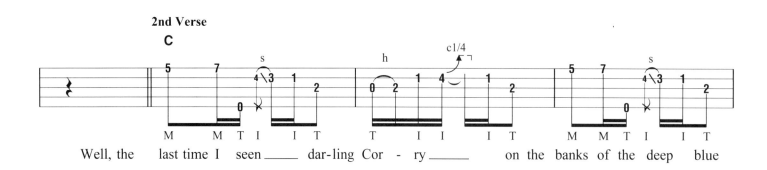

Well, the   last time I   seen _____ dar-ling Cor - ry _____   on the banks of the deep   blue

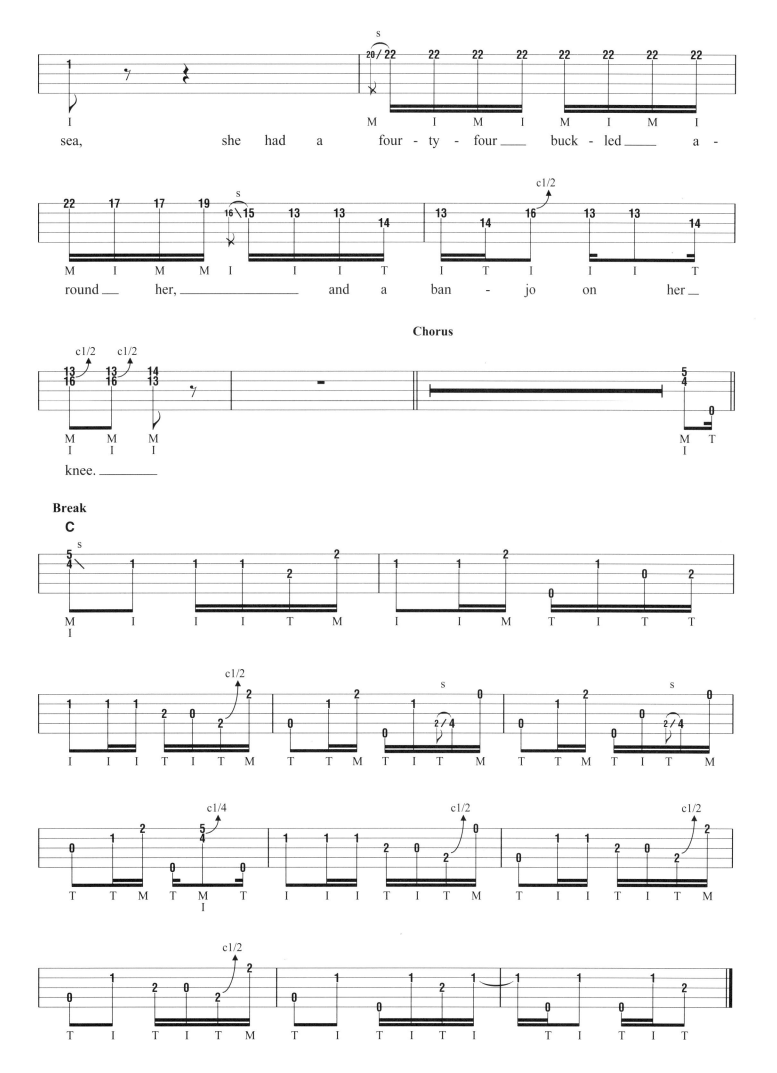

DOIN' MY TIME

Sound source—*The Complete Mercury Sessions - Flatt & Scruggs*

Words and Music by JIMMIE SKINNER

(G tuning)
Key of A: Capo at 2nd fret and hook the 5th string

Intro

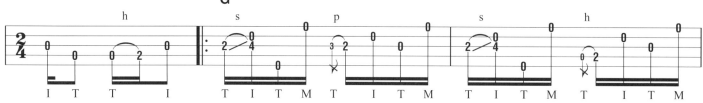

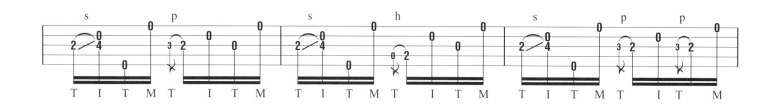

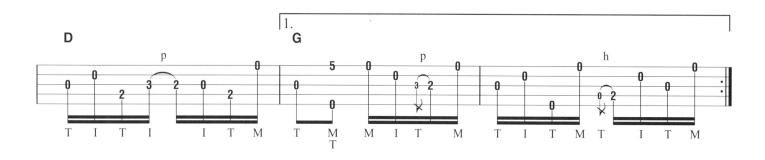

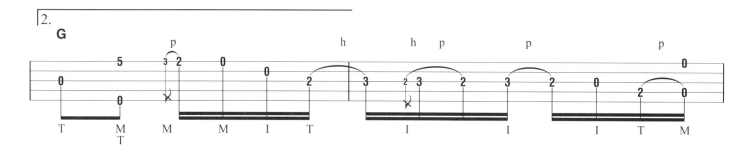

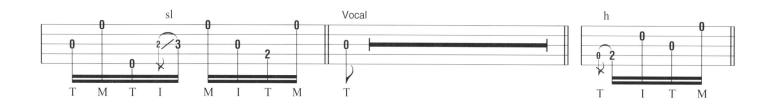

1st break

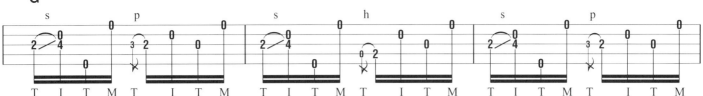

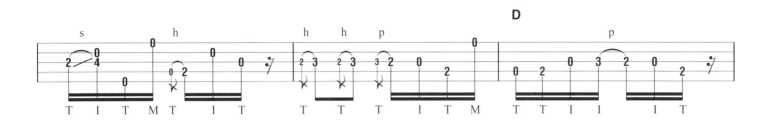

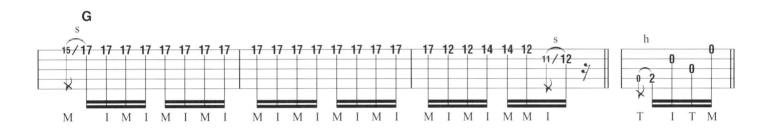

2nd break

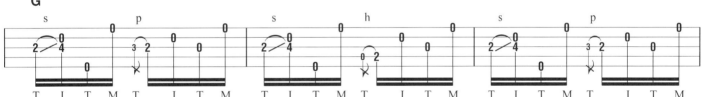

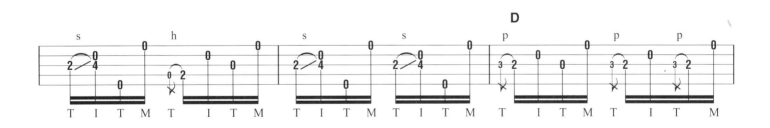

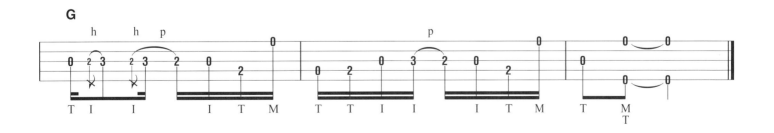

DON'T LET YOUR DEAL GO DOWN

Sound source—*The Essential Flatt & Scruggs - 'Tis Sweet to Be Remembered*

Words and Music by LOUISE CERTAIN, GLADYS STACEY FLATT,
JERRY ORGAN and WAYNE P. WALKER

(G tuning)
Key of F (Recorded in G# tuning)

Intro

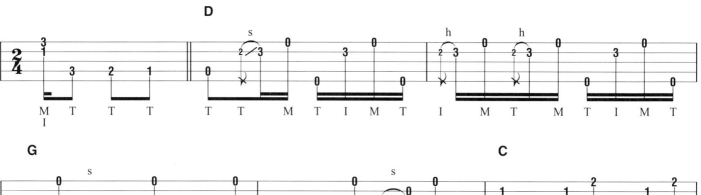

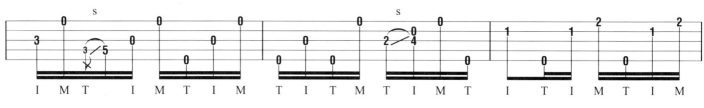

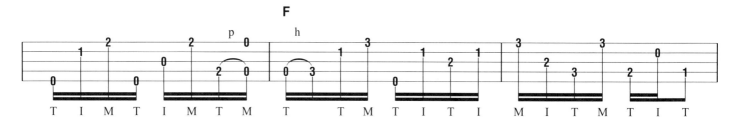

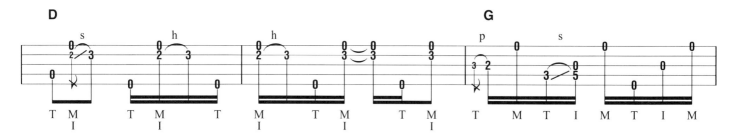

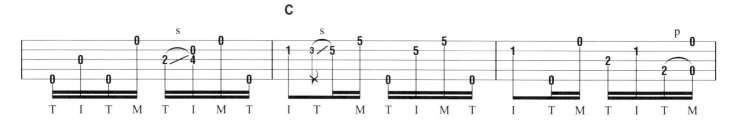

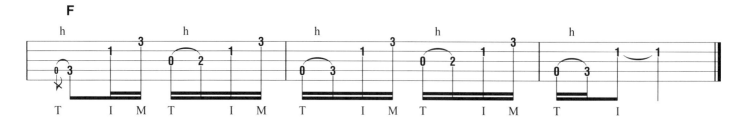

DOWN THE ROAD

Sound source—*The Essential Earl Scruggs*

By LESTER FLATT and EARL SCRUGGS

(G tuning)
Key of B: Capo at 4th fret and hook the 5th string

Intro

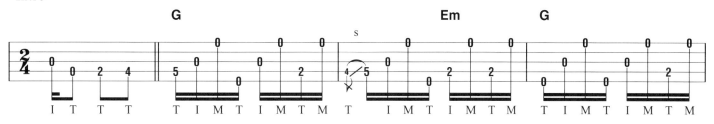

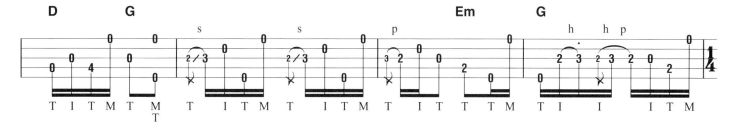

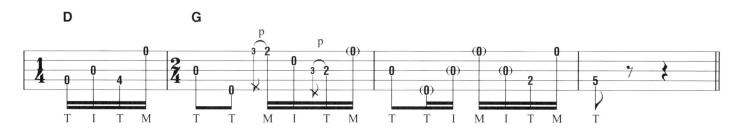

1st break

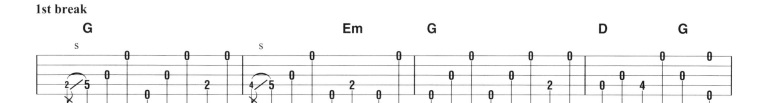

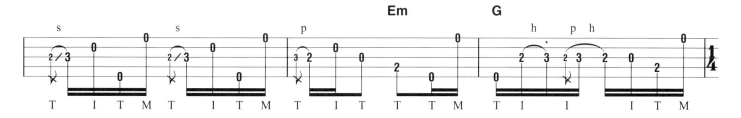

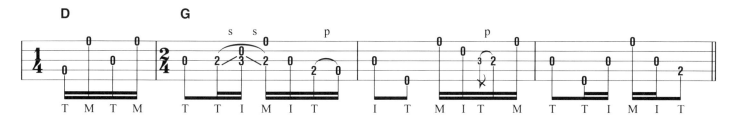

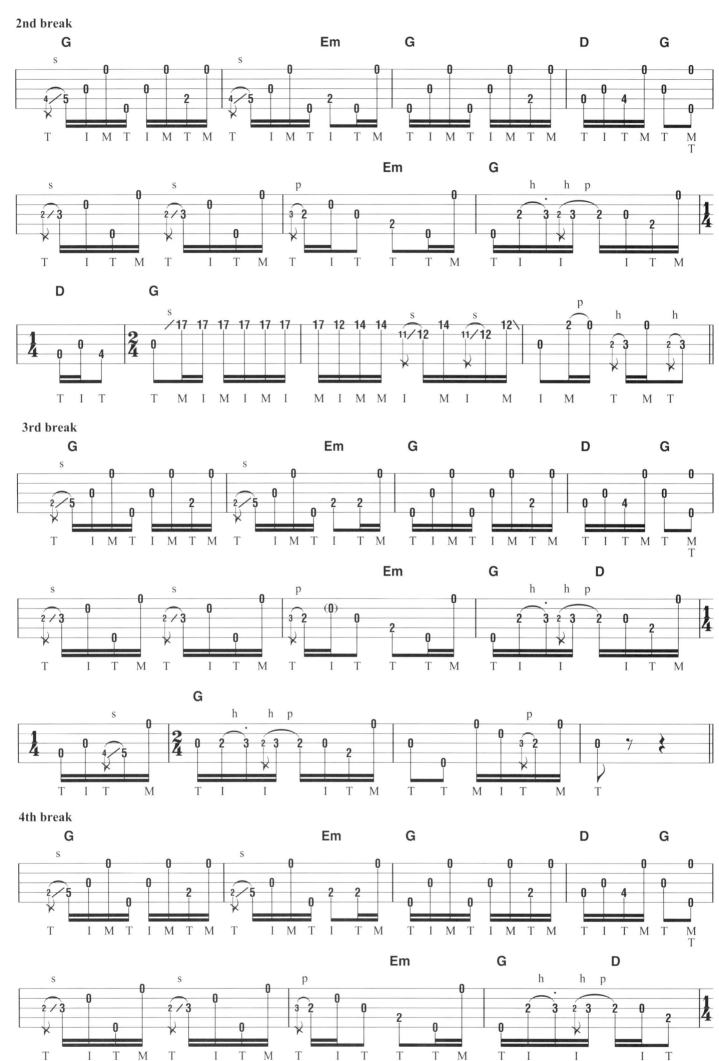

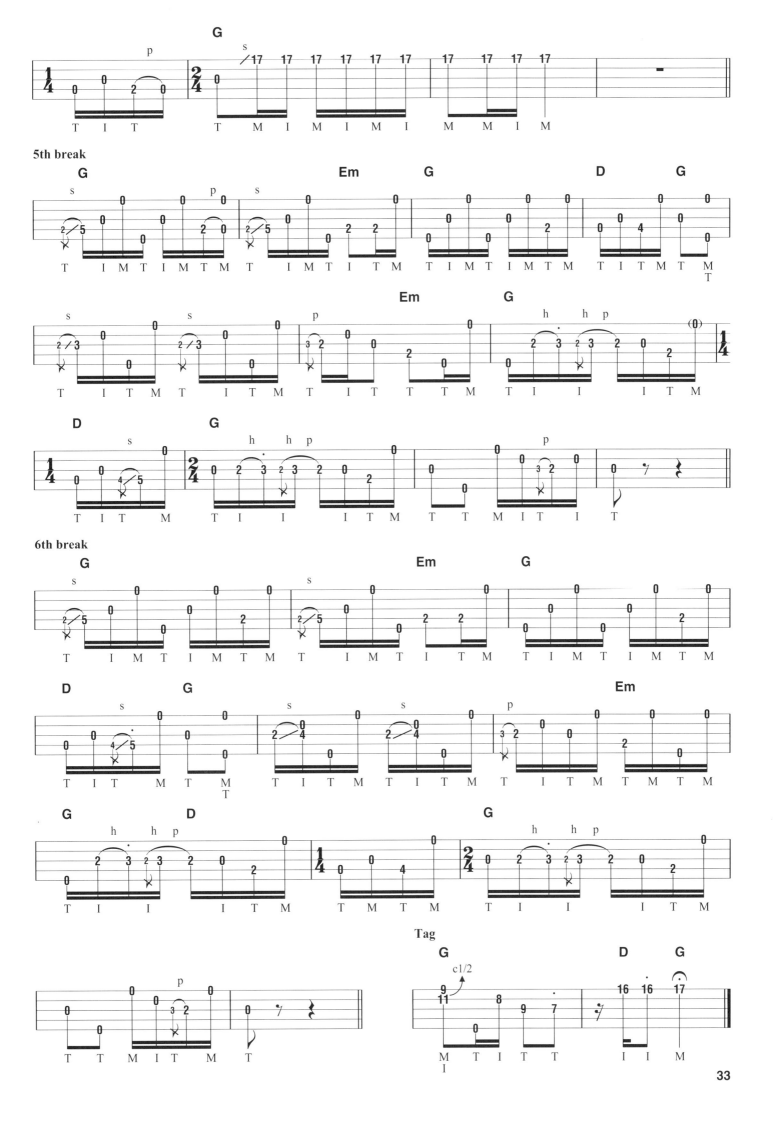

5th break

6th break

Tag

DUELIN' BANJOS

Sound source—*Dueling Banjos - Earl Scruggs*

By ARTHUR SMITH

(G tuning)
Key of G

Very slow and free
*N.C.
Guitar

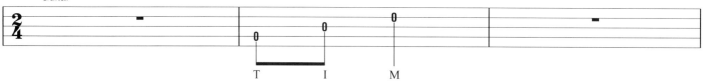

*No chord

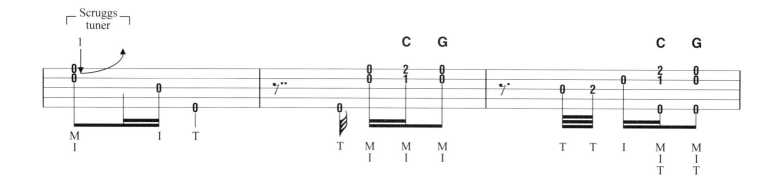

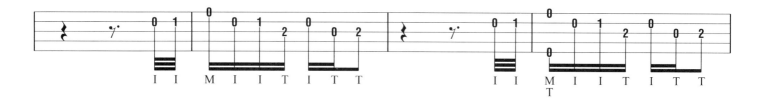

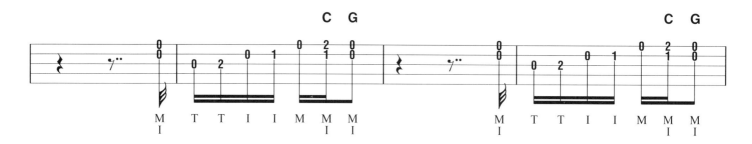

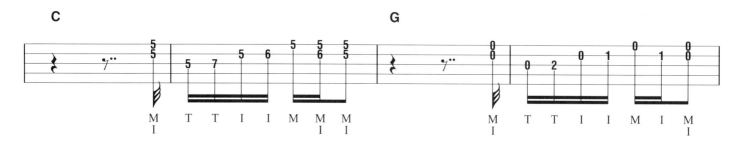

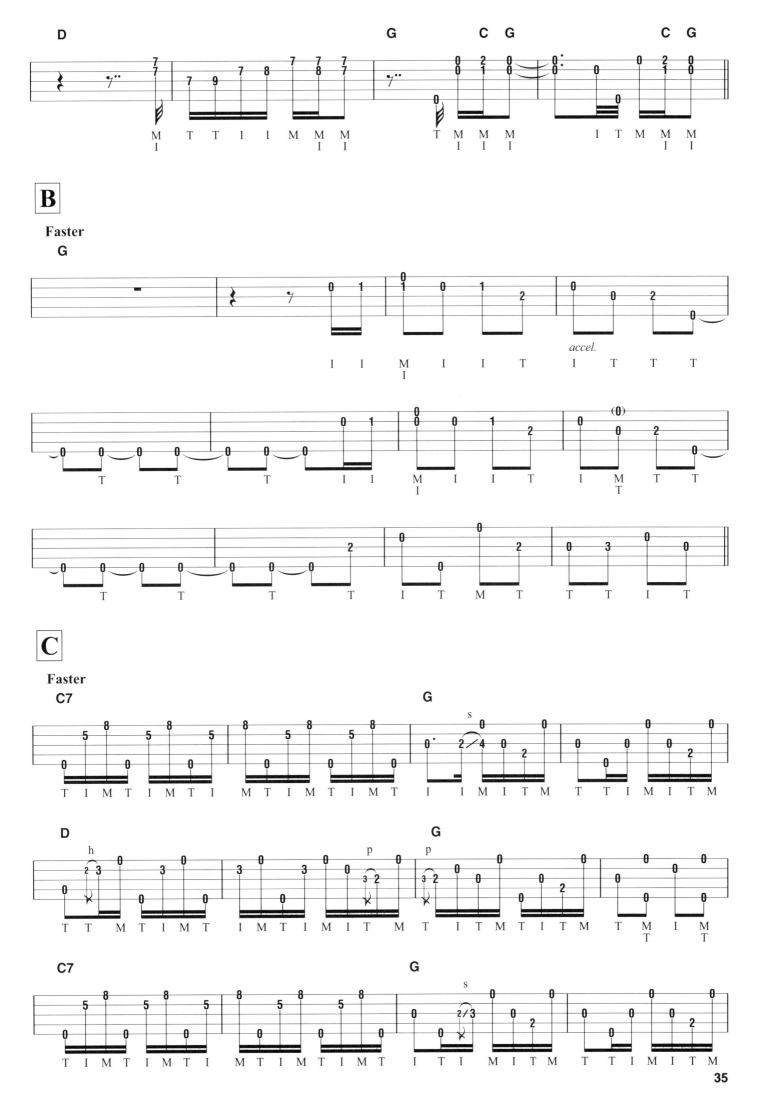

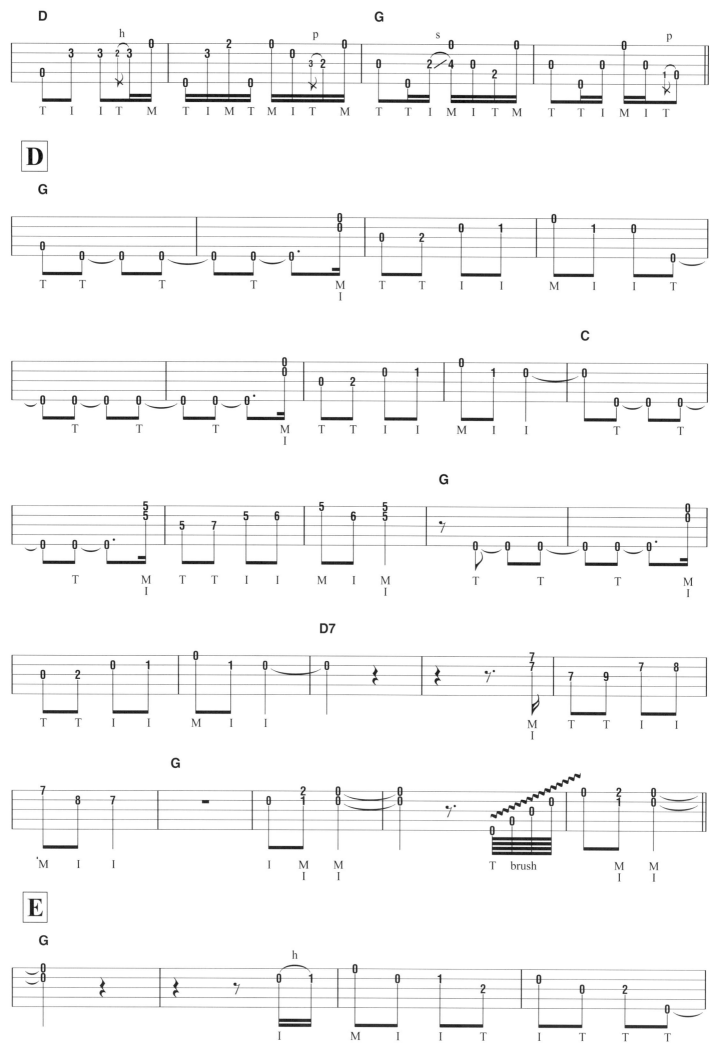

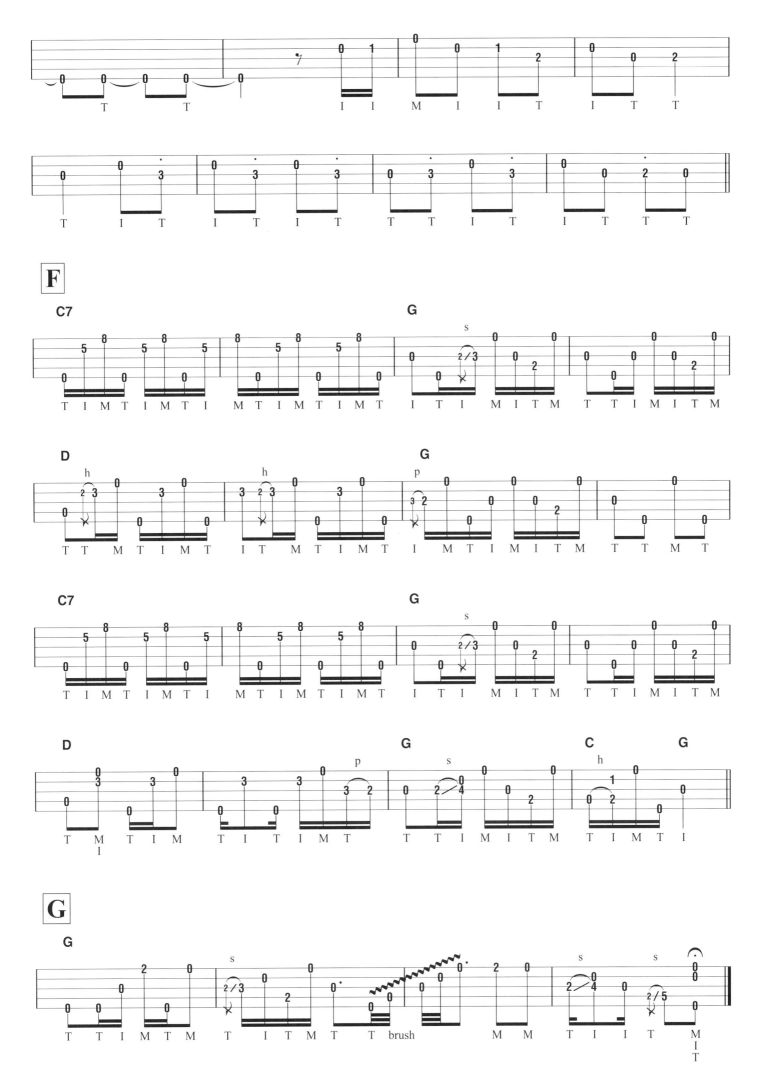

FIREBALL

Sound source—*Flatt & Scruggs' Greatest Hits*

Words and Music by LESTER FLATT,
BURKETT GRAVES and EARL SCRUGGS

(G tuning)
Key of G

1st break

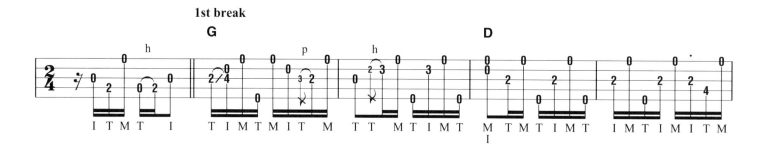

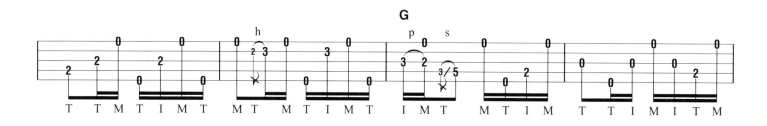

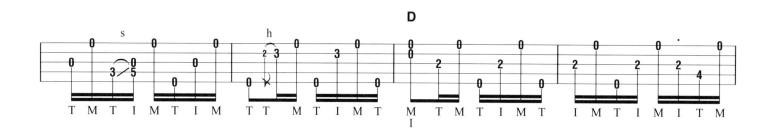

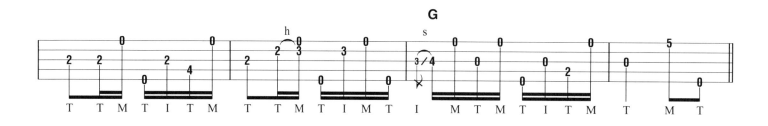

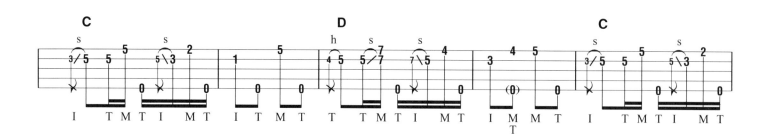

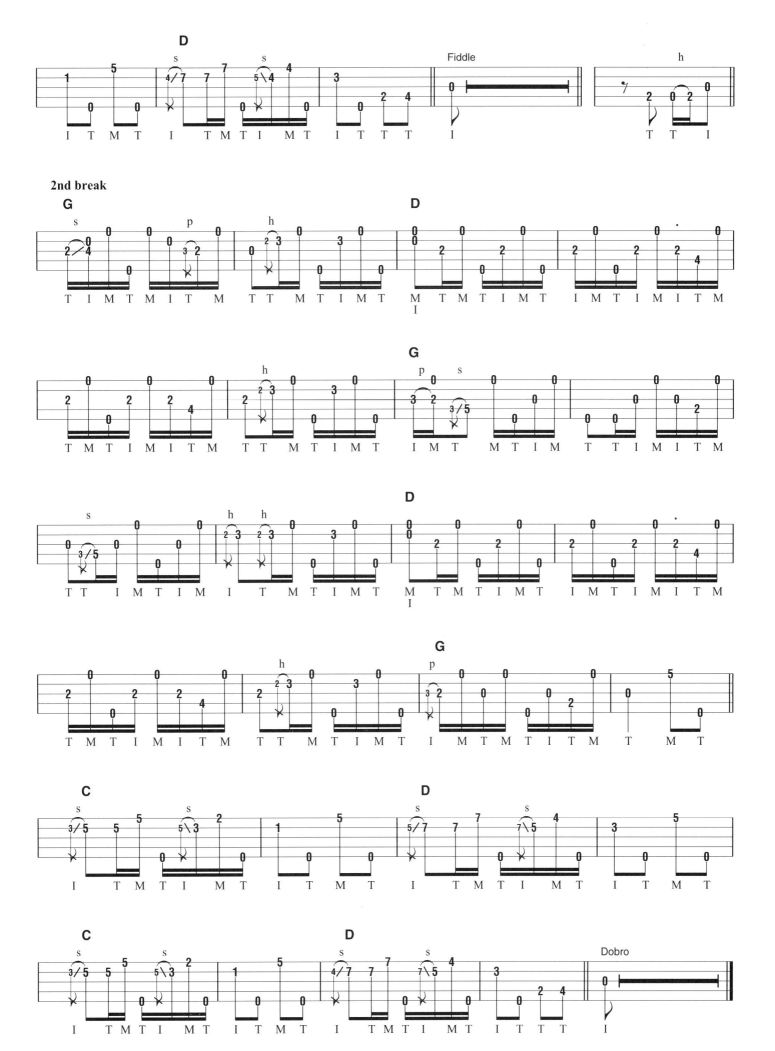

FIREBALL MAIL

Sound source—*Dueling Banjos–Earl Scruggs*

Words and Music by FRED ROSE

(G tuning)
Key of G

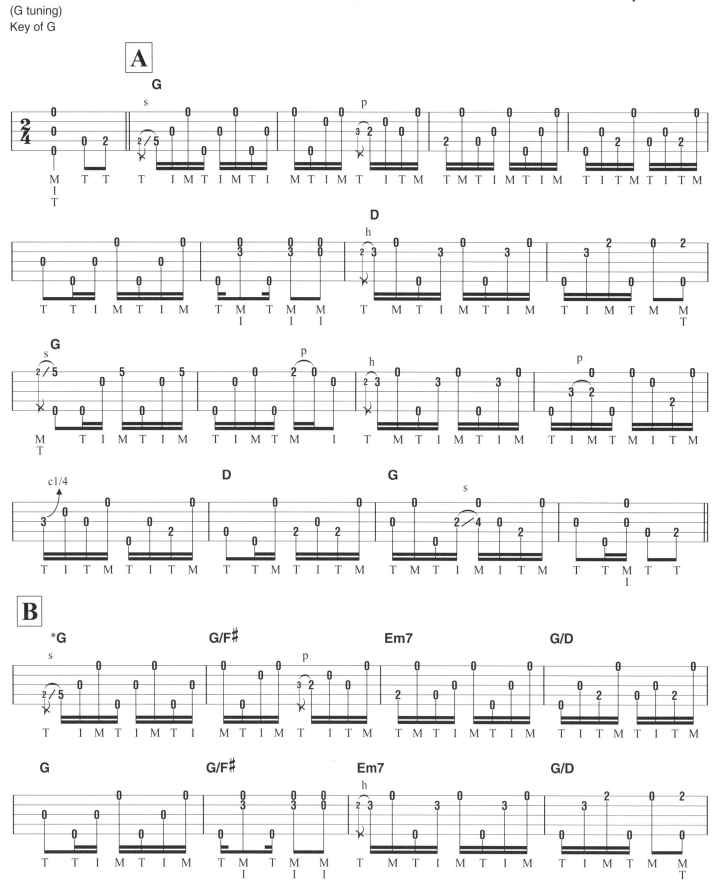

*Chord symbols reflect overall harmony w/ descending bassline.

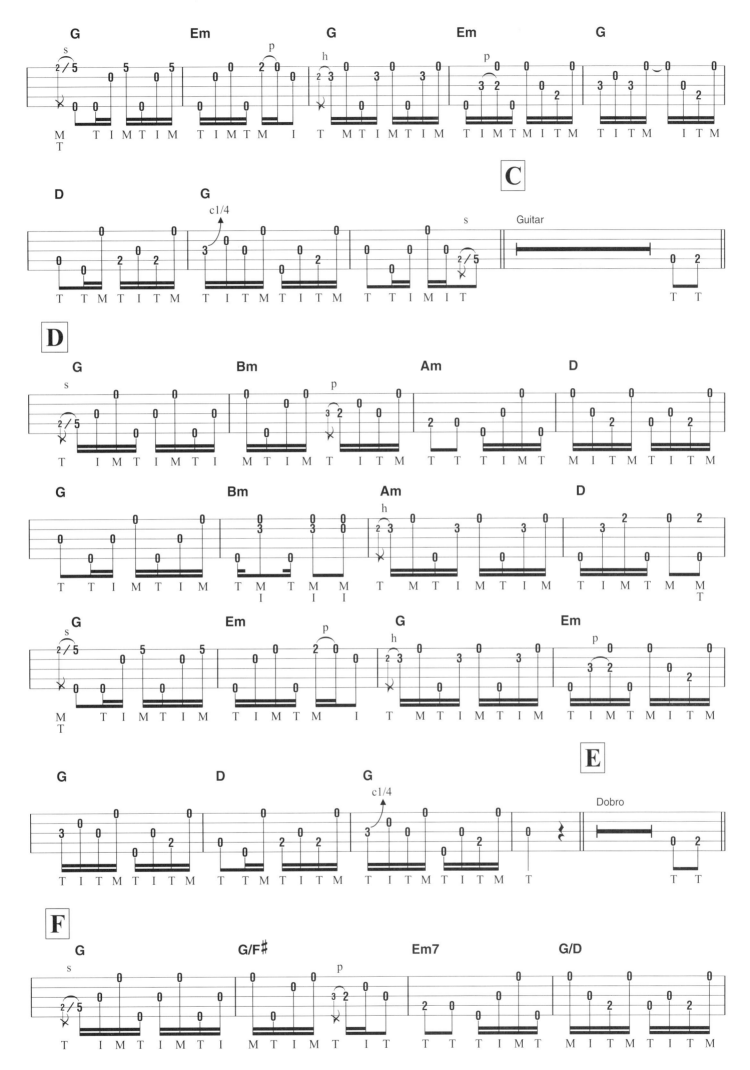

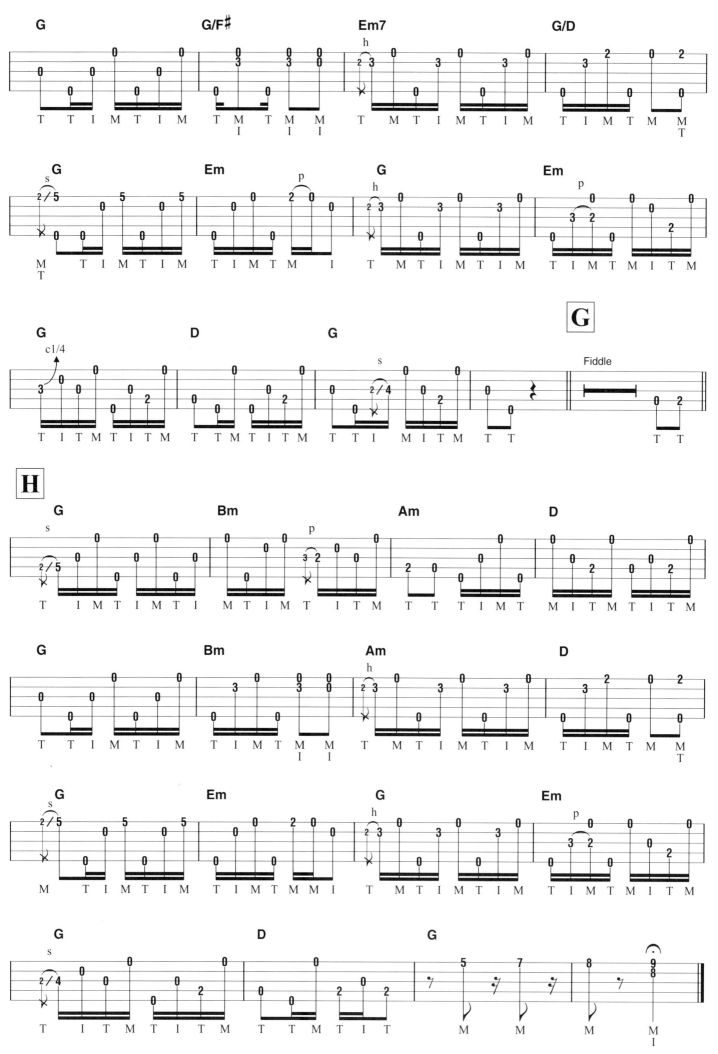

FAREWELL BLUES

Sound source—*The Complete Mercury Sessions–Flatt & Scruggs*

Words and Music by ELMER SCHOEBEL,
PAUL MARES and LEON ROPPOLO

(C tuning)
Key of C (Recorded in C♯ tuning)

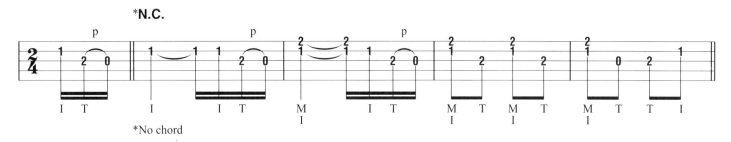

*No chord

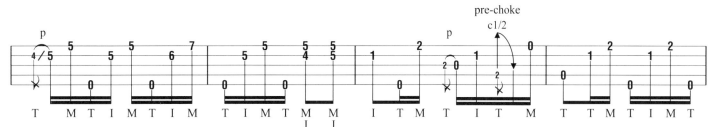

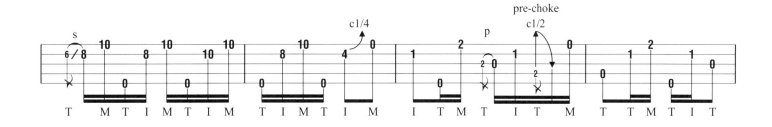

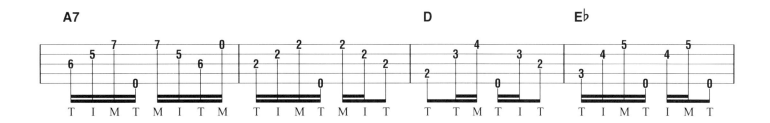

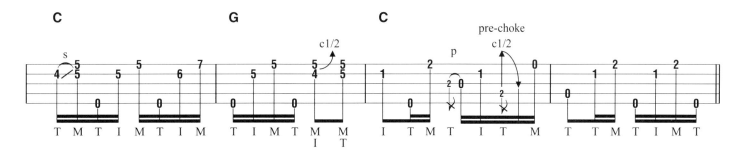

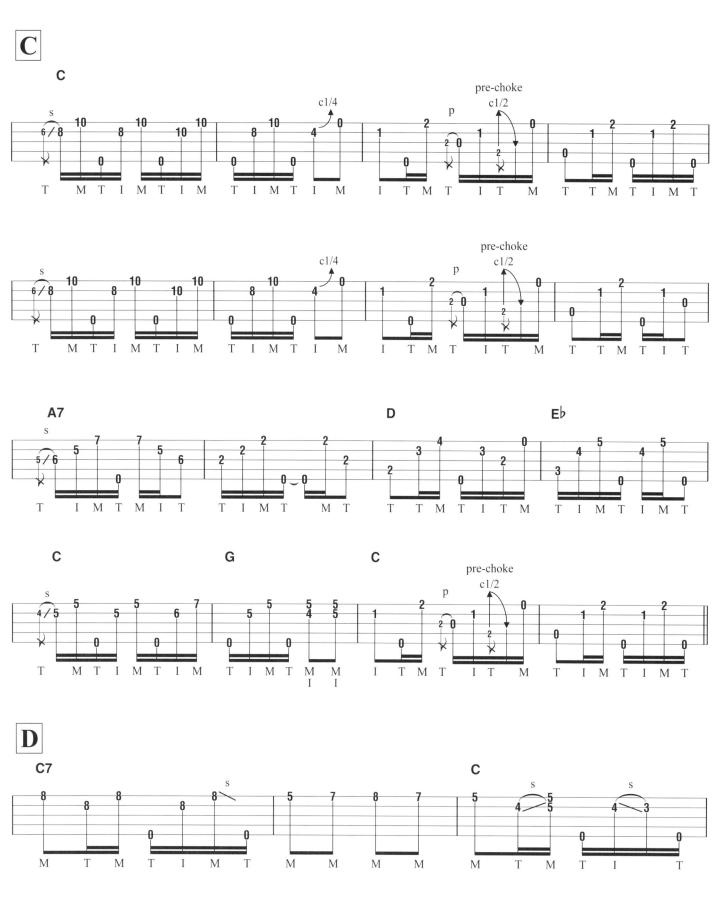

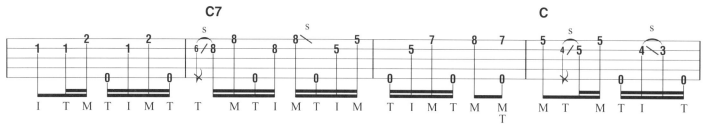

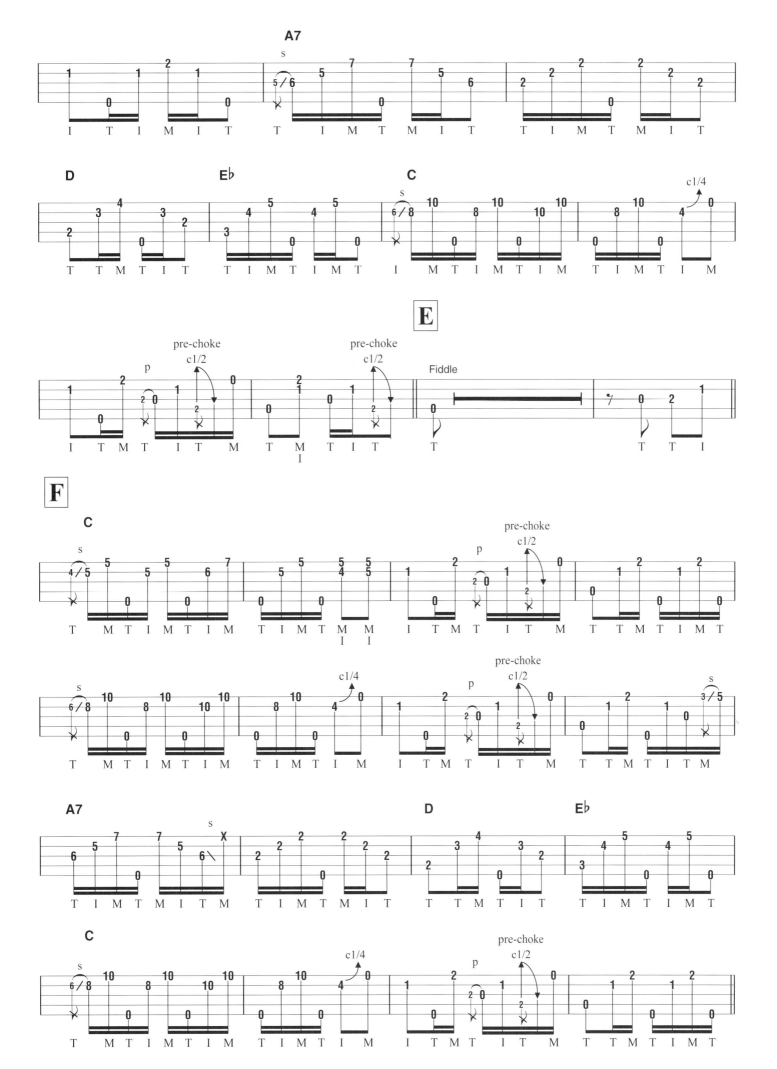

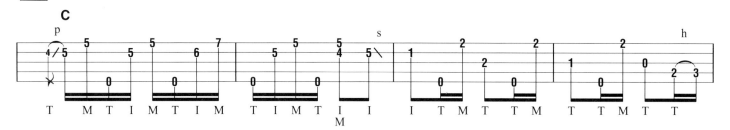

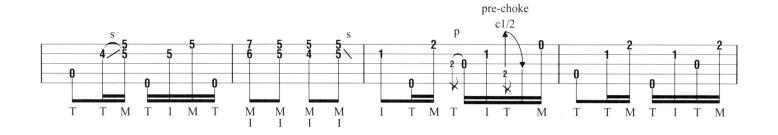

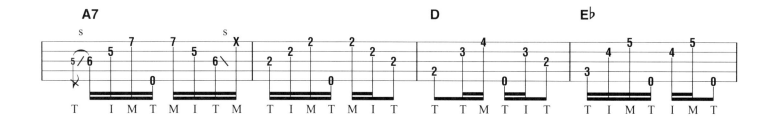

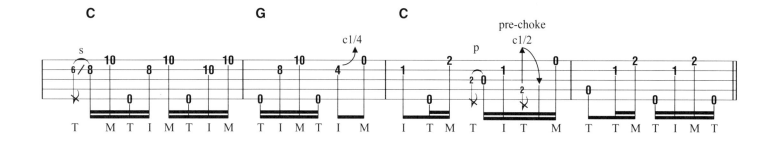

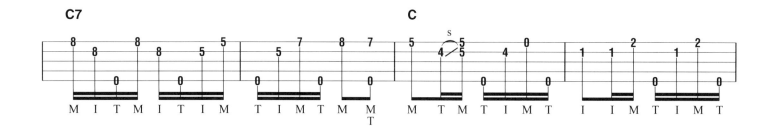

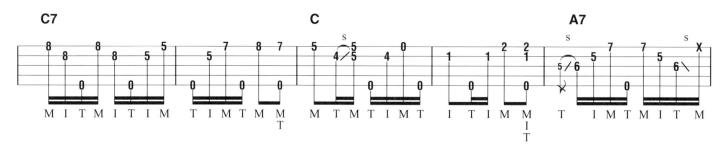

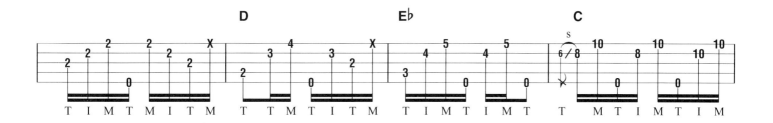

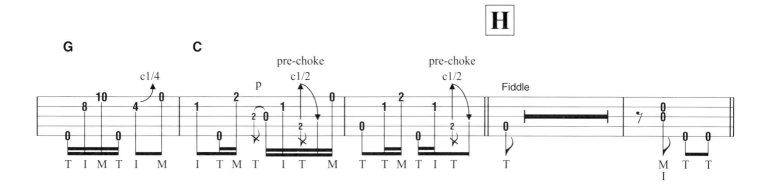

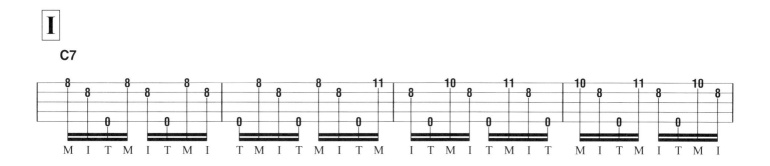

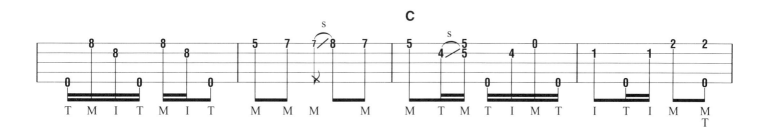

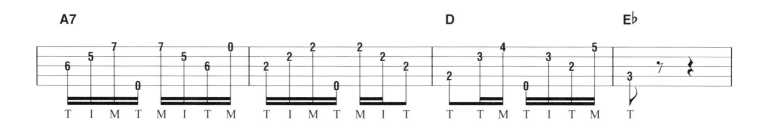

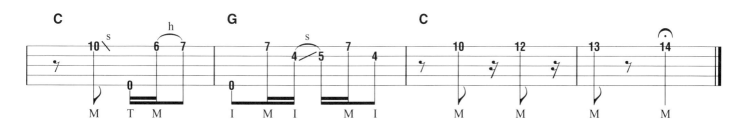

FOGGY MOUNTAIN ROCK

Sound source—*Breaking Out - Flatt & Scruggs*

Words and Music by LOUISE CERTAIN,
BURKETT GRAVES and GLADYS STACEY

(G tuning)
Key of C

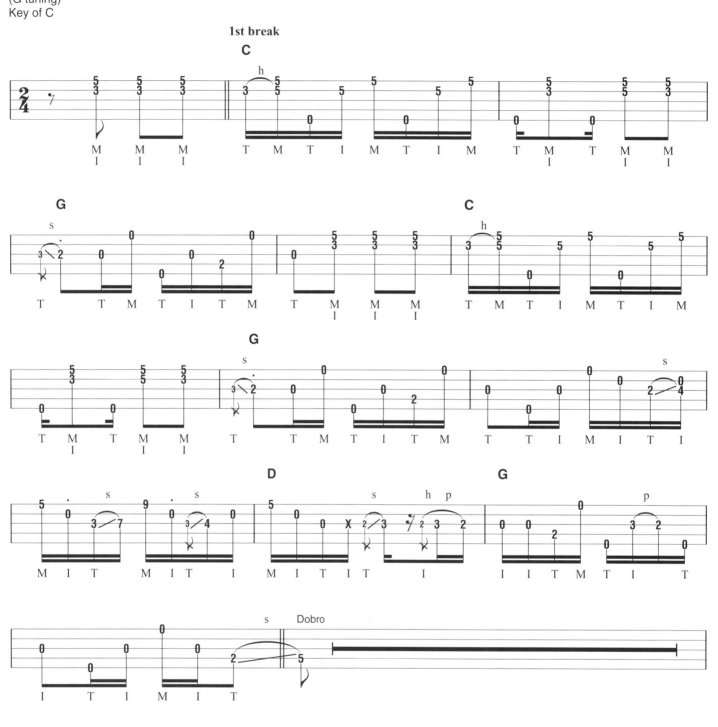

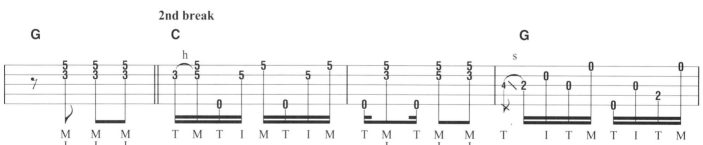

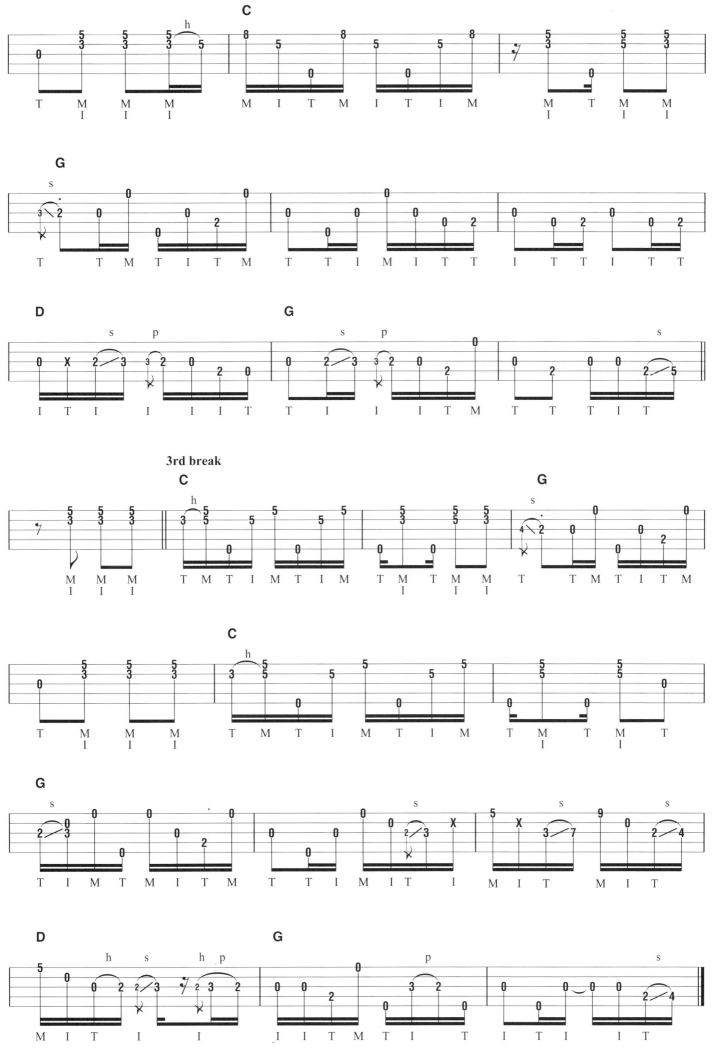

FOGGY MOUNTAIN SPECIAL
Sound source—*The Essential Earl Scruggs*

By ANNE LOUISE SCRUGGS and GLADYS STACEY FLATT

(G tuning)
Key of G (Recorded in G♯ tuning)

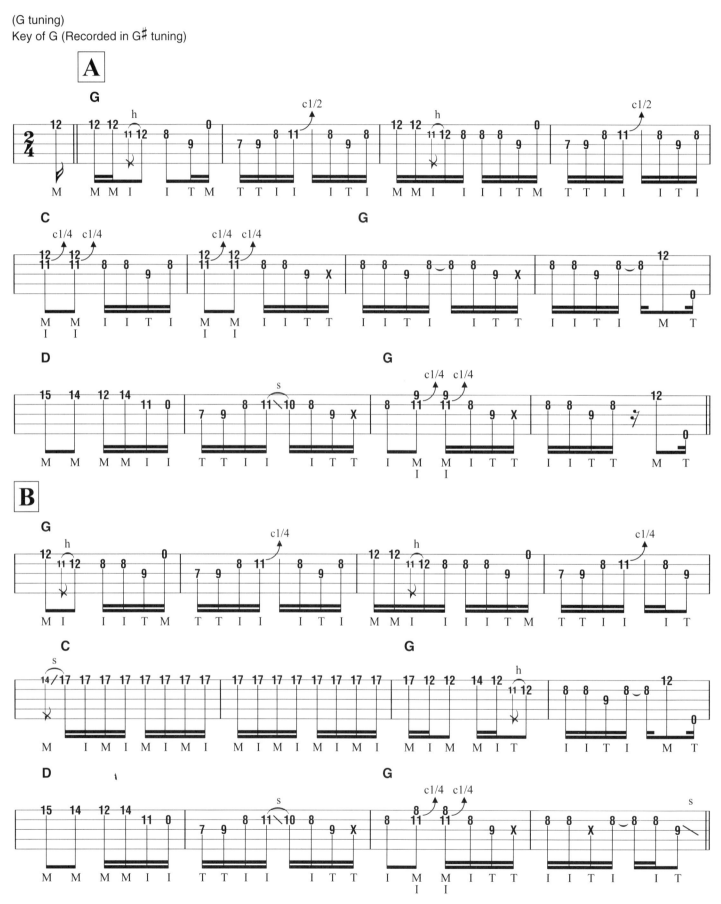

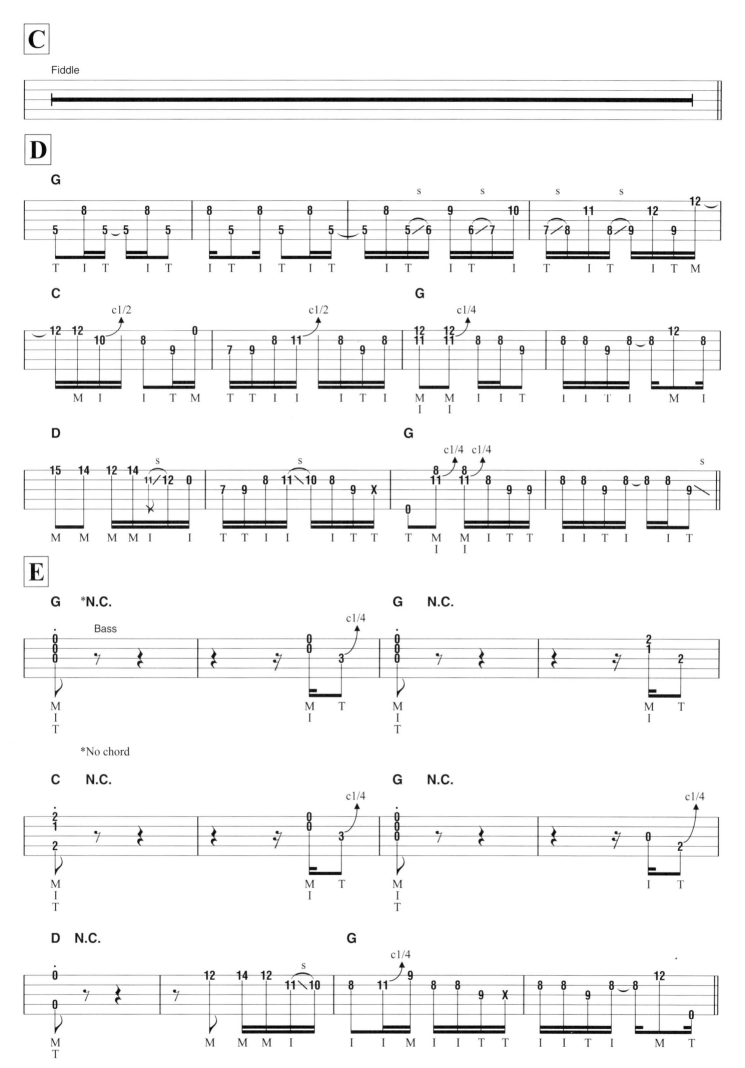

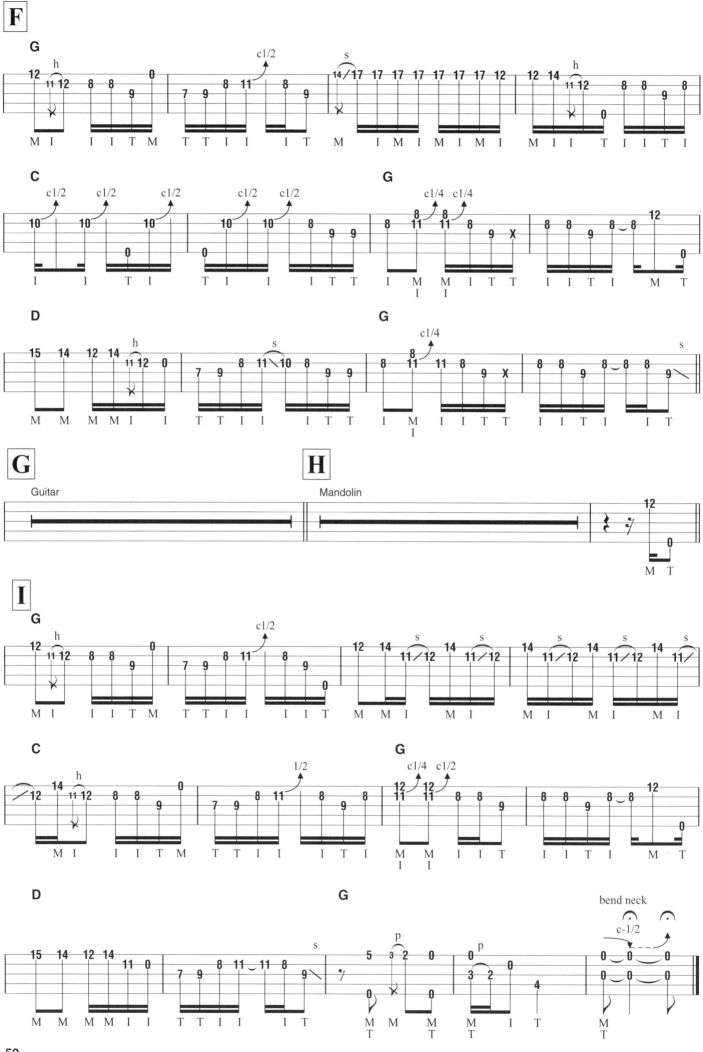

FLOP EARED MULE

Sound source—*Best of the Flatt & Scruggs TV Show, Vol. 10*

TRADITIONAL

(G tuning)
Key of G

A

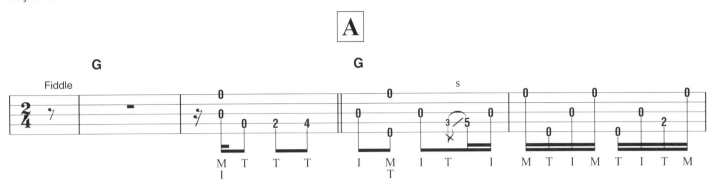

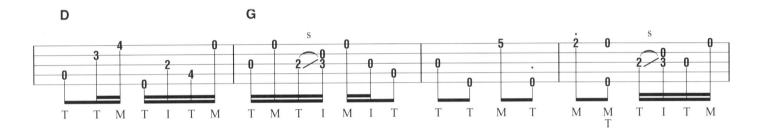

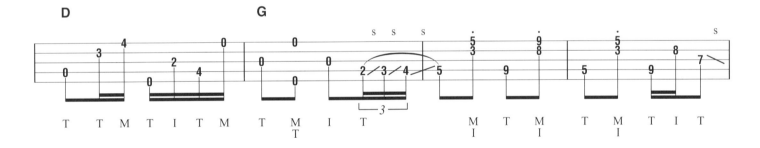

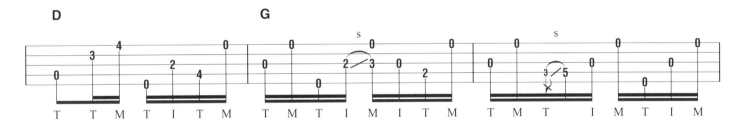

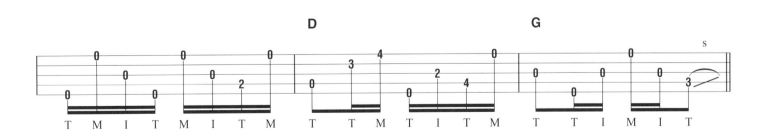

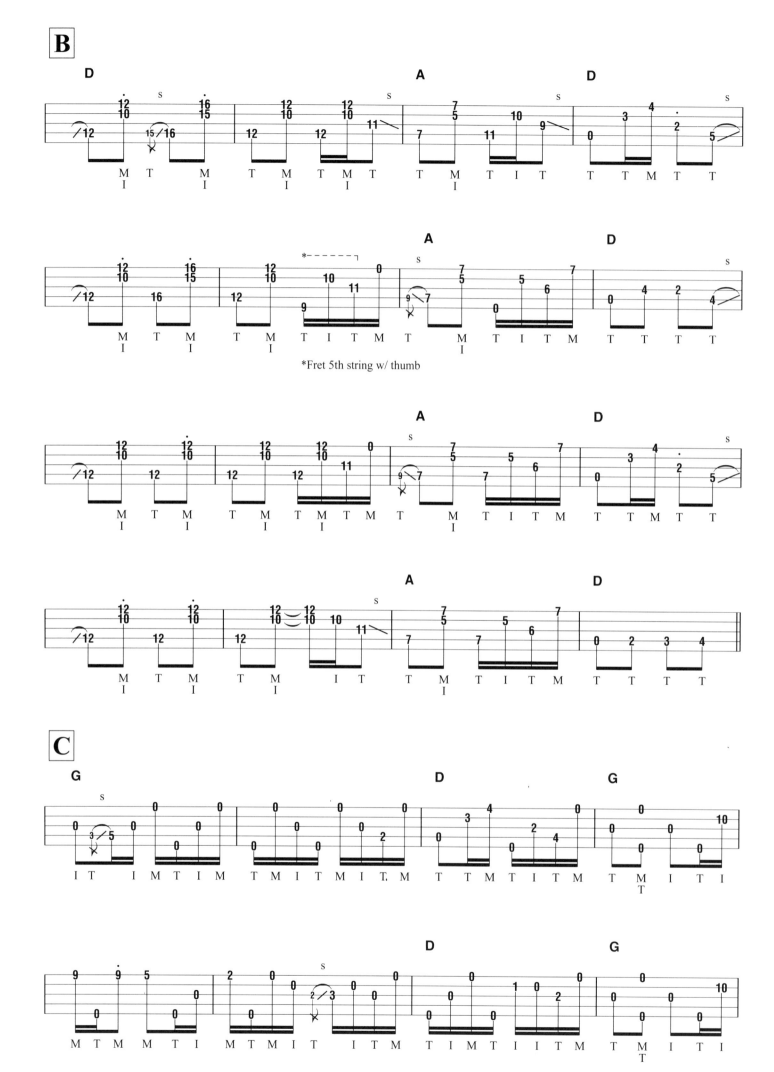

*Fret 5th string w/ thumb

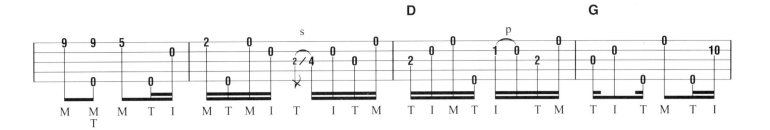

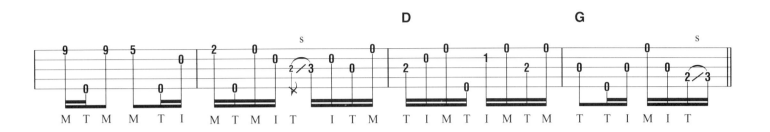

D

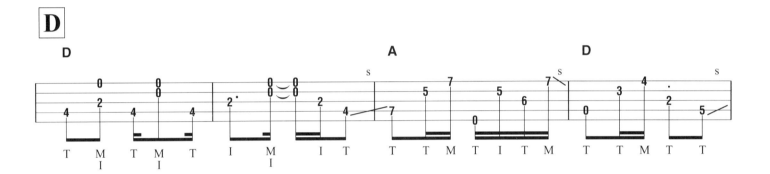

*Fret 5th string w/ thumb

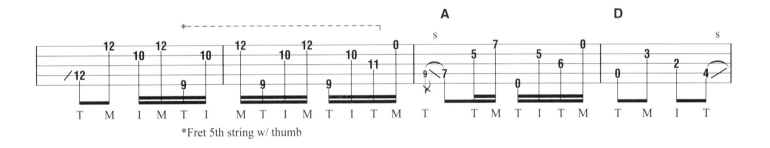

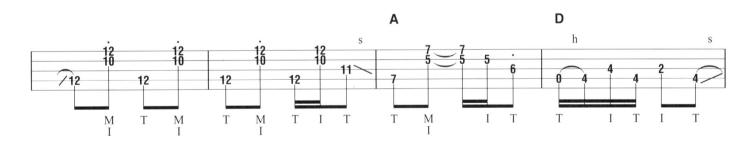

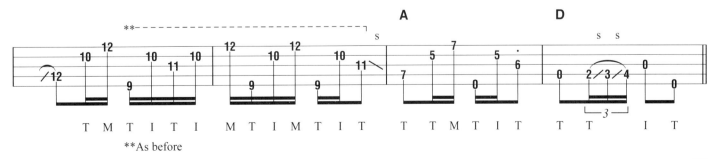

**As before

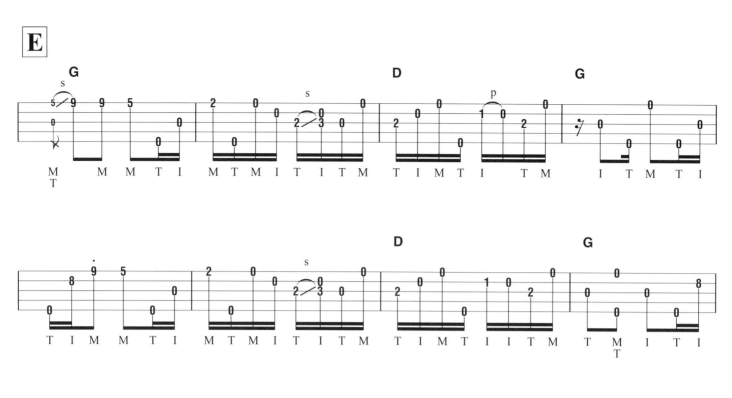

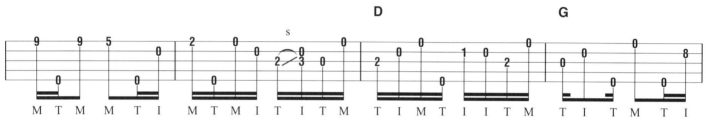

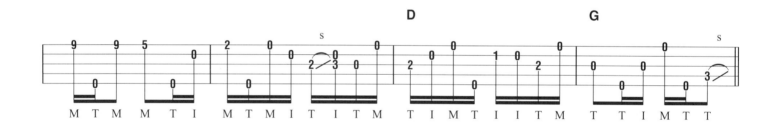

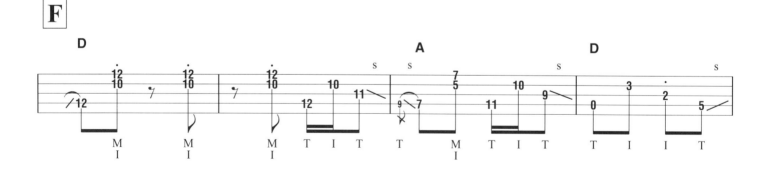

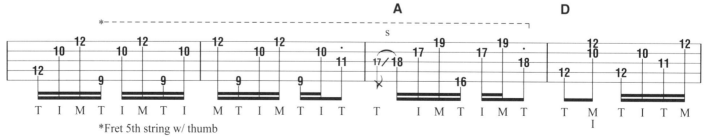

*Fret 5th string w/ thumb

56

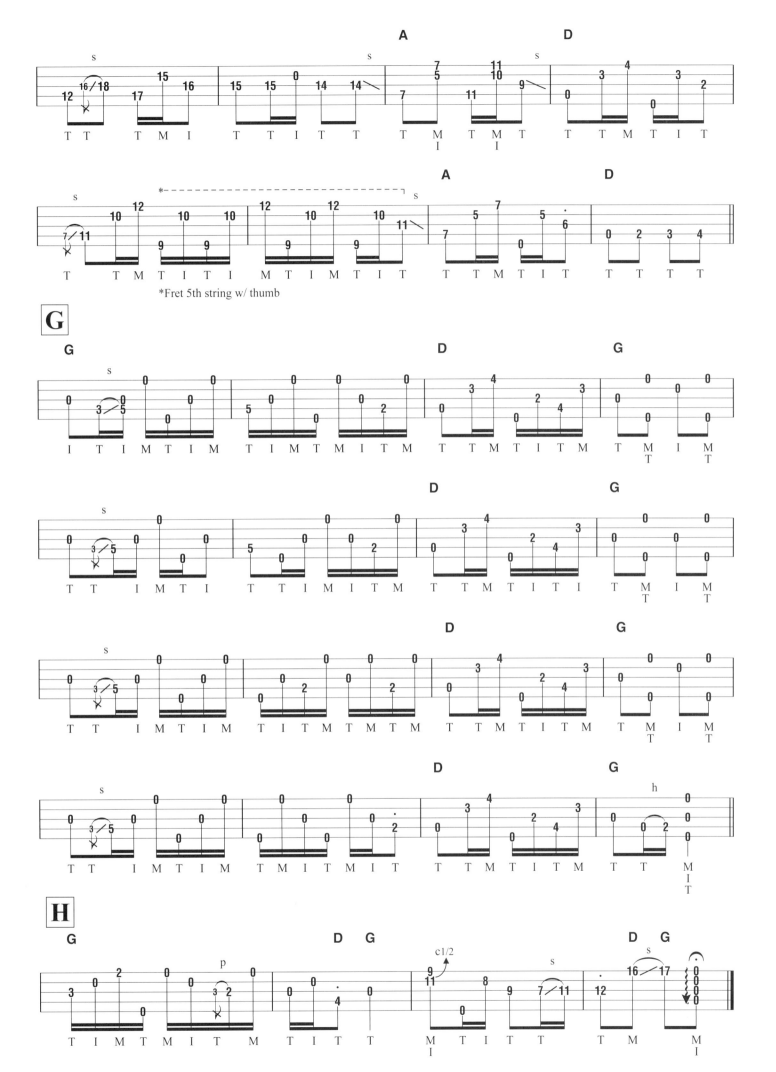

*Fret 5th string w/ thumb

FOGGY MOUNTAIN BREAKDOWN

Sound source—*The Essential Earl Scruggs*

By EARL SCRUGGS

(G tuning)
Key of G (Recorded in G♯ tuning)

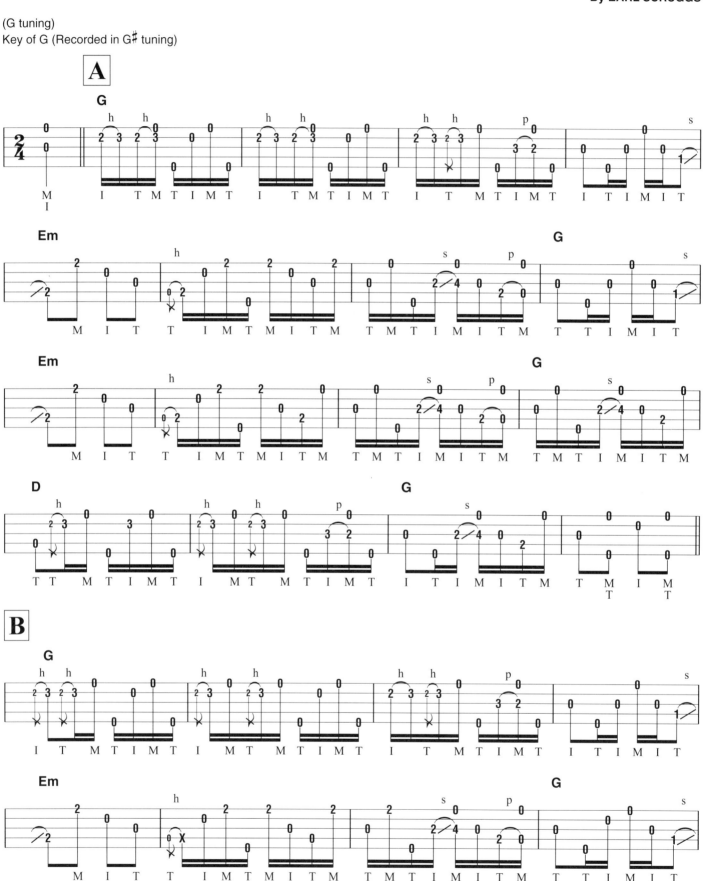

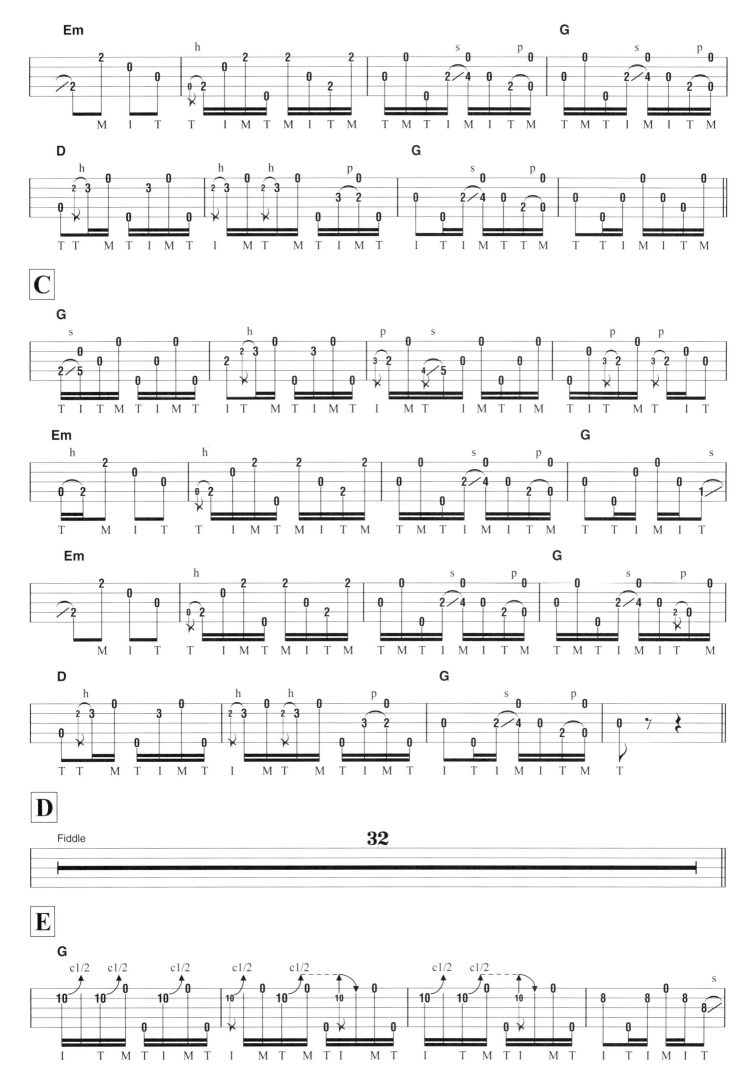

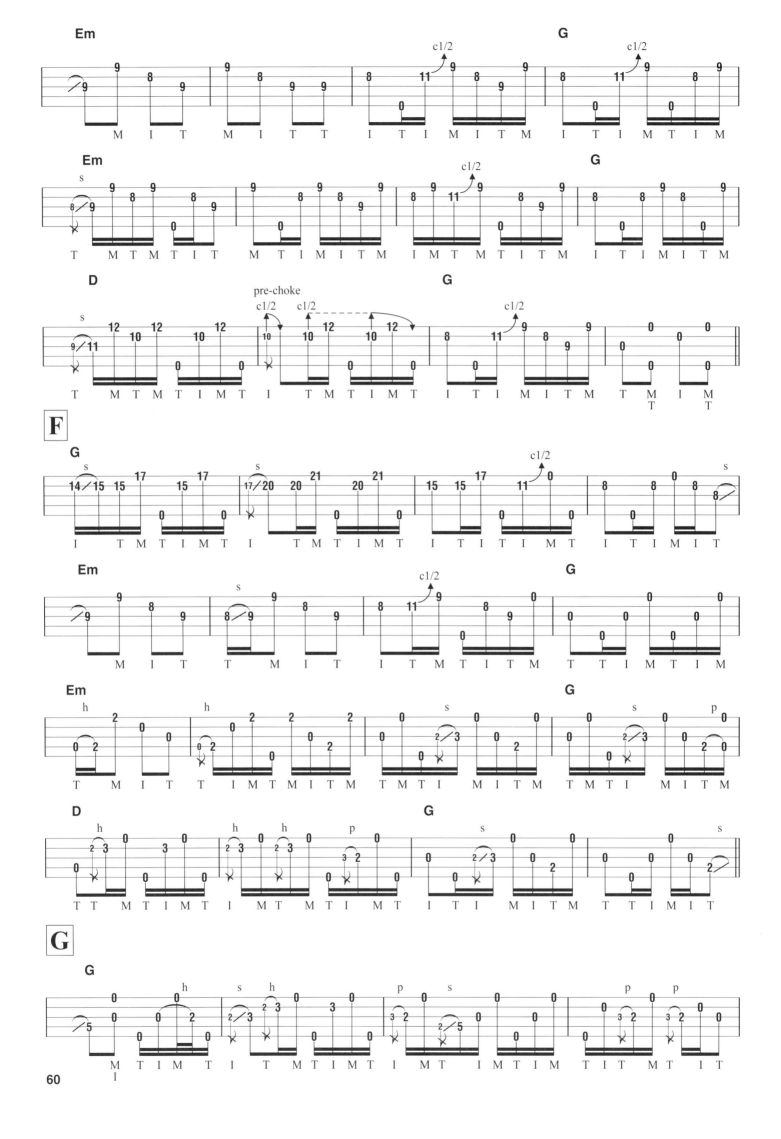

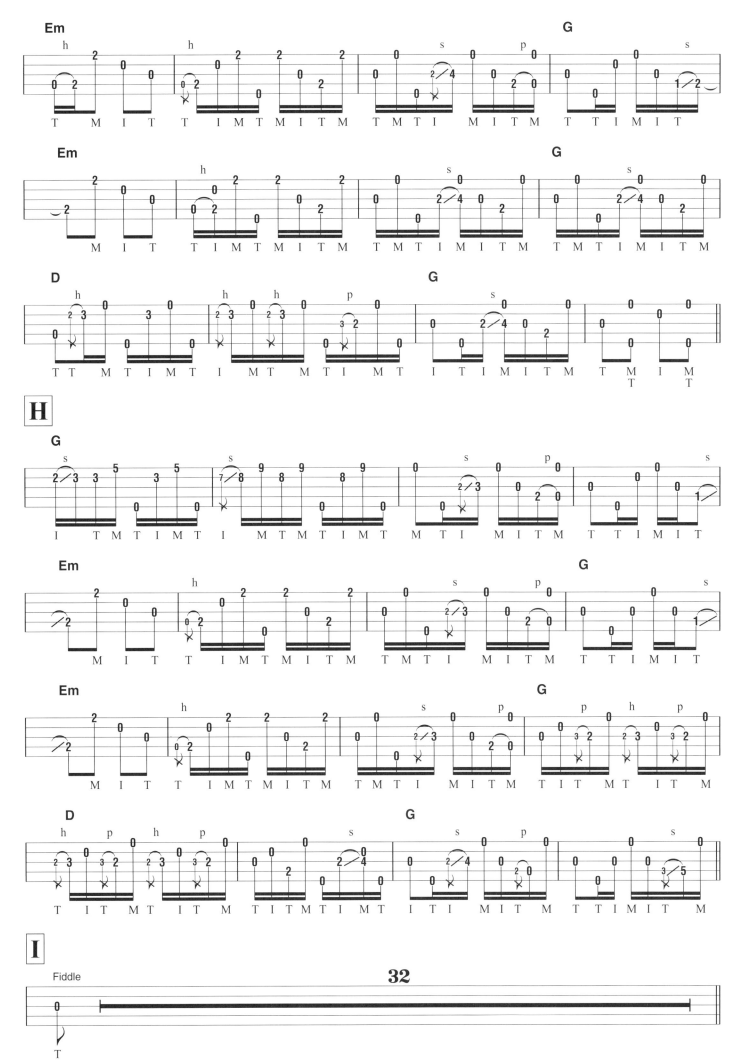

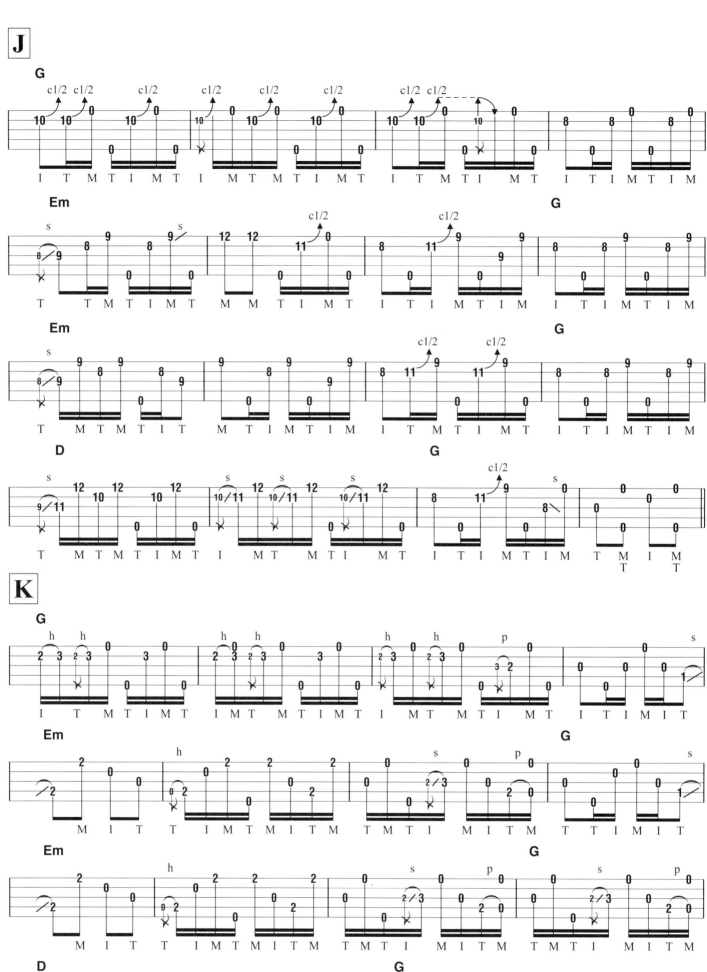

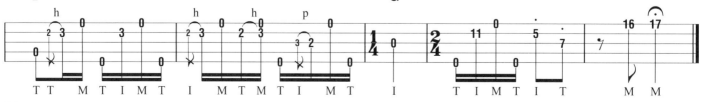

HAVE YOU COME TO SAY GOODBYE

Sound source—*Best of the Flatt & Scruggs TV Show, Vol. 2*

Words and Music by CLAUDE BOONE

(G tuning)
Key of A: Capo at 2nd fret and hook the 5th string

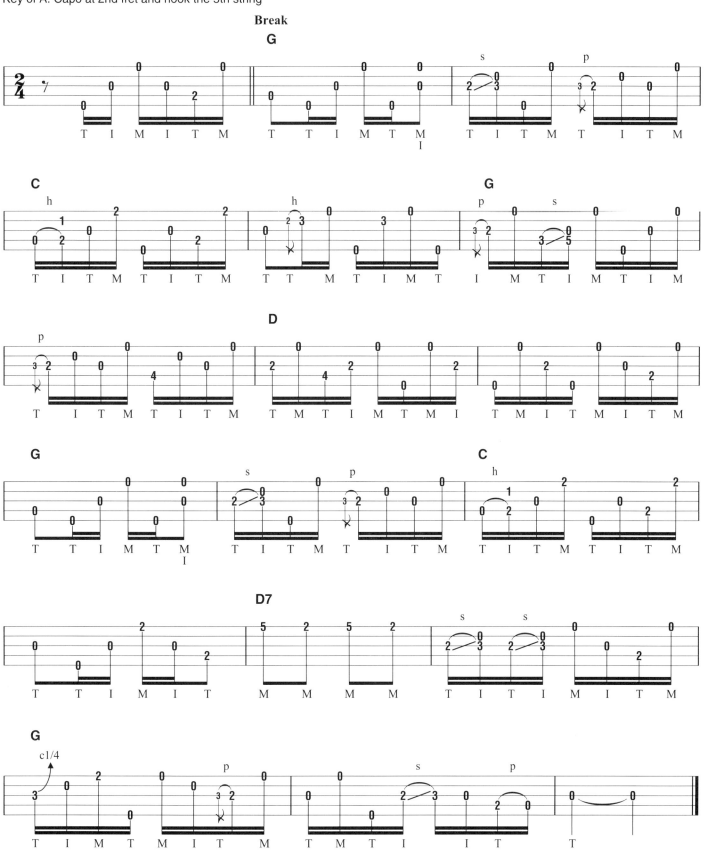

GET IN LINE BROTHER

Sound source—*The Essential Earl Scruggs*

Words and Music by LESTER FLATT

(G tuning)
Key of B♭: Capo at 3rd fret and hook the 5th string.
(Recorded in G♯ tuning, capoed at the 2nd fret)

Intro

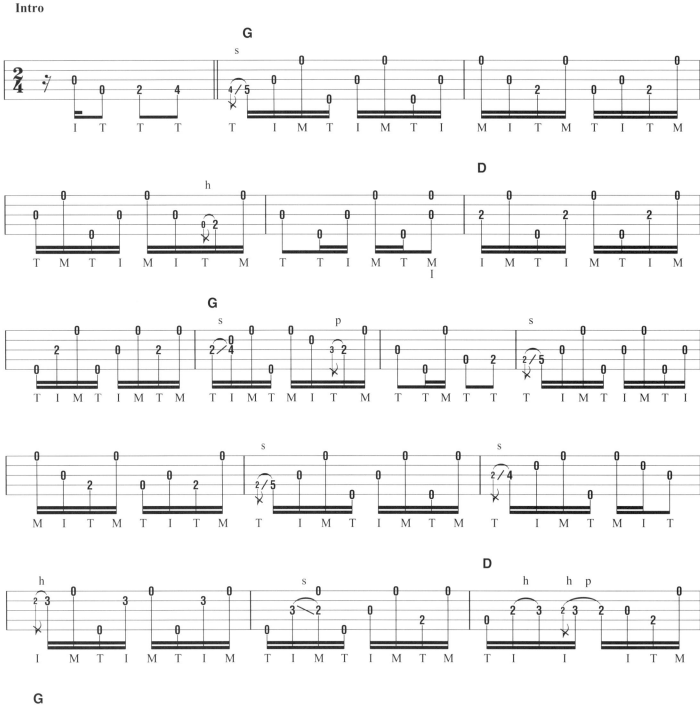

Break

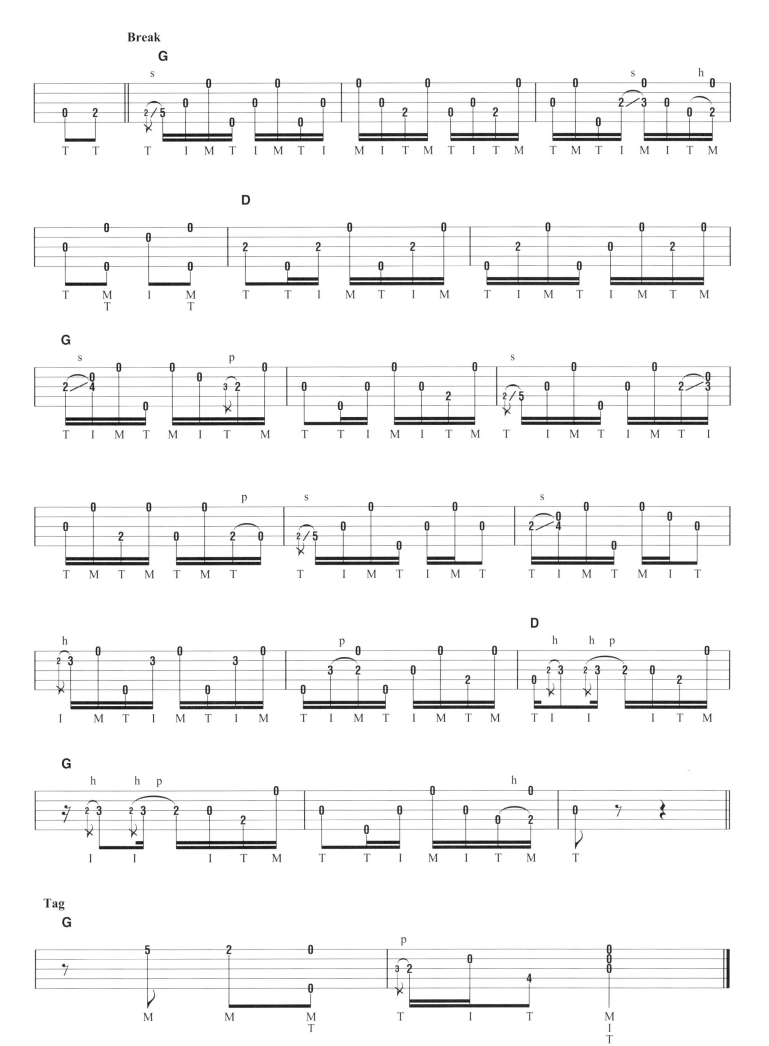

Tag

65

GOTTA TRAVEL ON

Sound source—*Flatt & Scruggs at Carnegie Hall! The Complete Concert*

Words and Music by PAUL CLAYTON,
LARRY EHRLICH, DAVID LAZAR and TOM SIX

(G tuning)
Key of G

Intro

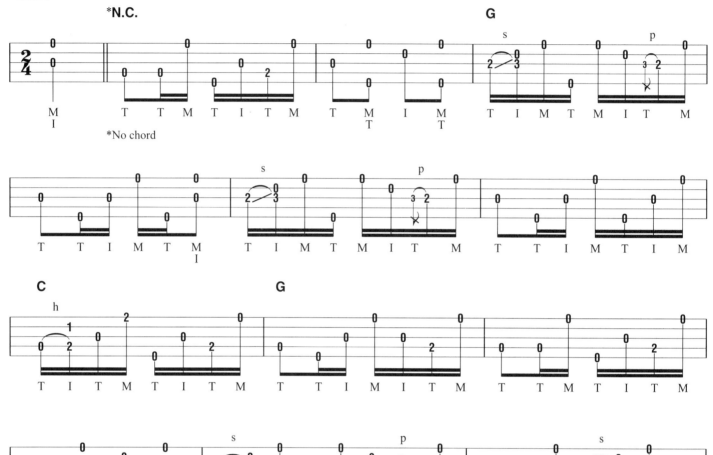

*No chord

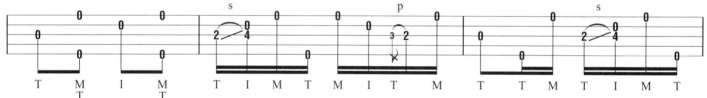

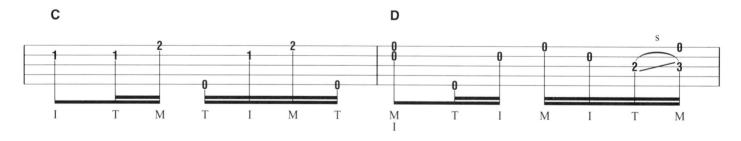

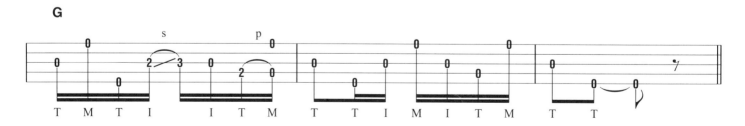

2nd Verse

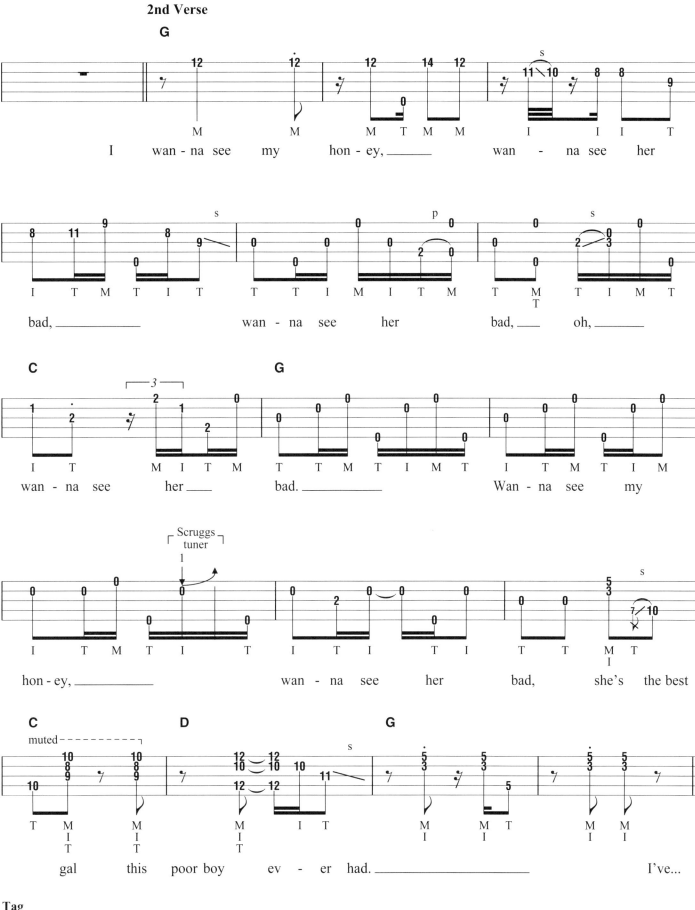

I wan-na see my hon-ey, _____ wan-na see her bad, _____ wan-na see her bad, ____ oh, _____ wan-na see her ____ bad. _____ Wan-na see my hon-ey, _____ wan-na see her bad, she's the best gal this poor boy ev-er had. _____ I've...

Tag

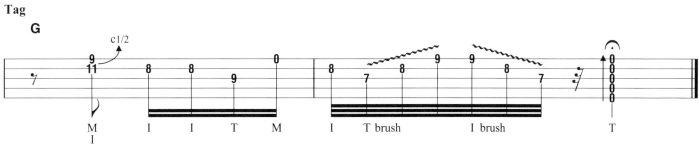

HAND ME DOWN MY WALKING CANE

Sound source—*Best of the Flatt & Scruggs TV Shows, Vol. 9*

Words and Music by JAMES A. BLAND

(G tuning)
Key of G

1st break

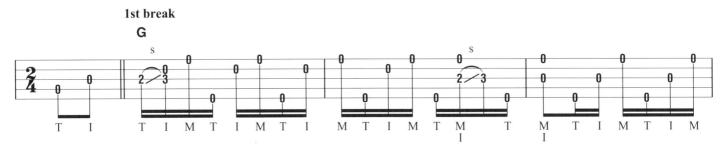

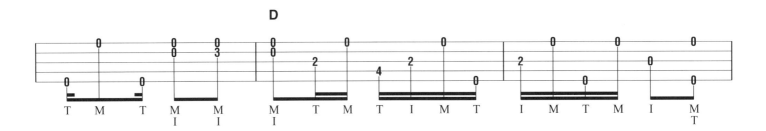

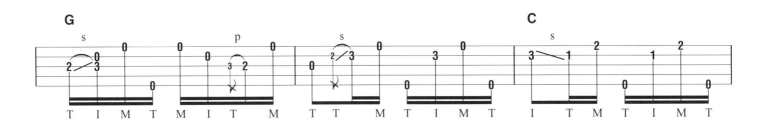

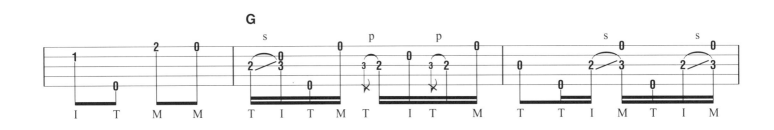

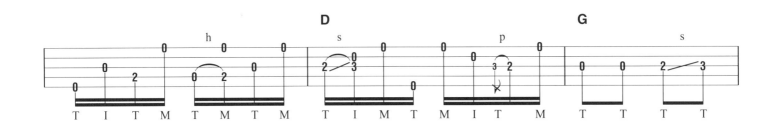

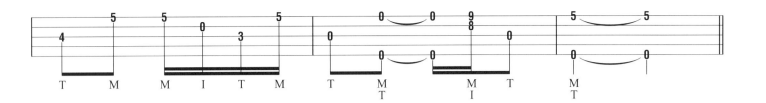

2nd break

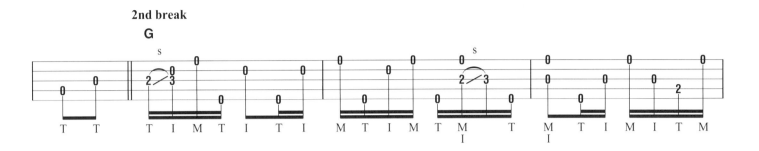

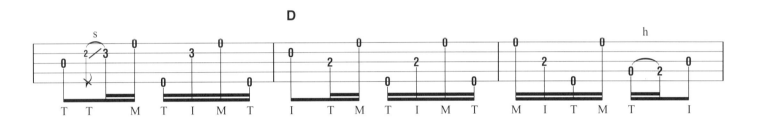

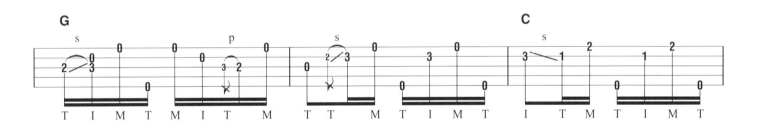

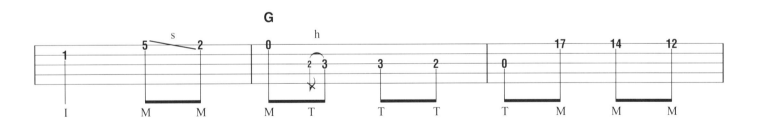

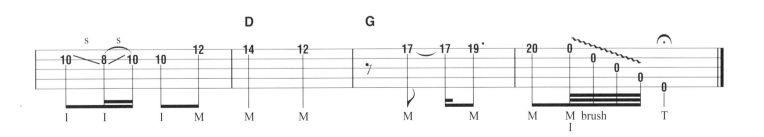

HEAR THE WHISTLE BLOW, ONE HUNDRED MILES

Sound source—*Flatt & Scruggs at Carnegie Hall! The Complete Concert*

Words and Music by LESTER FLATT
and EARL SCRUGGS

(G tuning)
Key of G

Intro

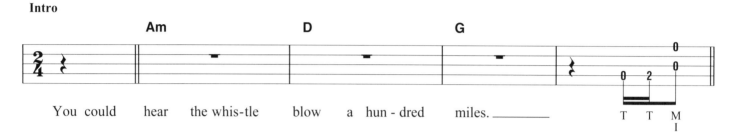

1st break

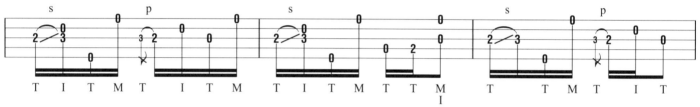

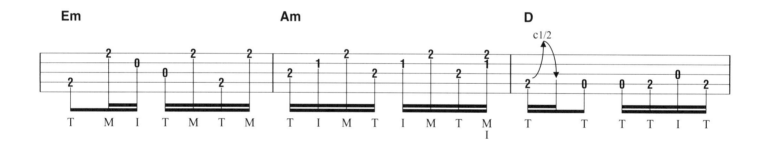

2nd break

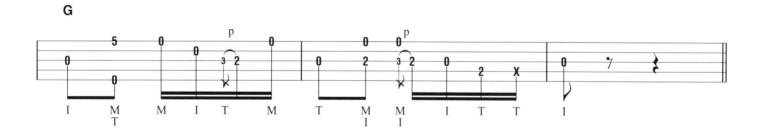

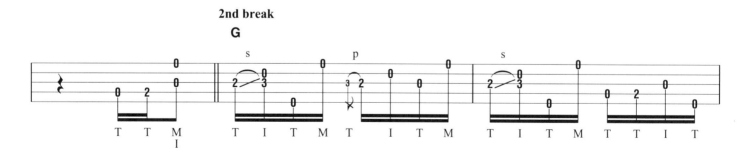

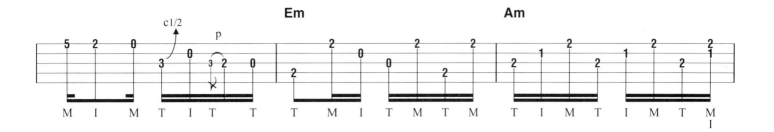

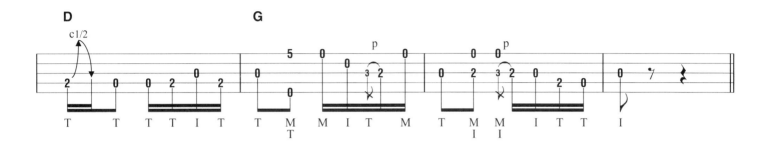

3rd break

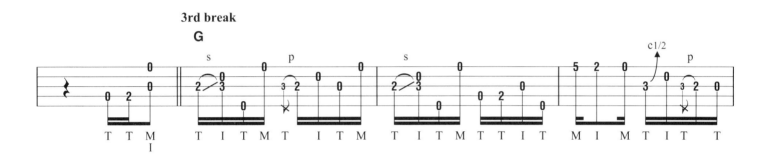

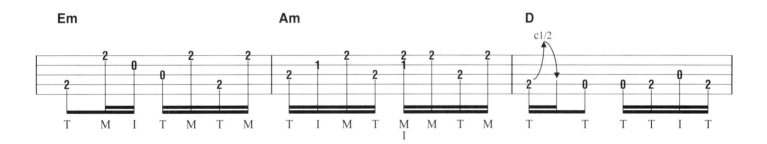

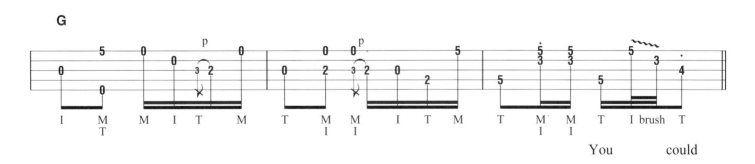

You could

Outro
*N.C.

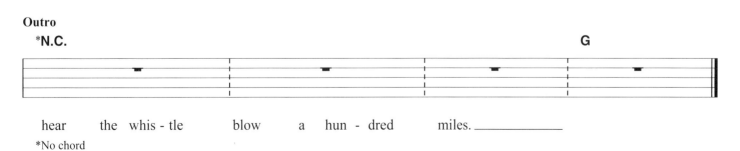

hear   the   whis - tle   blow   a   hun - dred   miles. _____

*No chord

HEAVY TRAFFIC AHEAD

Sound source—*The Essential Earl Scruggs*

Words and Music by BILL MONROE

(G tuning)
Key of A: Hook the 5th string at the 7th fret

Intro

***N.C.**

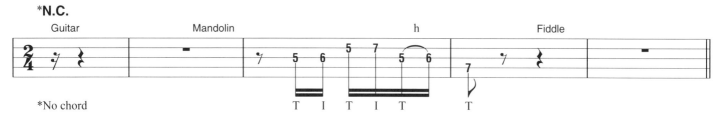

*No chord

1st break

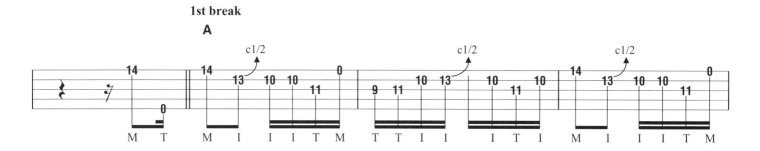

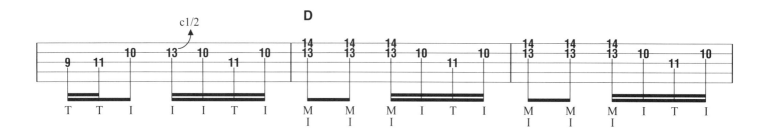

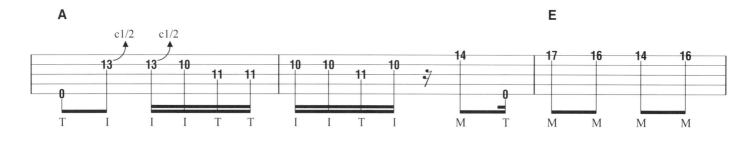

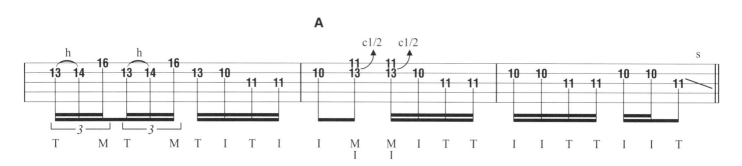

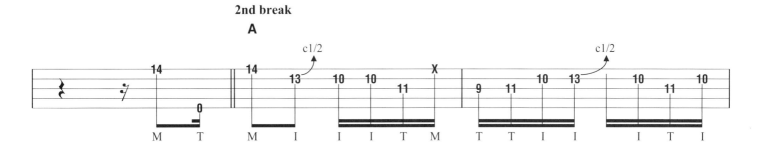

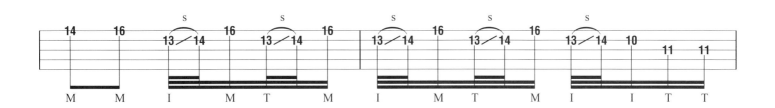

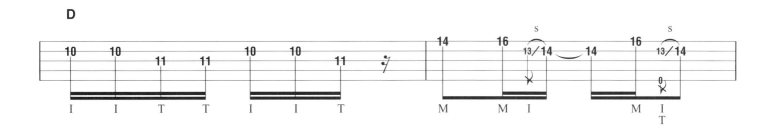

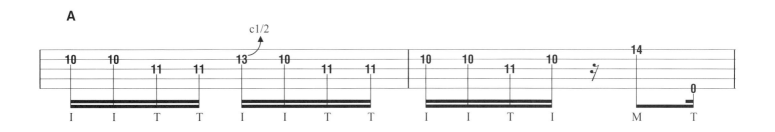

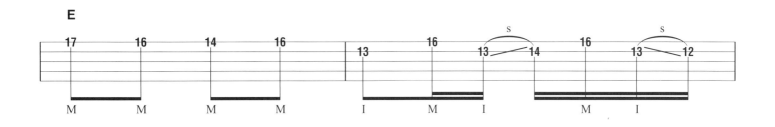

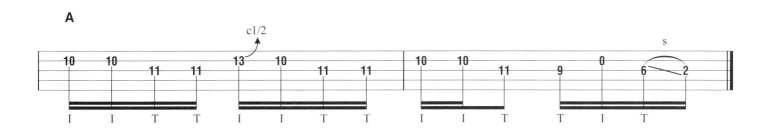

I AIN'T GOIN' TO WORK TOMORROW

Sound source—*60 Foggy Mountain Favorites–Flatt & Scruggs*

**Words and Music by A.P. CARTER,
LESTER FLATT and EARL SCRUGGS**

(C tuning)
Key of C

Intro

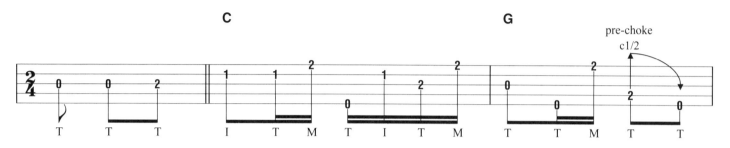

Verse

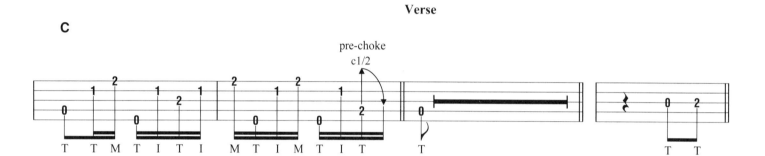

1st break

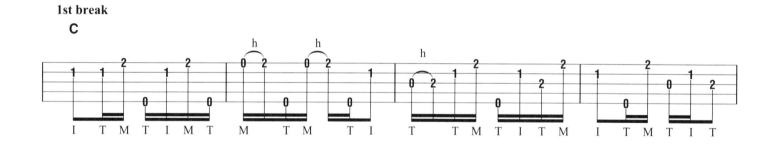

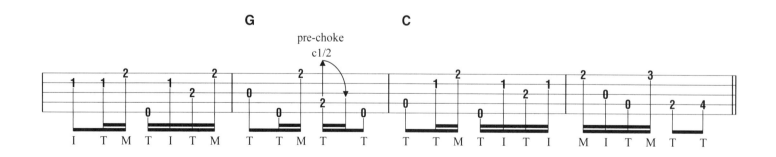

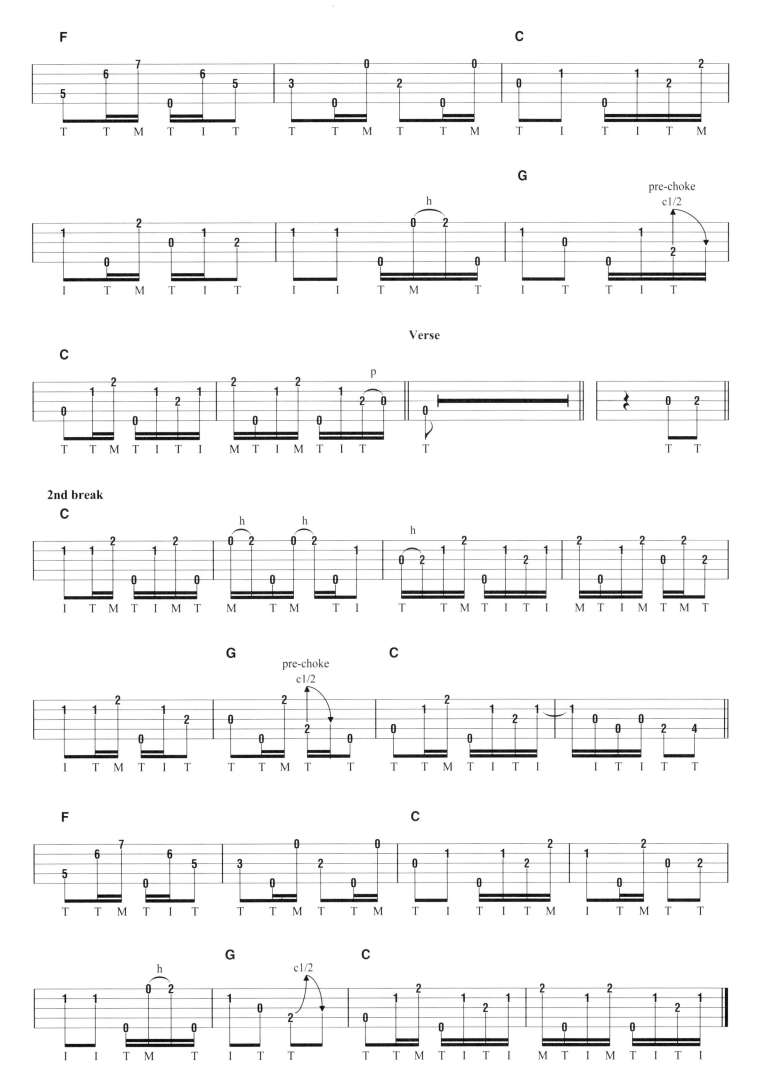

I SAW THE LIGHT

Sound source—*The Essential Earl Scruggs*

Words and Music by HANK WILLIAMS

(G tuning)
Key of A: Capo at 2nd fret and hook 5th string

Intro

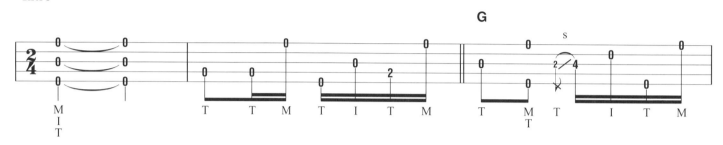

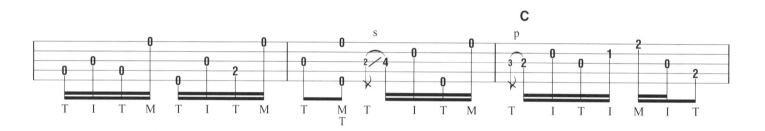

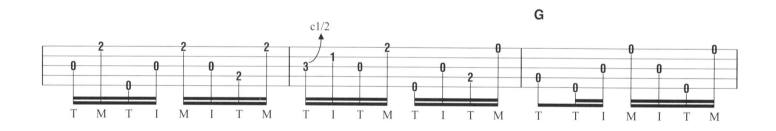

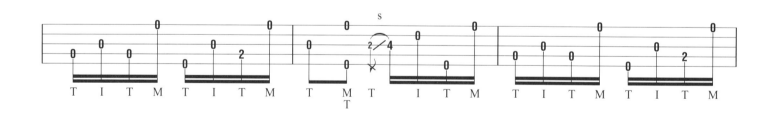

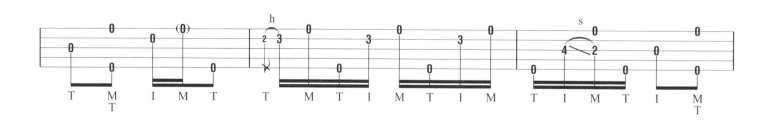

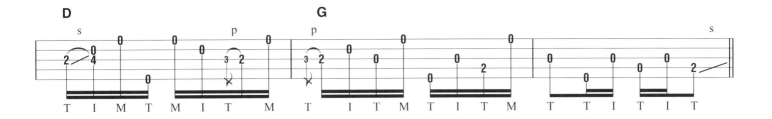

Break

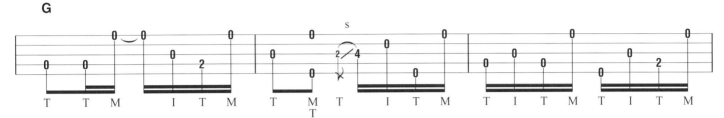

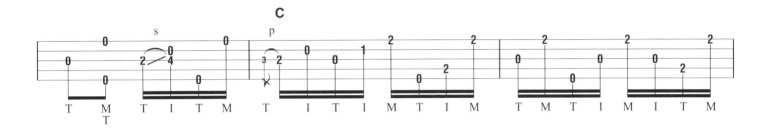

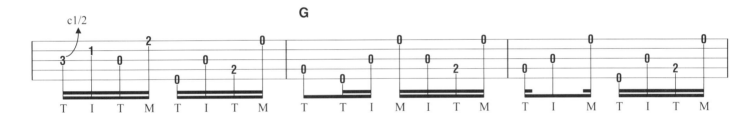

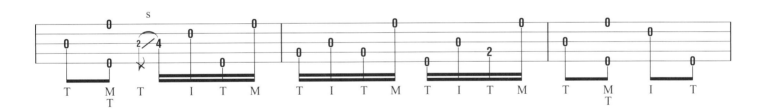

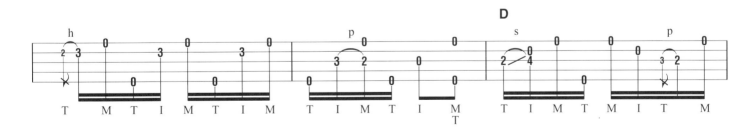

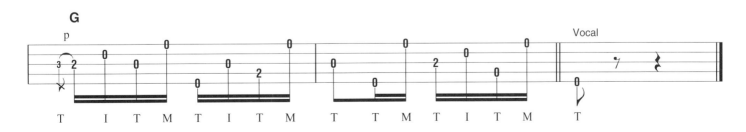

I WANT TO BE LOVED (BUT ONLY BY YOU)

Sound source—*Best of the Flatt & Scruggs TV Show, Vol. 7*

Words and Music by JOHN BAILES and WALTER BAILES

(G tuning)

Key of A: Capo at 2nd fret and hook the 5th string

Break

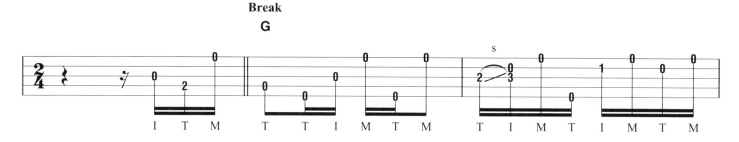

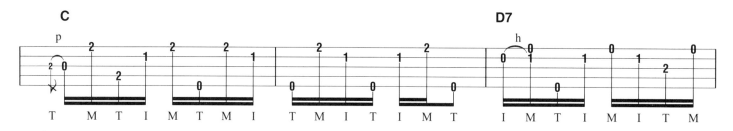

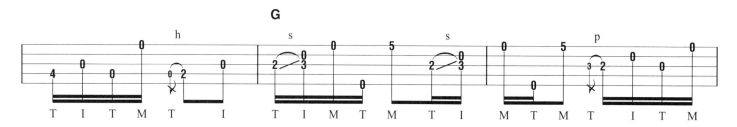

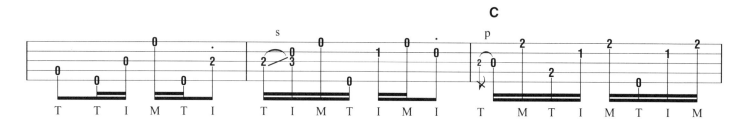

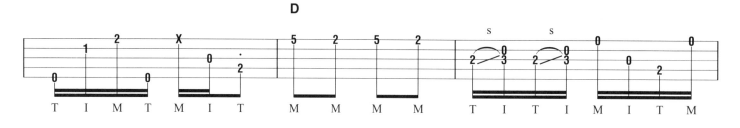

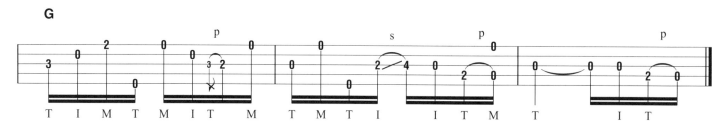

I'LL GO STEPPING TOO

Sound source—*Earl Scruggs: The Ultimate Collection, 1924-2012*

Words and Music by TOM JAMES and JERRY ORGAN

(G tuning)
Key of B♭: Capo at 3rd fret and hook the 5th string
(Recorded in G♯ tuning, capoed at the 2nd fret)

1st, 2nd & 3rd breaks

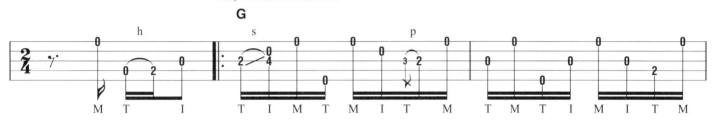

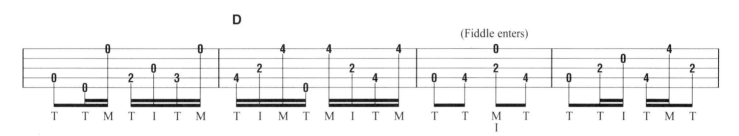

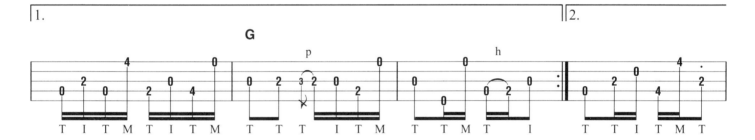

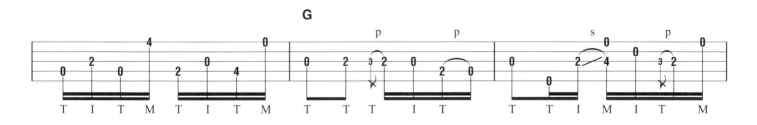

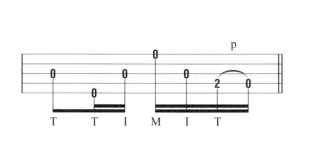

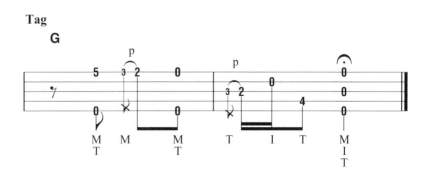

I Wonder Where You Are Tonight

Sound source—*Flatt and Scruggs at Carnegie Hall! The Complete Concert*

Words and Music by JOHNNY BOND

(G tuning)
Key of E: Hook 5th string at the 6th fret
(Earl tuned the 5th string up to G♯)

1st break

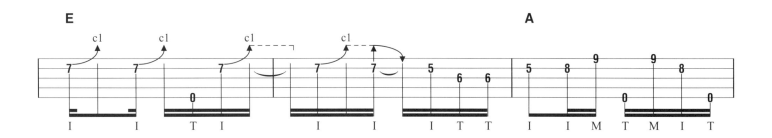

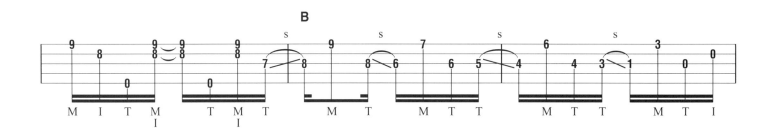

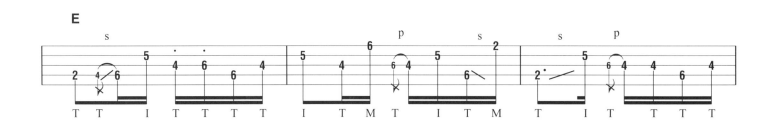

2nd break

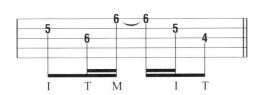

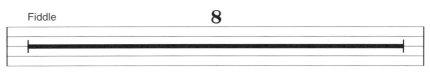

Fiddle

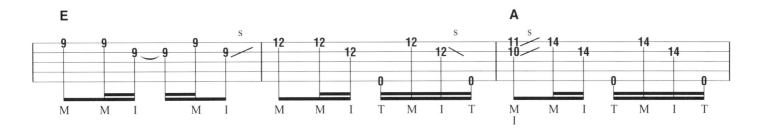

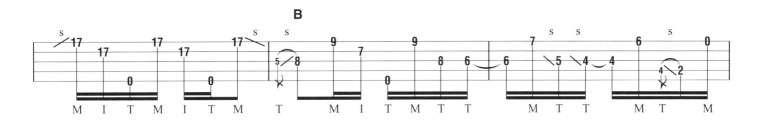

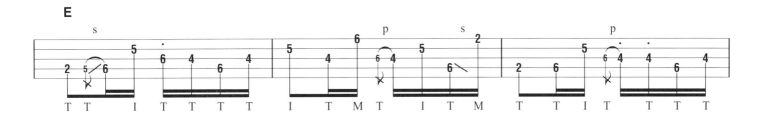

Tag

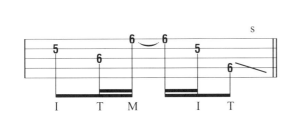

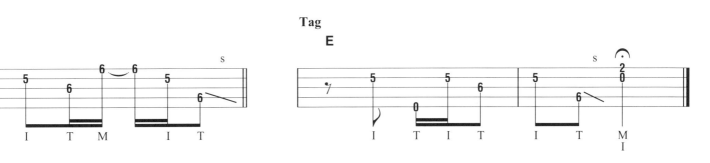

I'D RATHER BE ALONE

Sound source—*Earl Scruggs: The Ultimate Collection, 1924-2012*

**Words and Music by TOM JAMES,
JAMES WEST and TONY LEE**

(G tuning)
Key of F (Recorded in G♯ tuning)

Intro

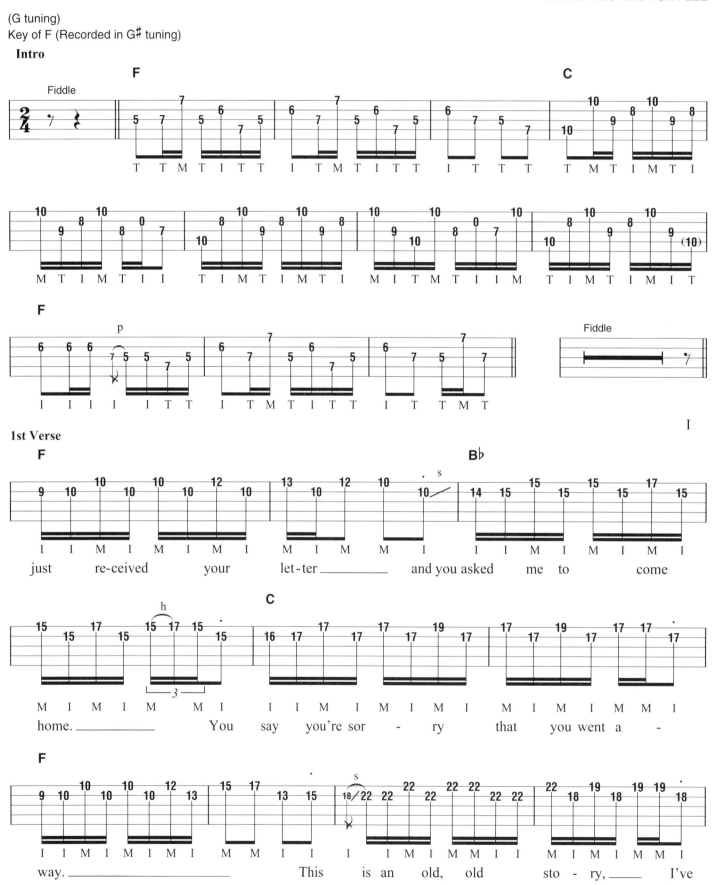

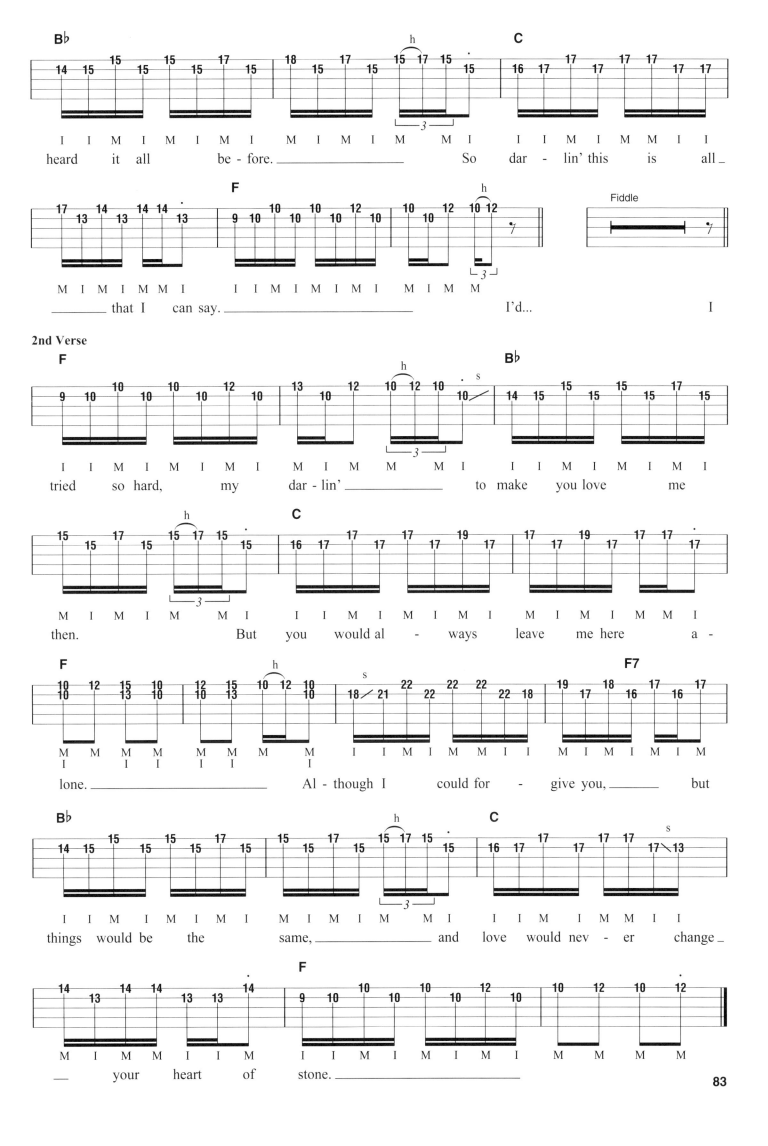

I'LL JUST PRETEND

Sound source—*The Complete Mercury Sessions—Flatt & Scruggs*

Words and Music by JESSE MAE MARTIN

(G tuning)
Key of C (Recorded in G# tuning)

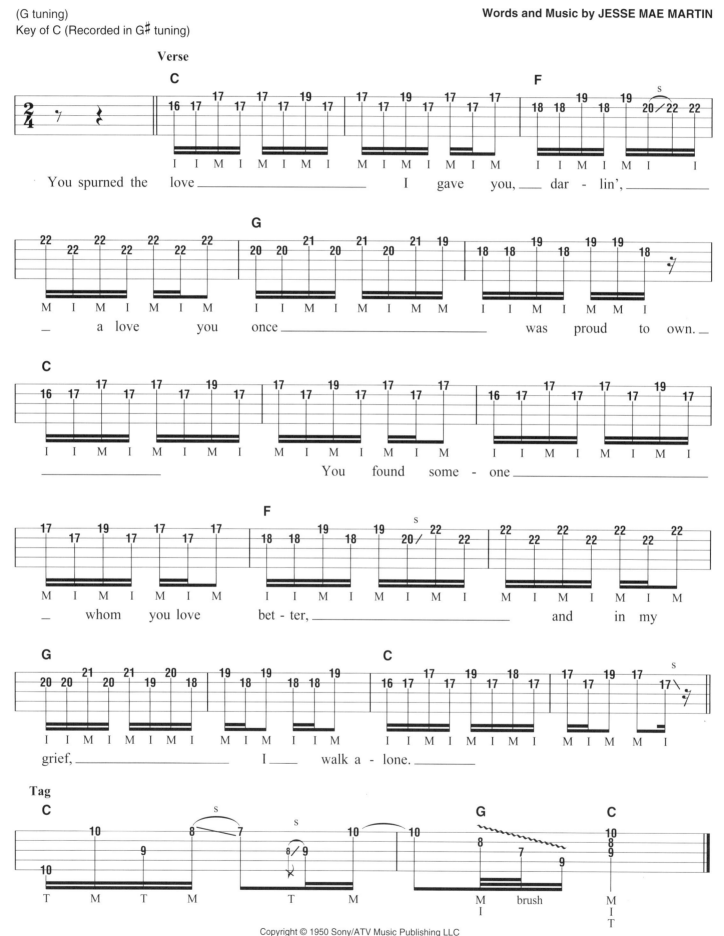

I'LL STAY AROUND

Sound source—*Earl Scruggs: The Ultimate Collection, 1924-2012*

Words and Music by LESTER FLATT

(G tuning)
Key of G (Recorded in G# tuning)

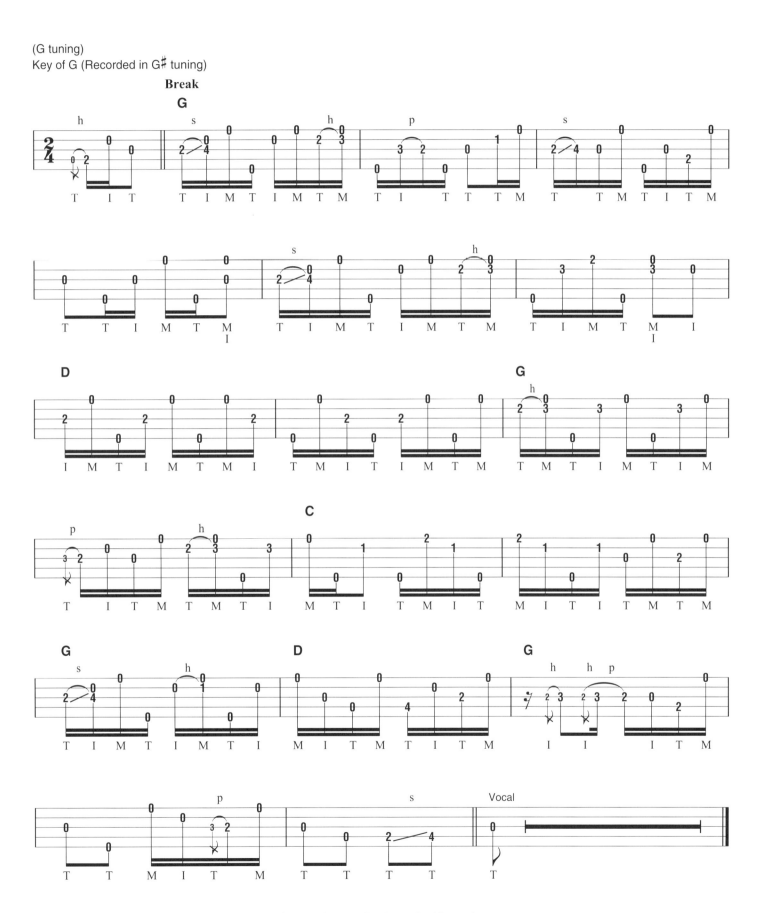

I'LL NEVER SHED ANOTHER TEAR

Sound source—*The Complete Mercury Sessions–Flatt & Scruggs*

Words and Music by LESTER FLATT

(G tuning)
Key of G (Recorded in G# tuning)

Intro

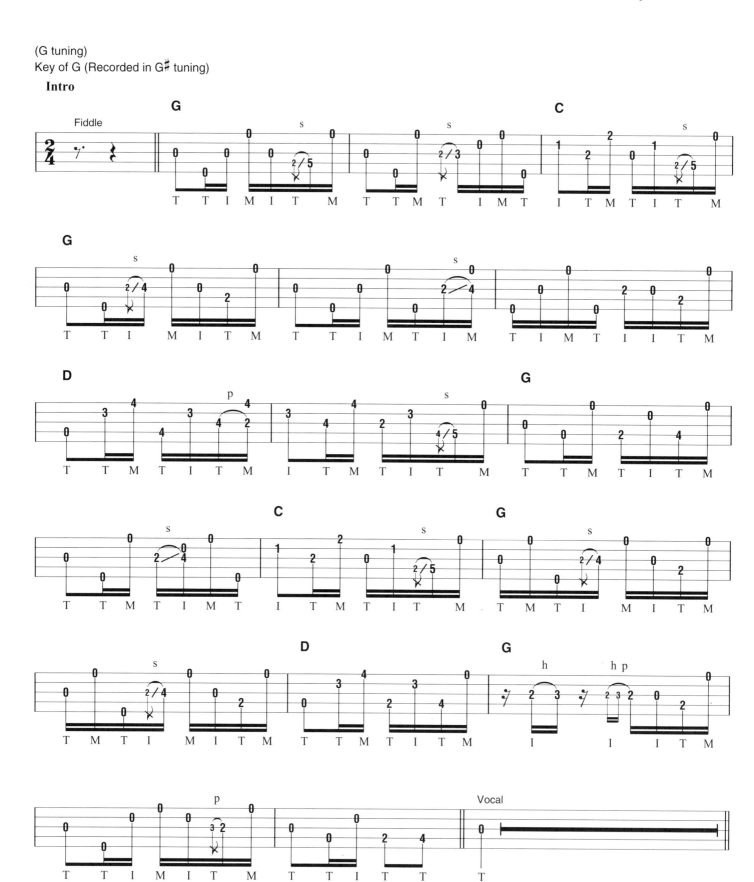

1st break

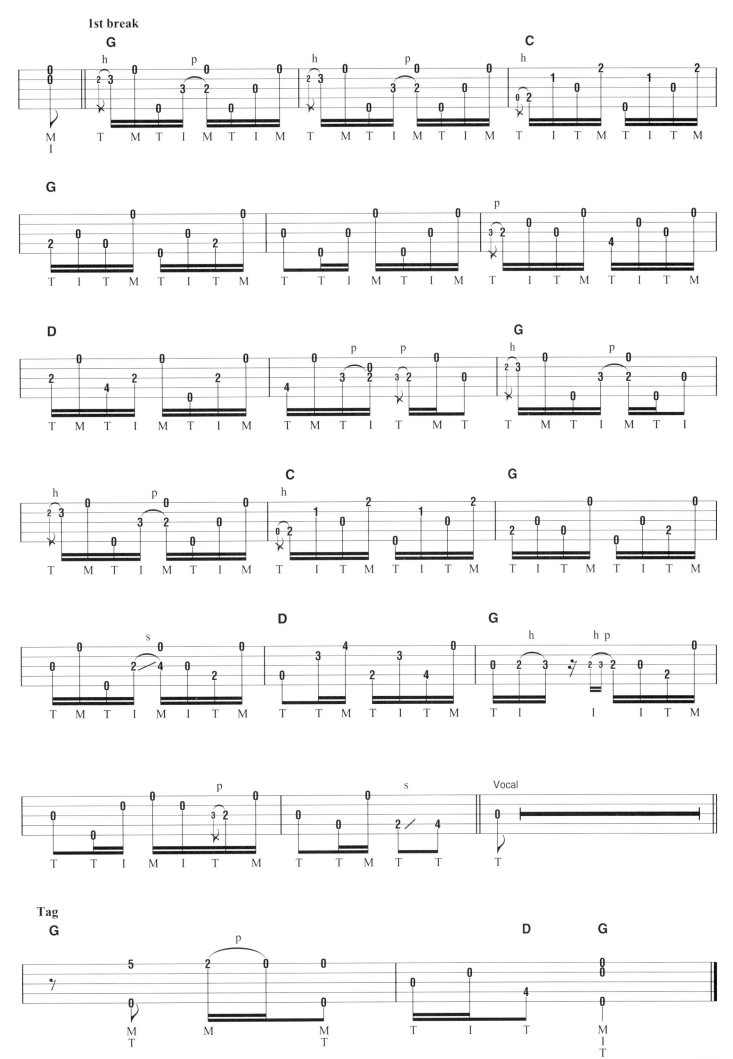

Tag

I'M GOIN' BACK TO OLD KENTUCKY

Sound source—*The Essential Bill Monroe: 1945 - 1949*

Words and Music by BILL MONROE

(G tuning)
Key of A: Capo at 2nd fret and hook the 5th string

Break

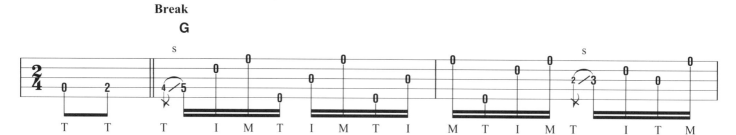

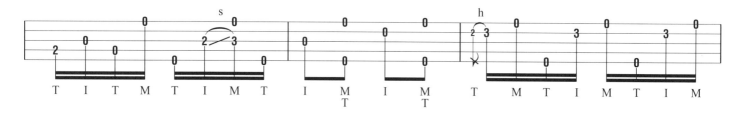

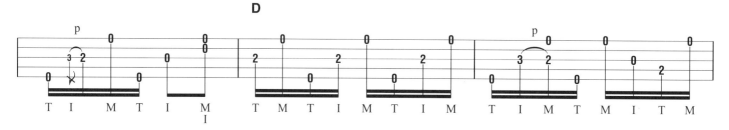

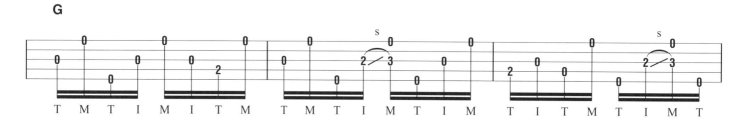

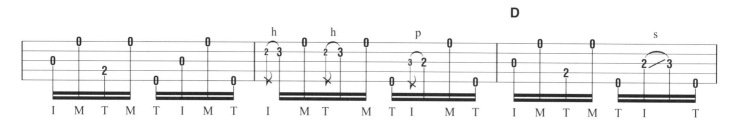

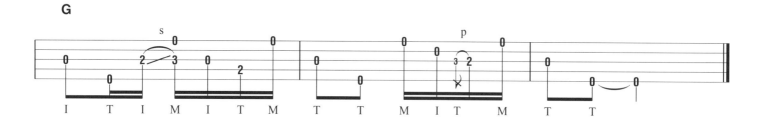

IF I SHOULD WANDER BACK TONIGHT

Sound source—*Earl Scruggs: The Ultimate Collection, 1924-2012*

**Words and Music by LESTER FLATT
and EARL SCRUGGS**

(G tuning)
Key of G (Recorded in G♯ tuning)

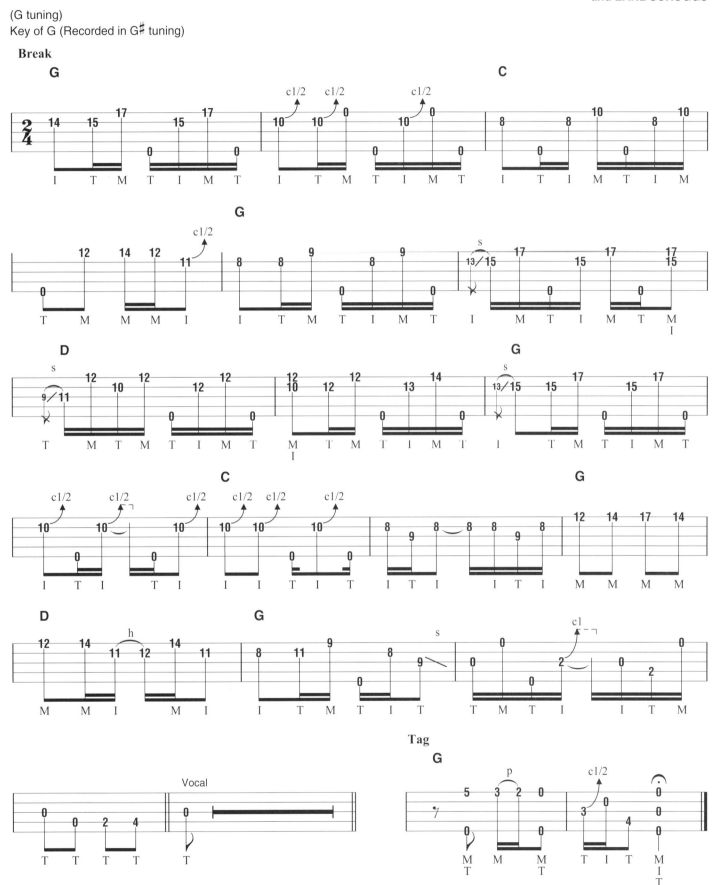

I'M HEAD OVER HEELS IN LOVE

Sound source—*The Essential Flatt & Scruggs–'Tis Sweet to Be Remembered*

Words and Music by LESTER FLATT

(G tuning)
Key of G

Intro & 1st break

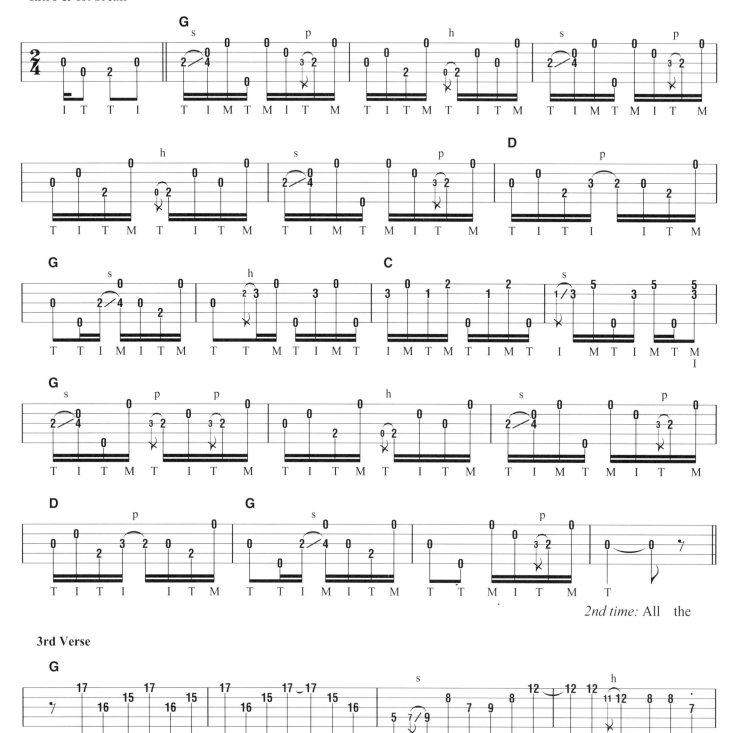

2nd time: All the

3rd Verse

nights   are long   and   drear - y.   All   I   do ___   is   sit   and   wor   - ry   I   just

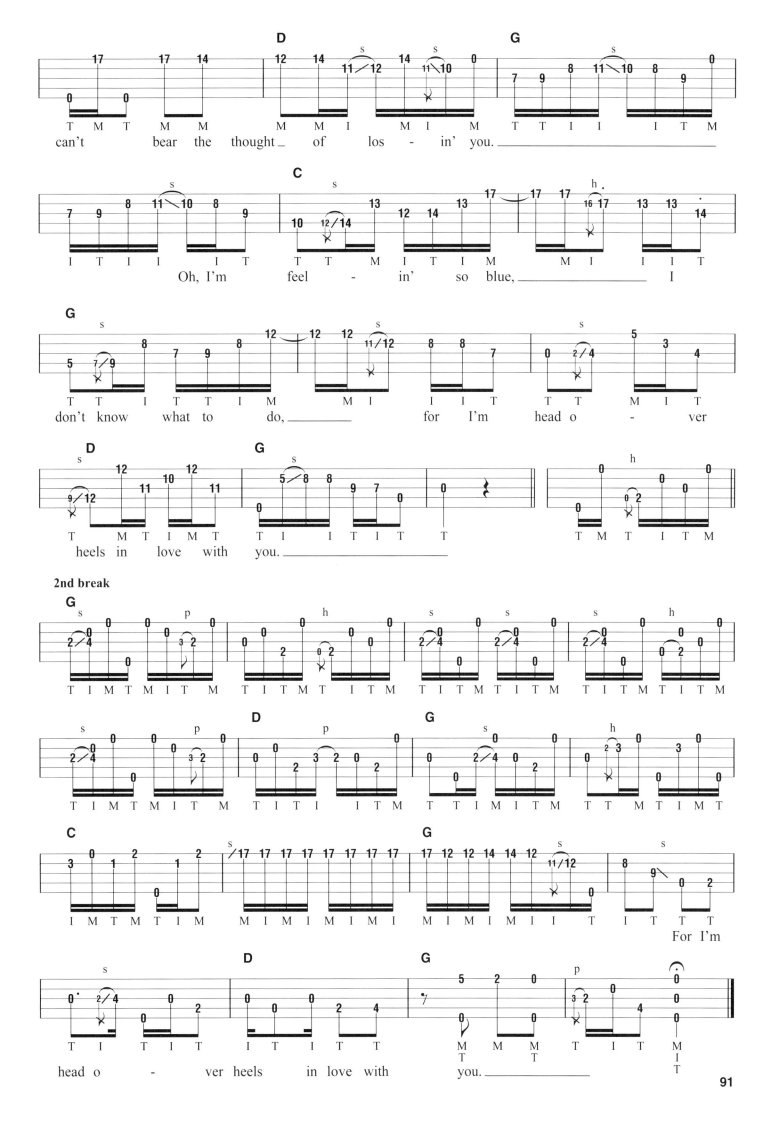

2nd break

JINGLE BELLS

Sound source—*A Very Special Acoustic Christmas–Assorted Artists*

Words and Music by J. PIERPONT

(G tuning)
Key of G

1st break

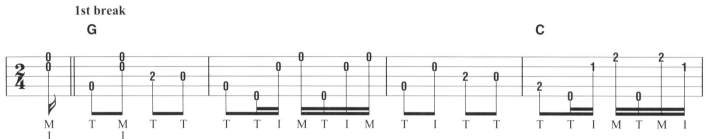

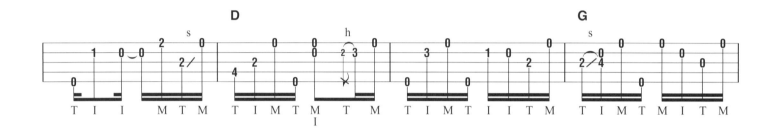

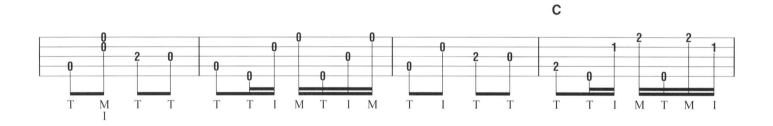

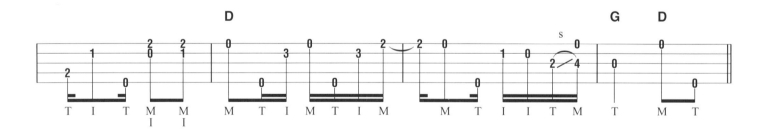

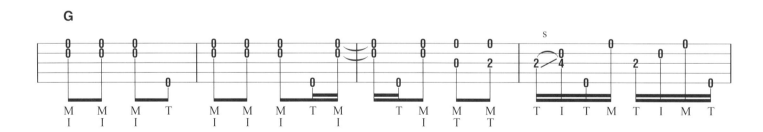

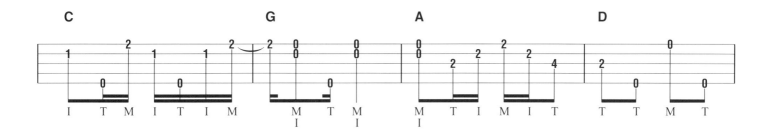

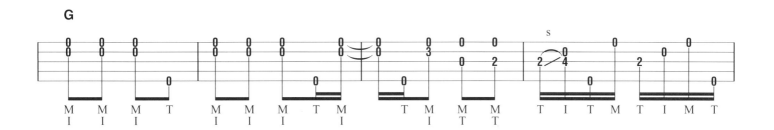

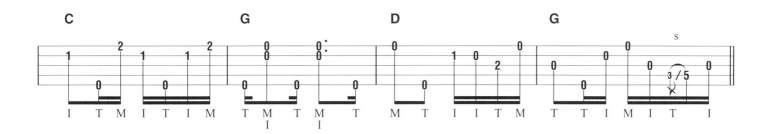

2nd break

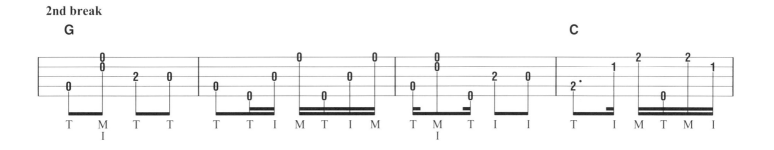

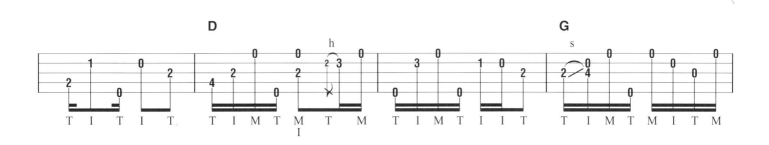

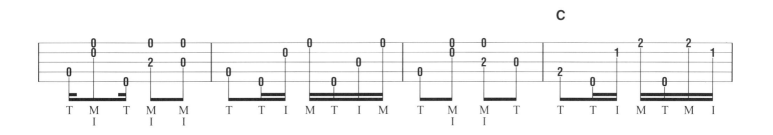

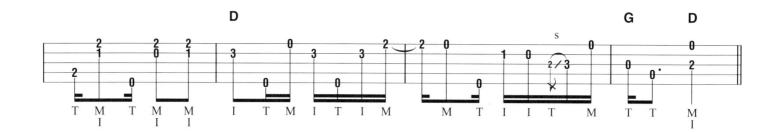

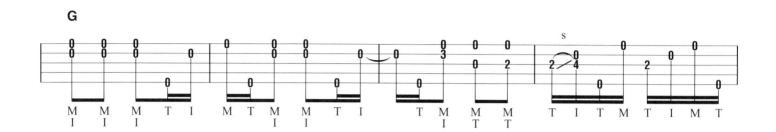

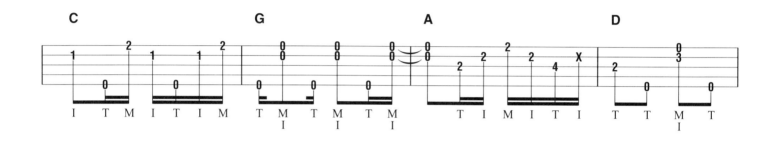

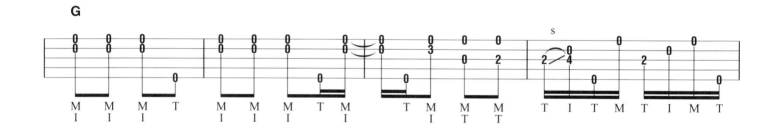

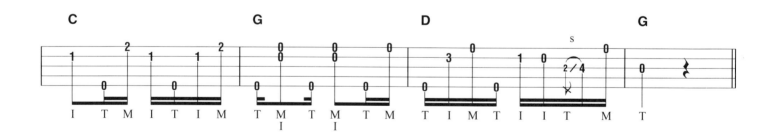

Tag

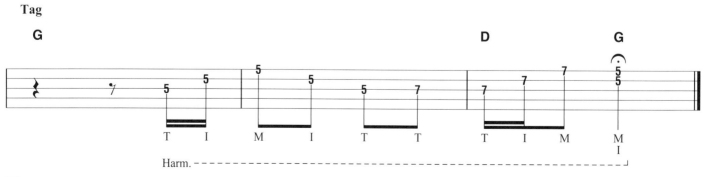

Harm. -

94

IT'S MIGHTY DARK TO TRAVEL

Sound source—*The Essential Earl Scruggs*

Words and Music by BILL MONROE

(G tuning)
Key of G

Break

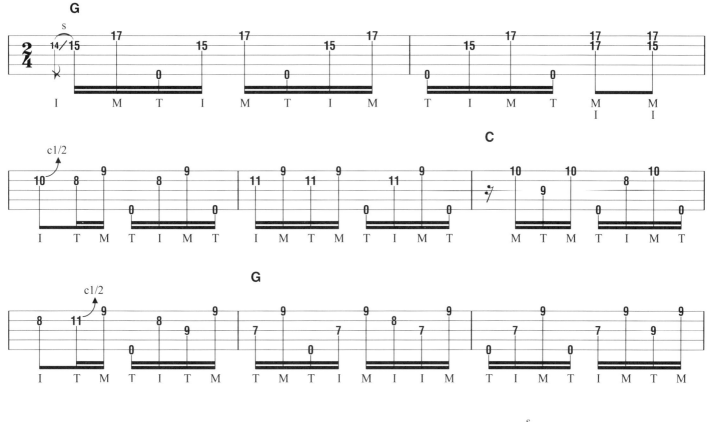

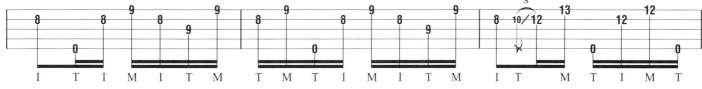

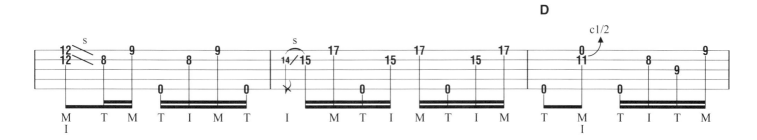

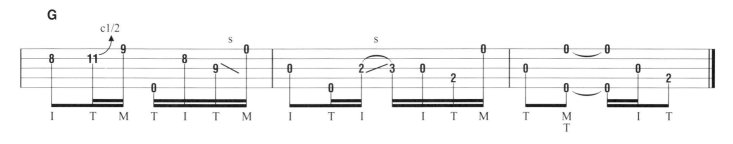

JAZZING

Sound source—*Strictly Instrumental–Flatt & Scruggs with Doc Watson*

Words and Music by LESTER FLATT
and EARL SCRUGGS

(G tuning)
Key of G

1st break

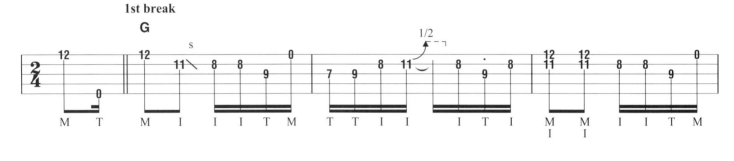

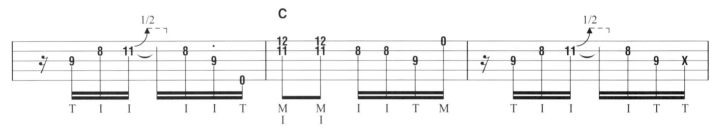

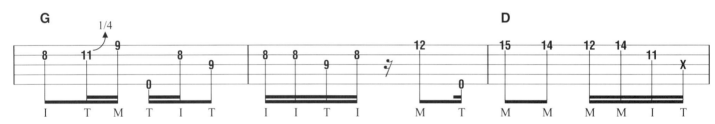

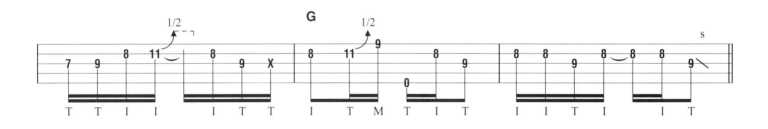

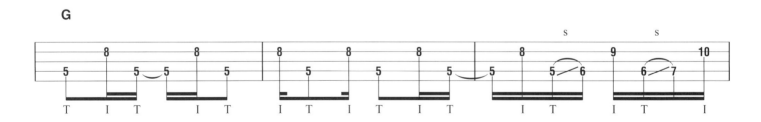

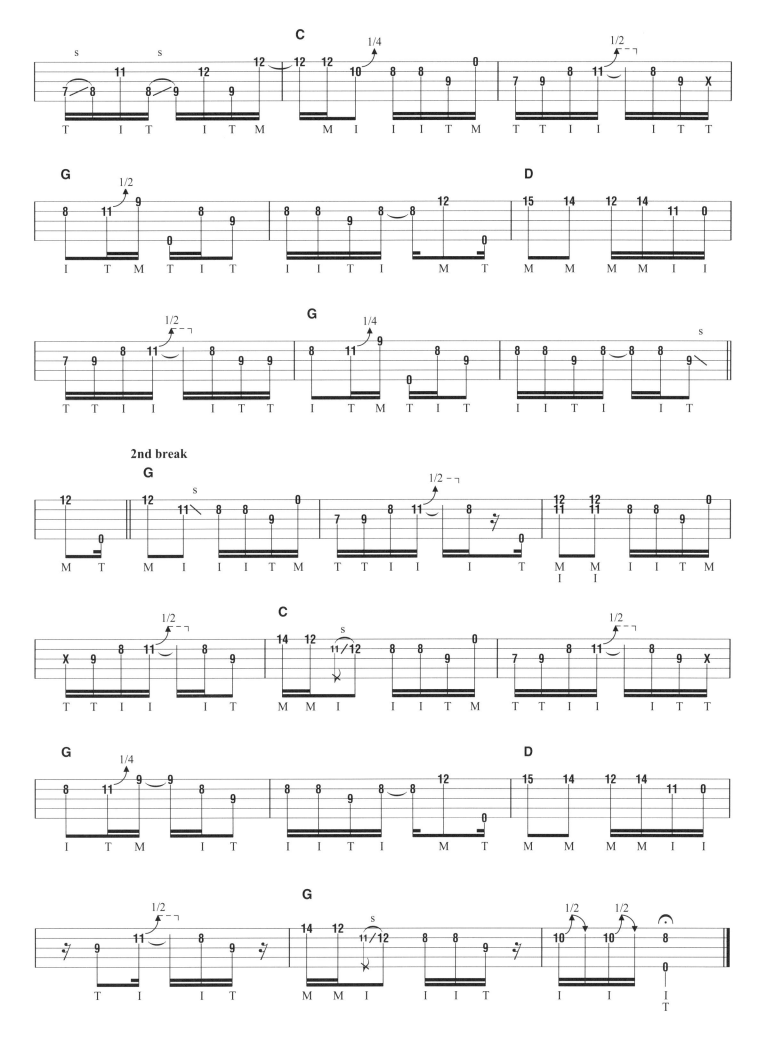

JOHN HARDY WAS A DESPERATE LITTLE MAN

Sound source—*The Essential Earl Scruggs*

Words and Music by A.P. CARTER

(G tuning)
Key of G

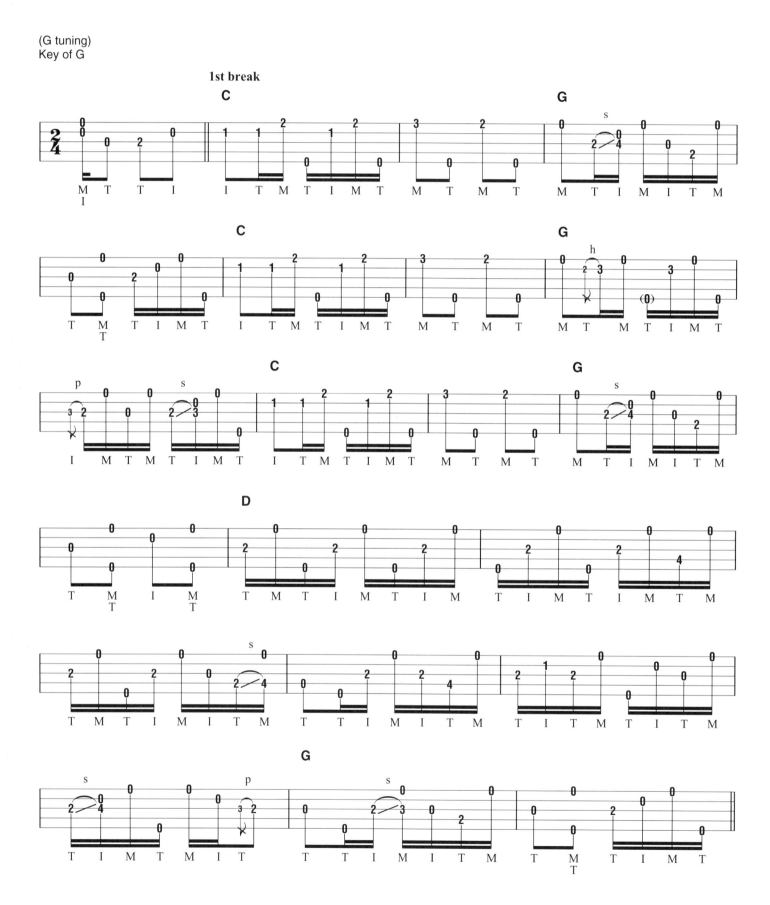

2nd break

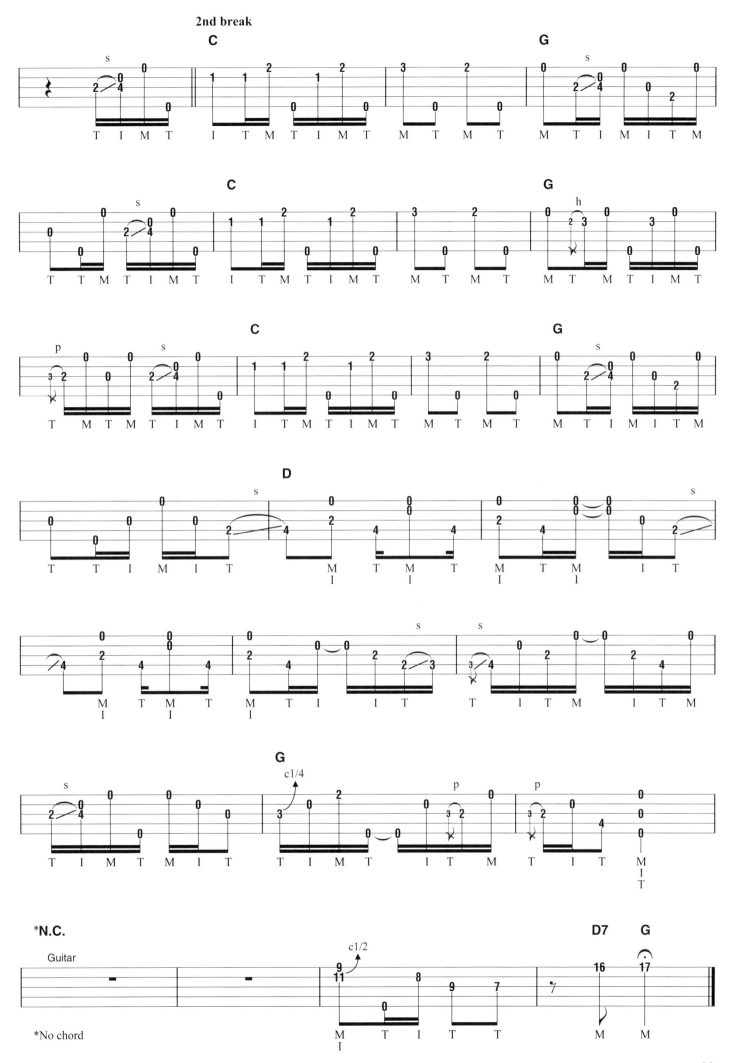

JUST JOSHIN'

Sound source—*Dueling Banjos–Earl Scruggs*

By BURKETT GRAVES and ENGLISH P. TULLOCK

(G tuning)
Key of G

Break

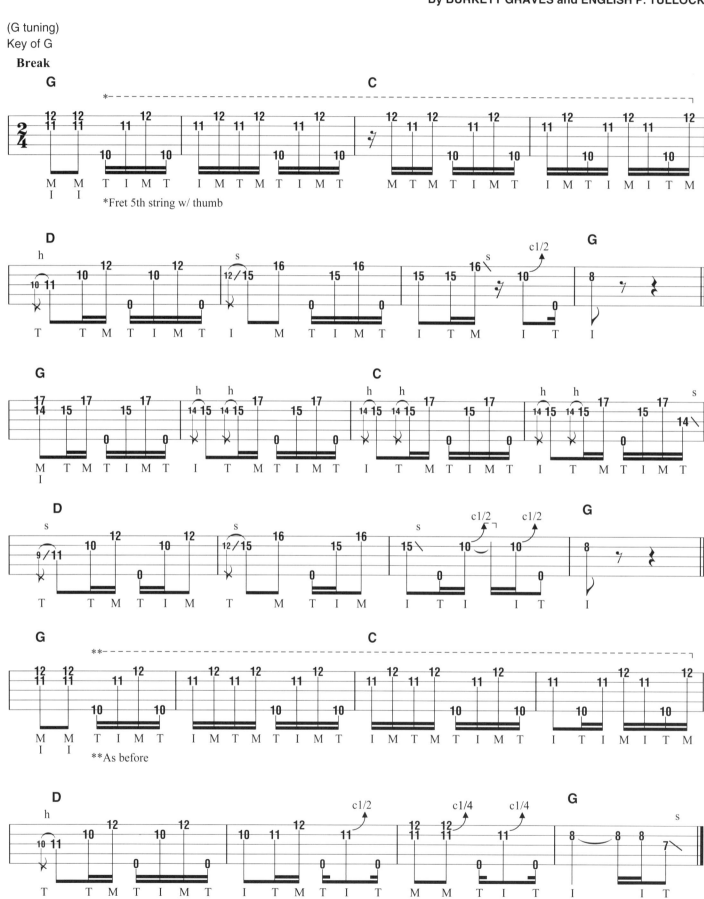

LONESOME ROAD BLUES

Sound source—*A Boy Named Sue–Flatt & Scruggs*

By EARL SCRUGGS

(G tuning)
Key of G

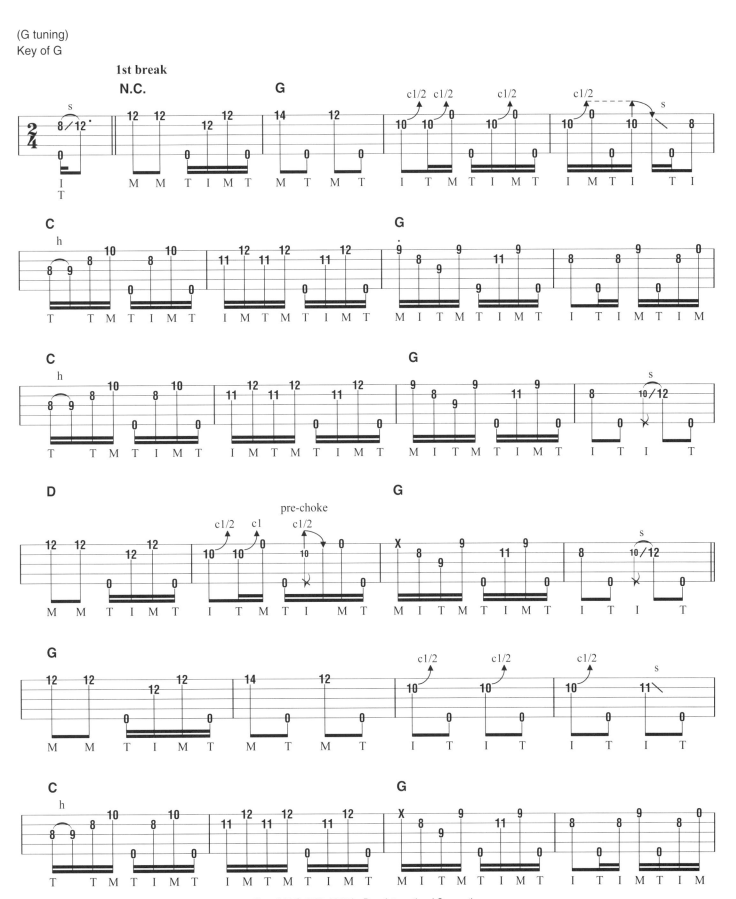

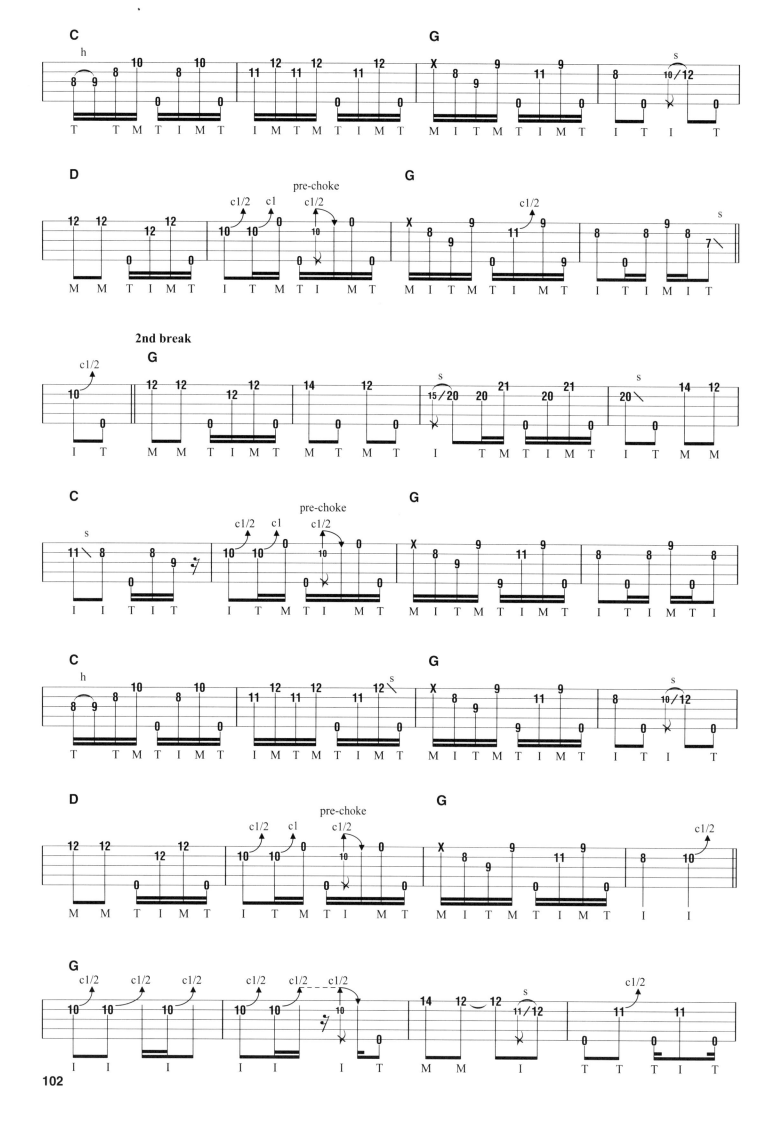

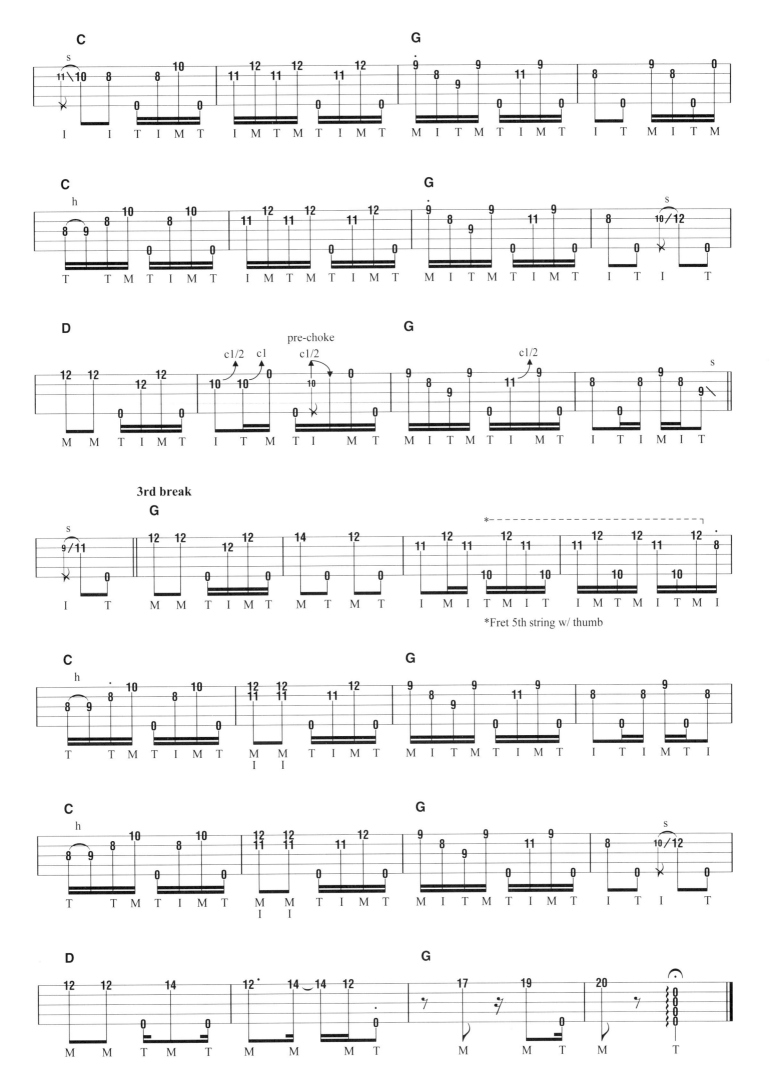

*Fret 5th string w/ thumb

103

LOVE AND WEALTH

Sound source—*Best of the Flatt & Scruggs TV Show, Vol. 7*

Words and Music by CHARLES LOUVIN and IRA LOUVIN

(G tuning)
Key of A: Capo at 2nd fret and hook the 5th string

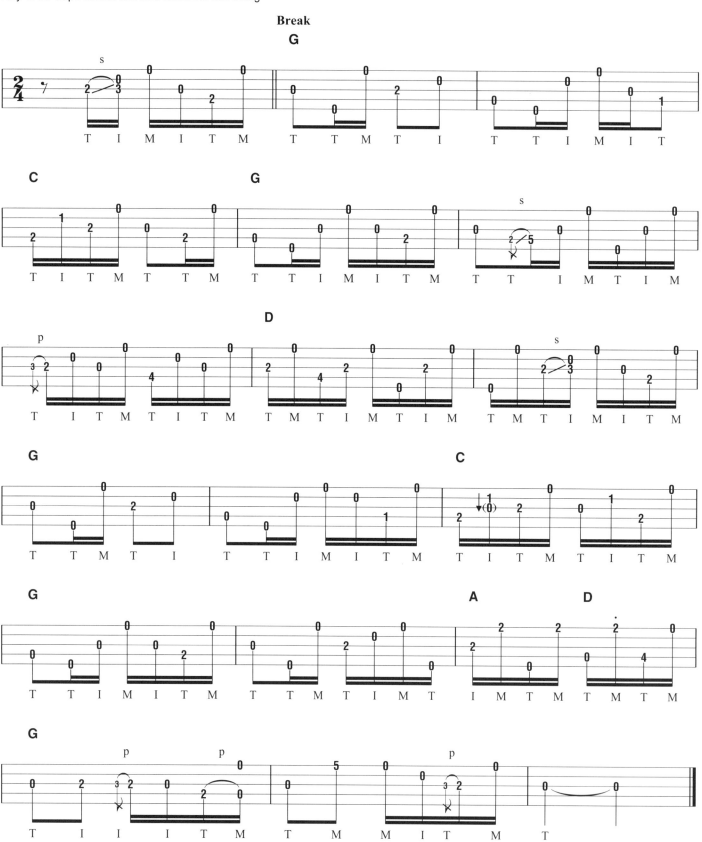

LOVE IS JUST A FOUR LETTER WORD
Sound source—*Nashville's Rock–Earl Scruggs*

Words and Music by BOB DYLAN

(G tuning)
Key of G

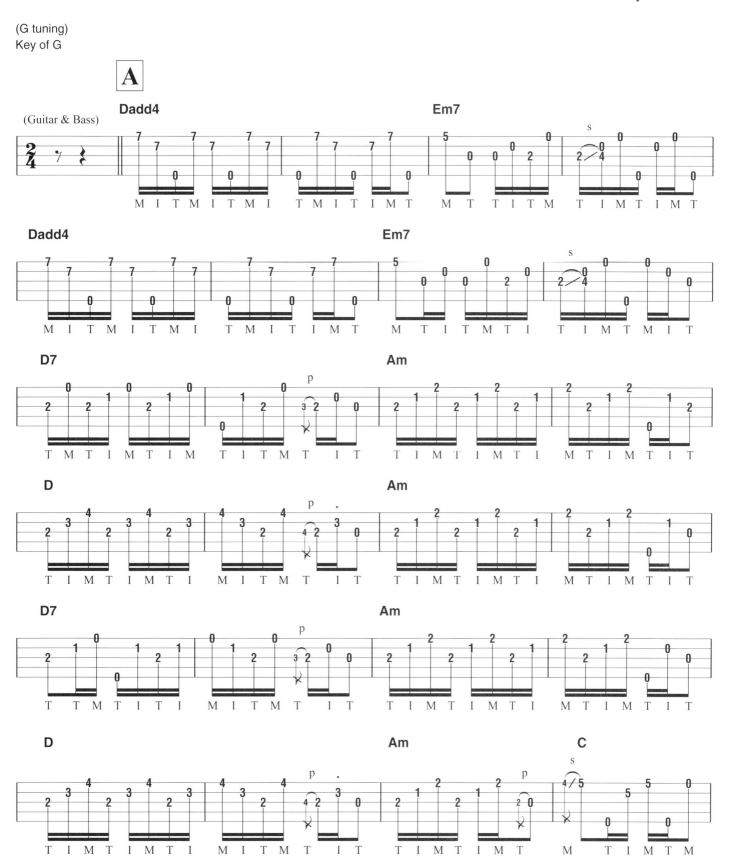

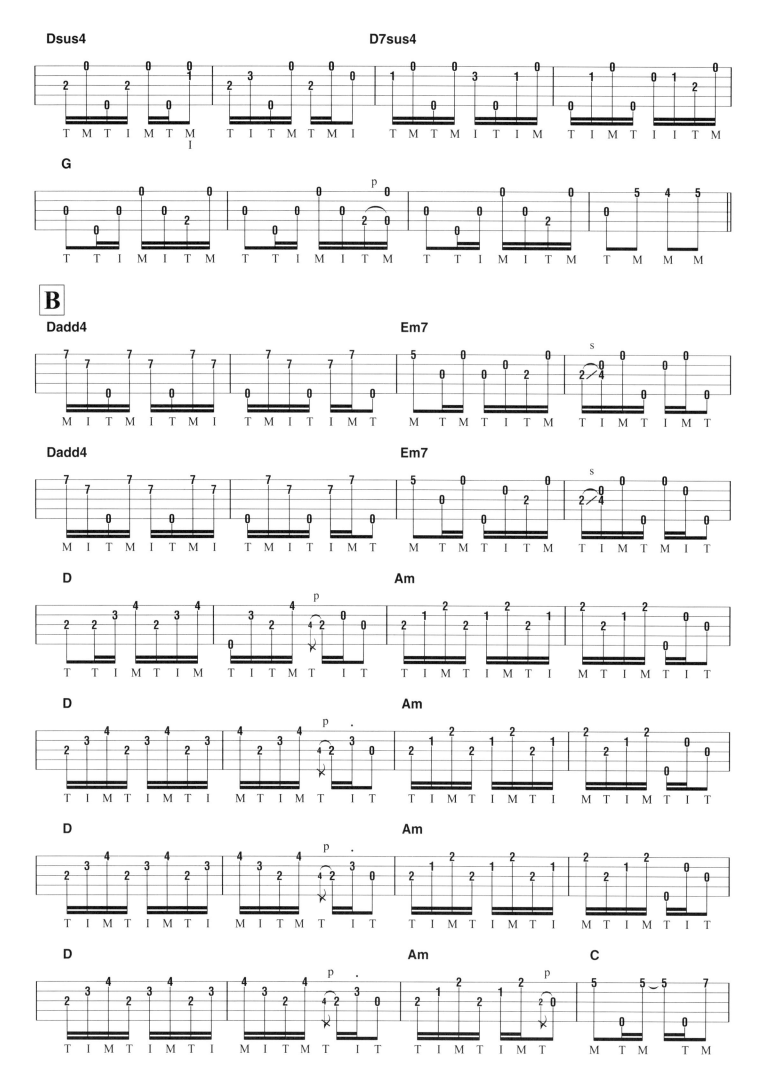

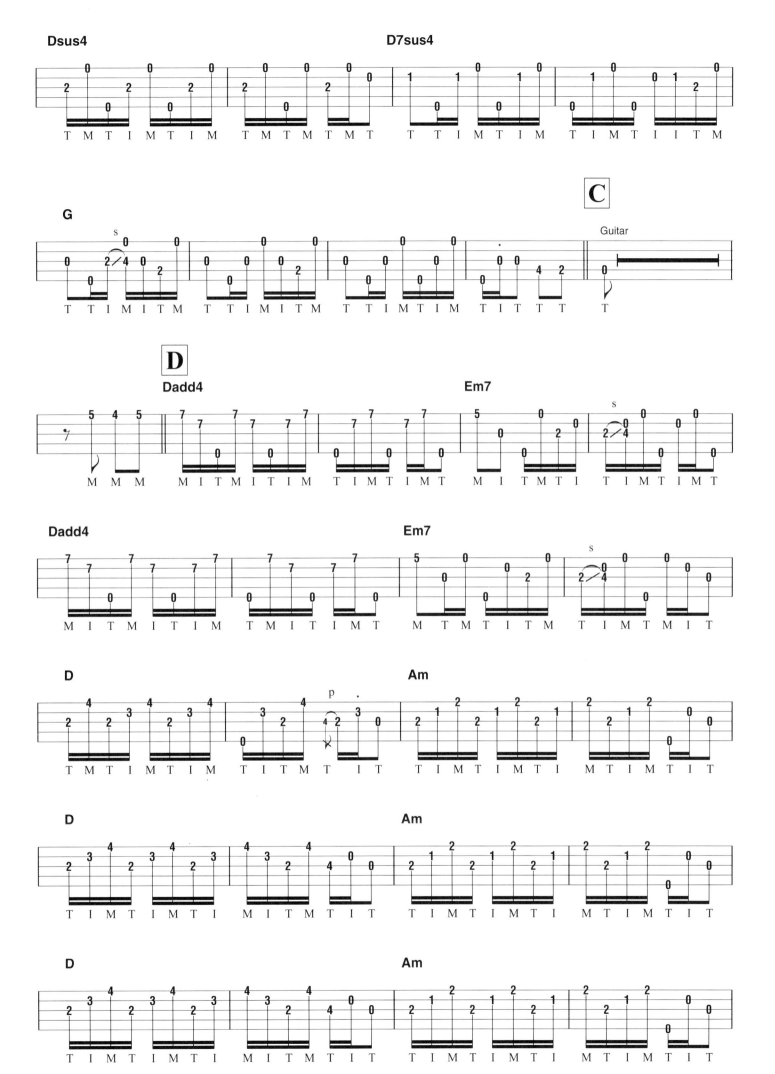

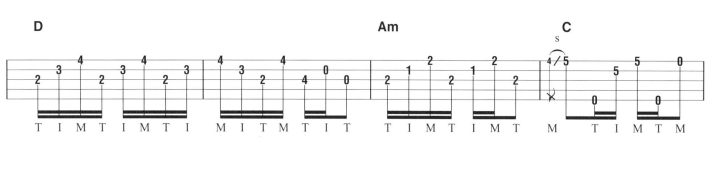

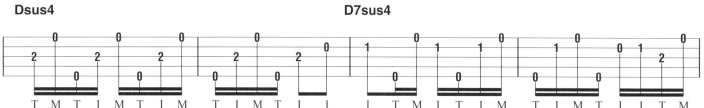

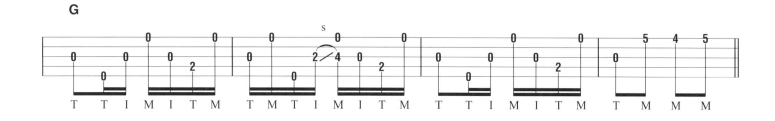

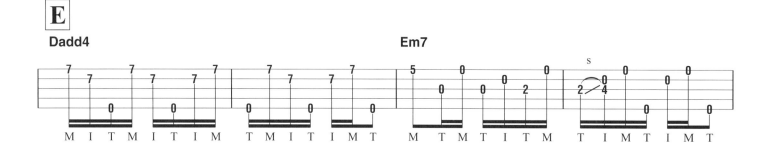

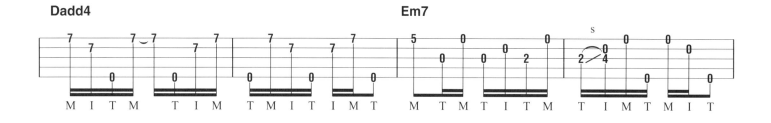

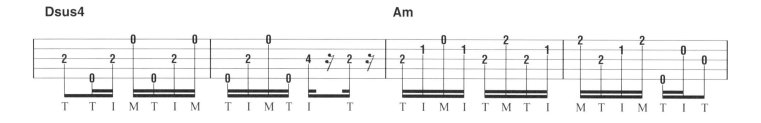

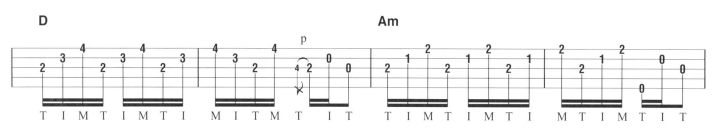

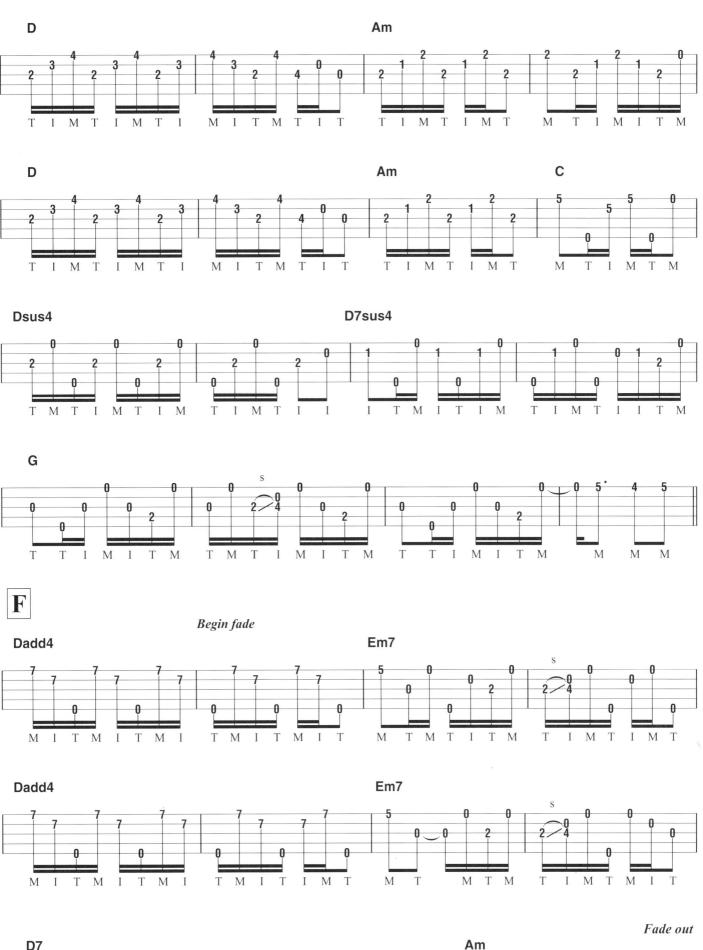

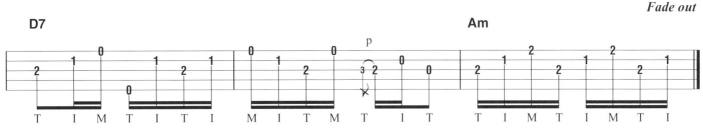

MAMA BLUES

Sound source—*Flatt & Scruggs at Carnegie Hall! The Complete Concert*

Words and Music by EARL SCRUGGS

(D tuning)
Key of D

Intro

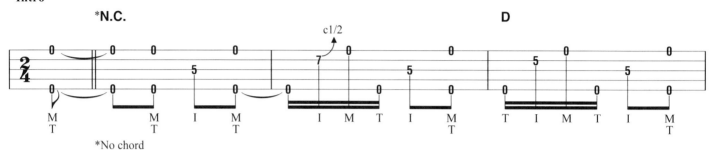

*No chord

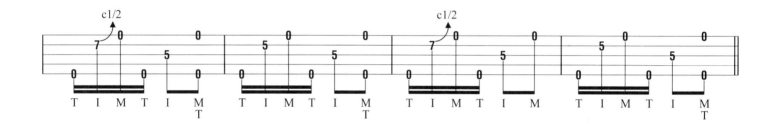

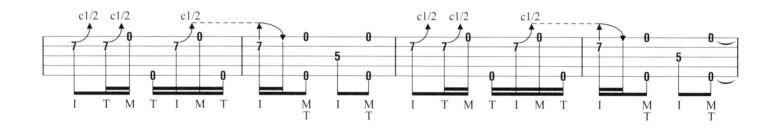

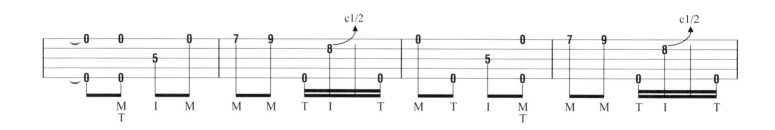

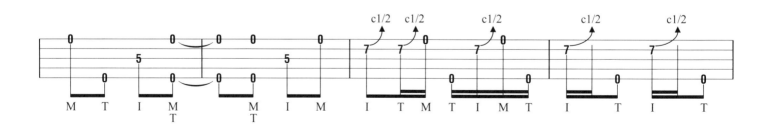

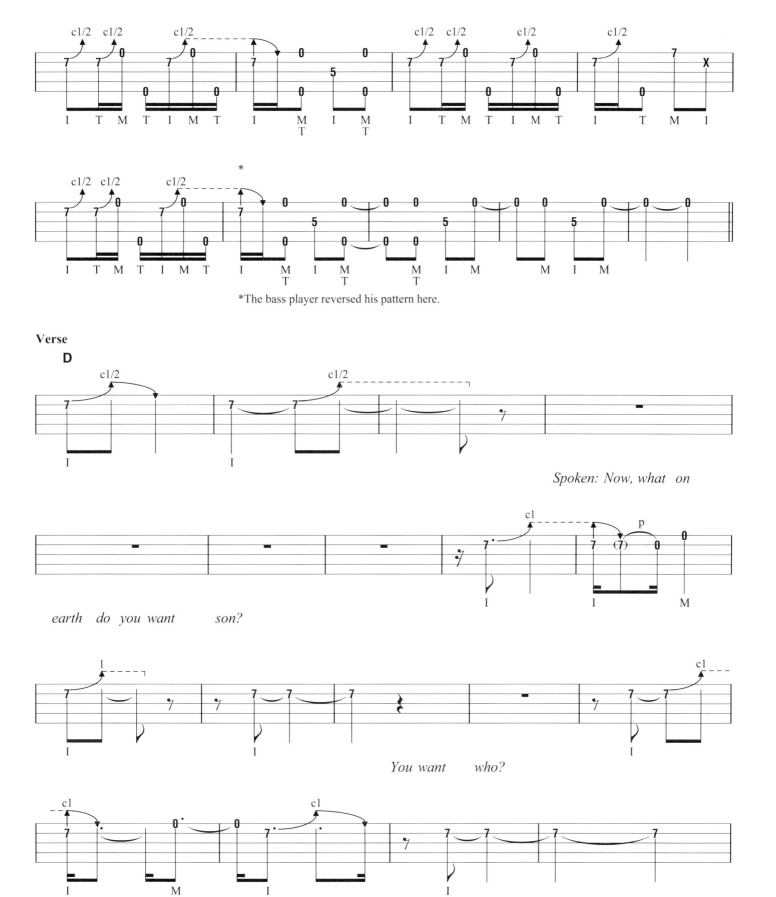

*The bass player reversed his pattern here.

Verse

D

Spoken: Now, what on

earth do you want son?

You want who?

You want your ma -

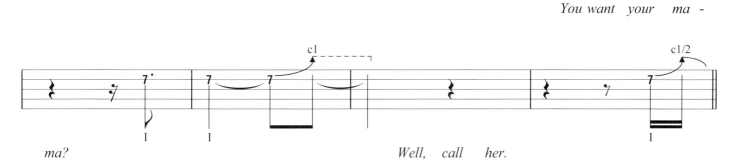

ma?　　　　　　Well, call her.

1st break

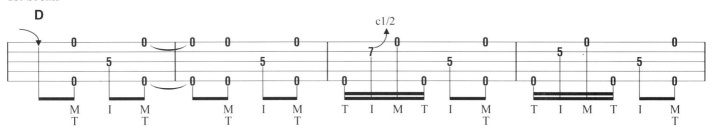

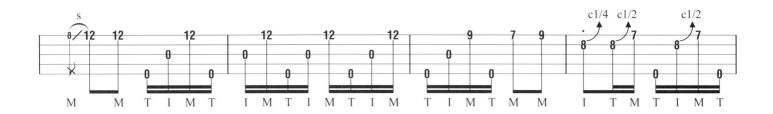

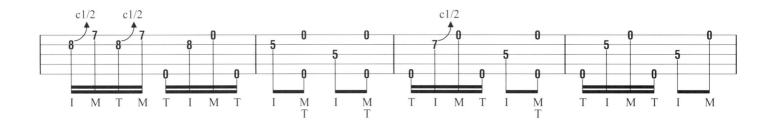

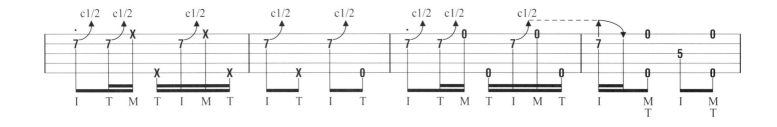

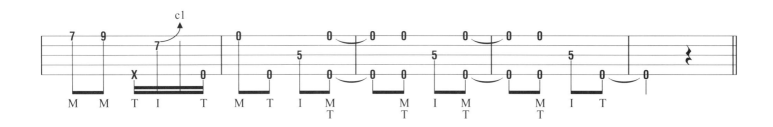

Verse

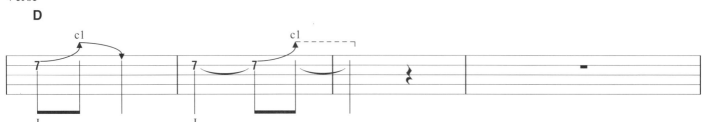

Spoken: Now,   what   do   you   want

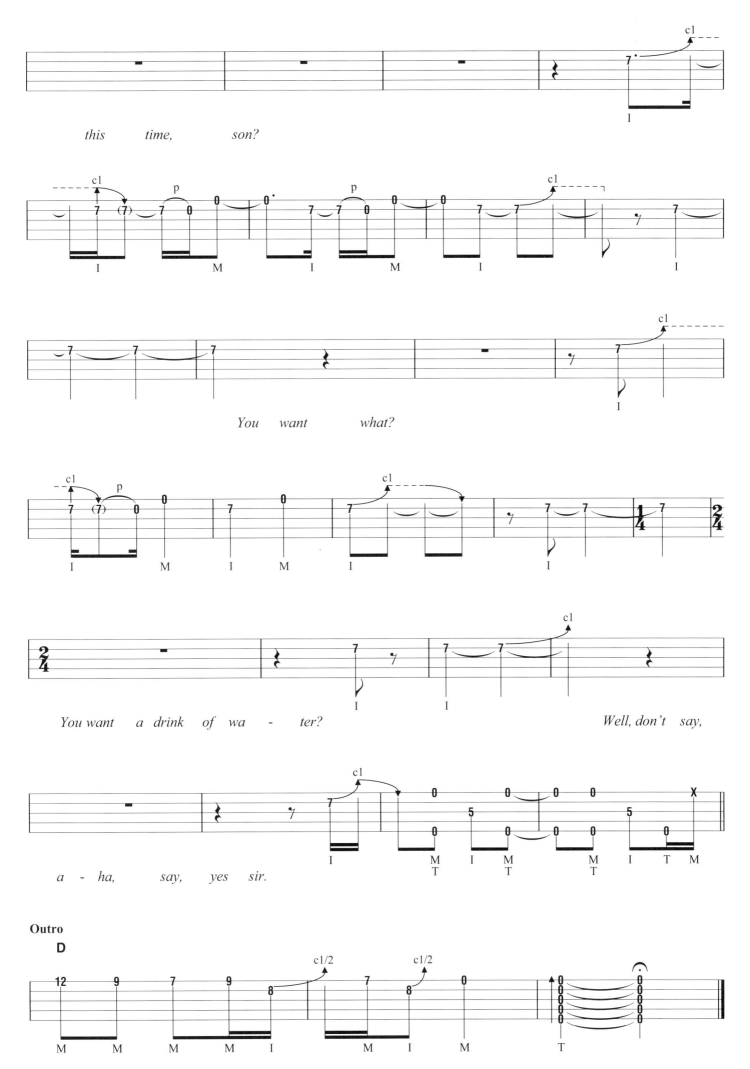

this time,   son?

You   want   what?

You want   a   drink   of   wa - ter?   Well, don't   say,

a - ha,   say,   yes   sir.

Outro

D

MOLLY AND TENBROOKS

Sound source—*The Essential Earl Scruggs*

Words and Music by BILL MONROE

(G tuning)
Key of B: Capo at 4th fret and hook the 5th string

Intro

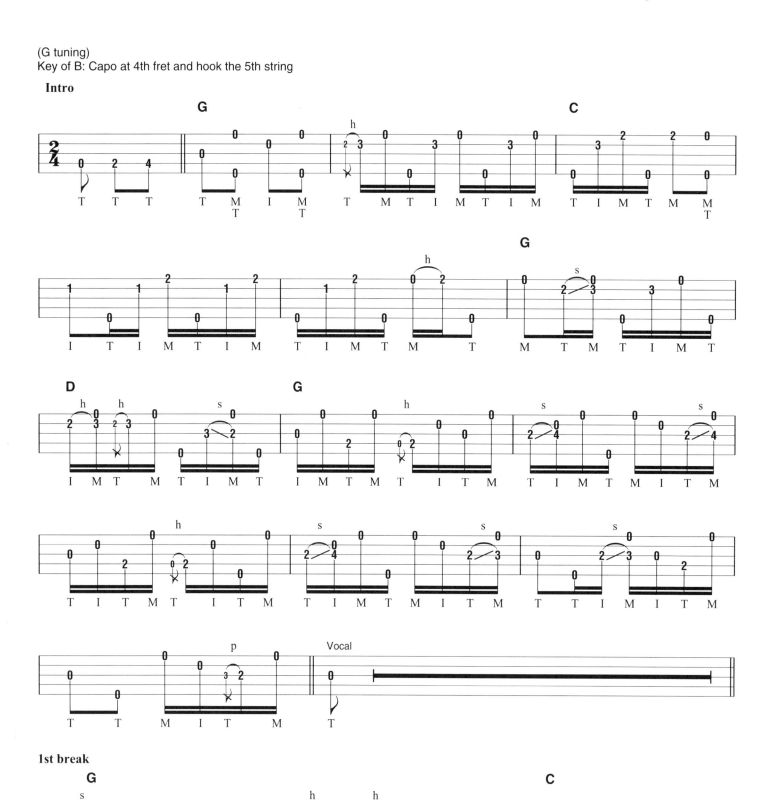

1st break

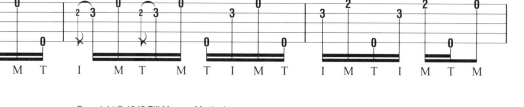

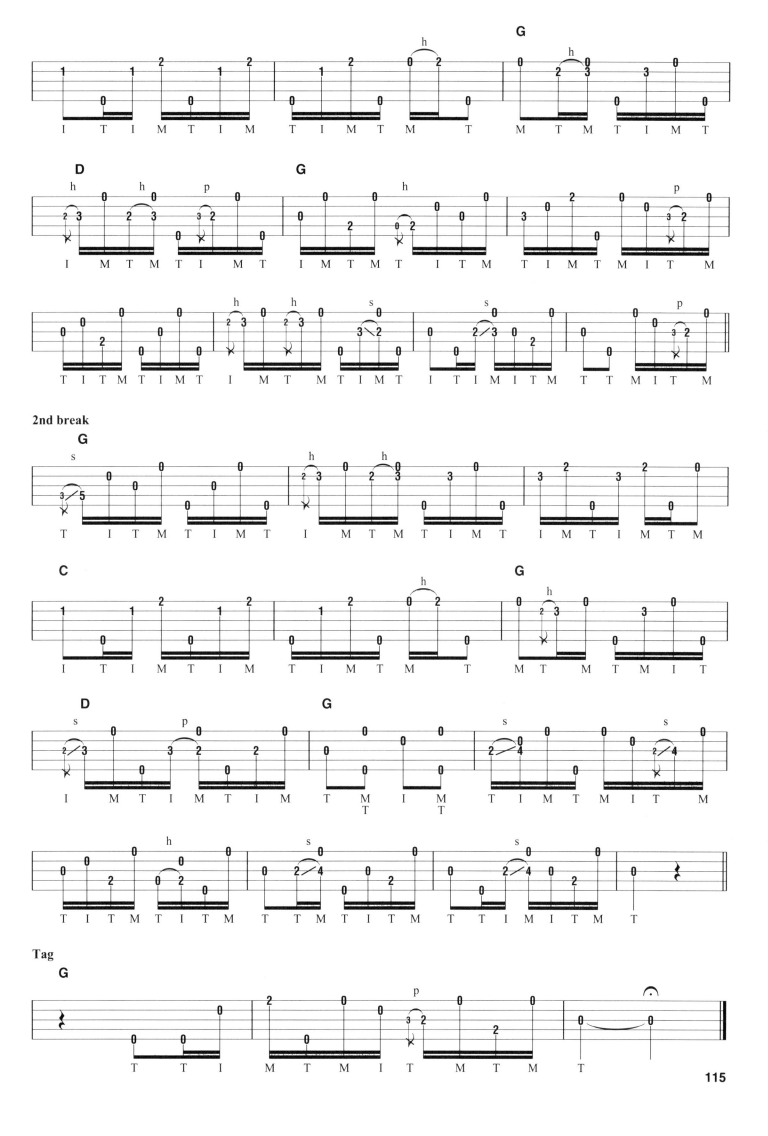

2nd break

Tag

115

MOUNTAIN DEW

Sound source—*Flatt & Scruggs at Carnegie Hall! The Complete Concert*

Words and Music by SCOTT WISEMAN
and BASCOM LUNSFORD

(G tuning)
Key of A: Capo at 2nd fret and hook the 5th string

1st break

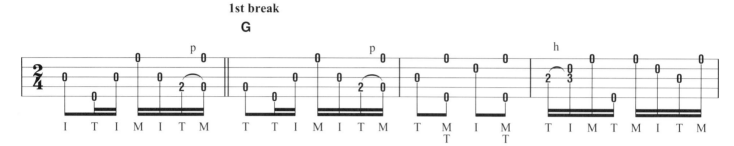

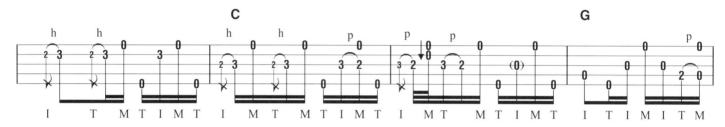

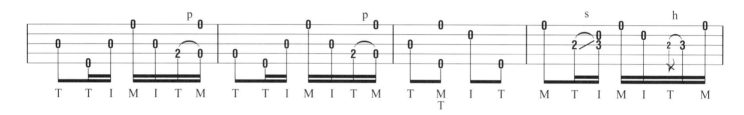

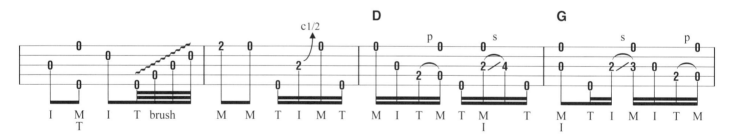

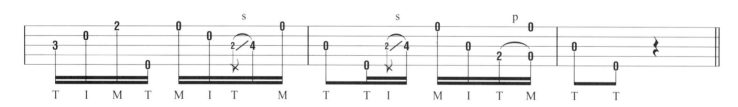

Tag

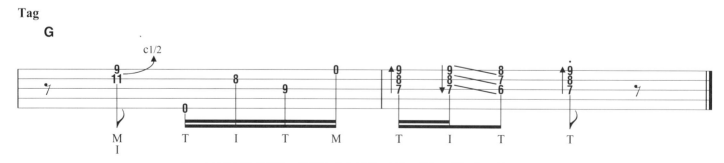

MY HOME'S ACROSS THE BLUE RIDGE MOUNTAINS

Sound source—*Earl Scruggs: His Family and Friends*

Words and Music by THOMAS ASHLEY

(G tuning)
Key of C

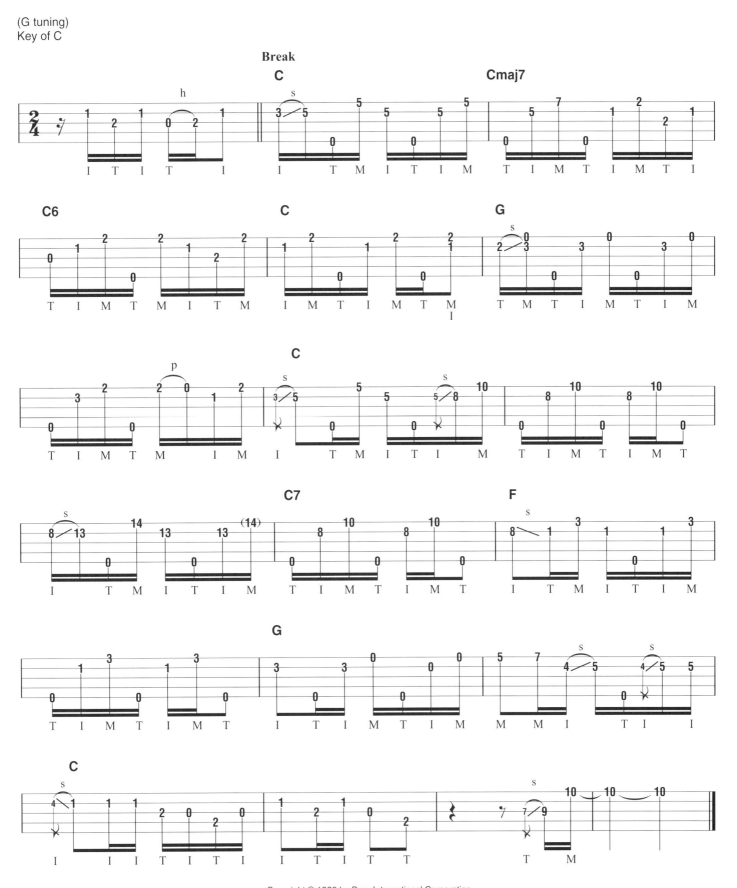

MY CABIN IN CAROLINE

Sound source—*The Complete Mercury Sessions - Flatt & Scruggs*

Words and Music by LESTER FLATT
and EARL SCRUGGS

(G tuning)
Key of G (Recorded in G♯ tuning)

Intro

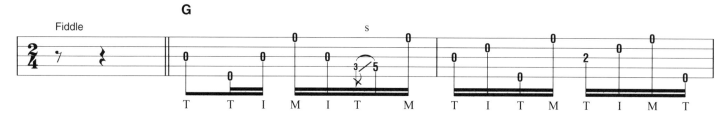

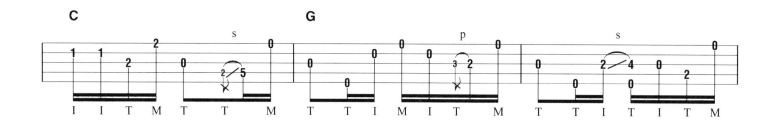

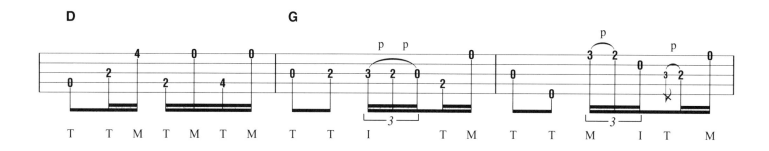

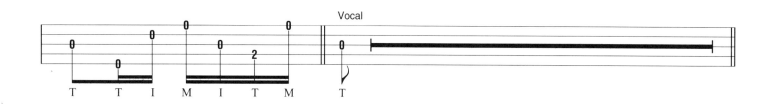

Break

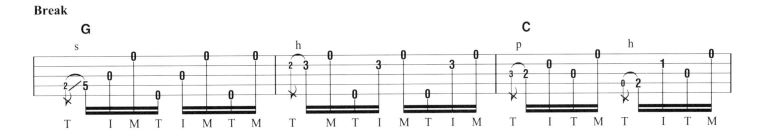

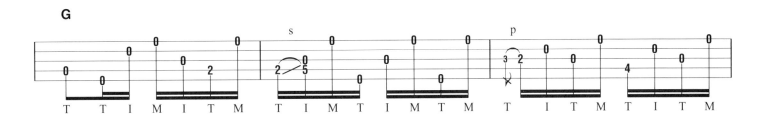

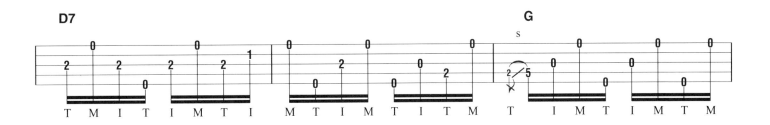

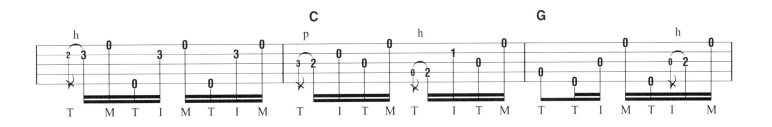

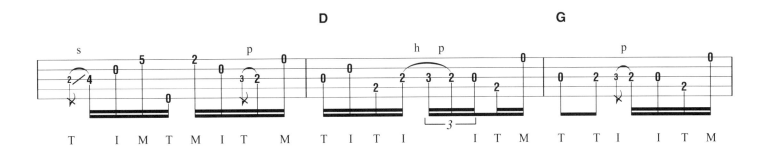

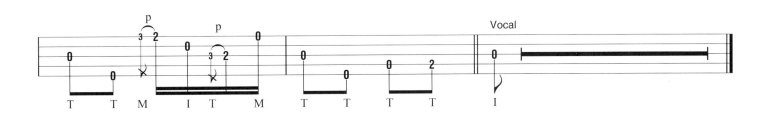

MY LITTLE GIRL IN TENNESSEE

Sound source—*The Complete Mercury Sessions - Flatt & Scruggs*

Words and Music by LESTER FLATT

(G tuning)
Key of G (Recorded in G# tuning)

Intro

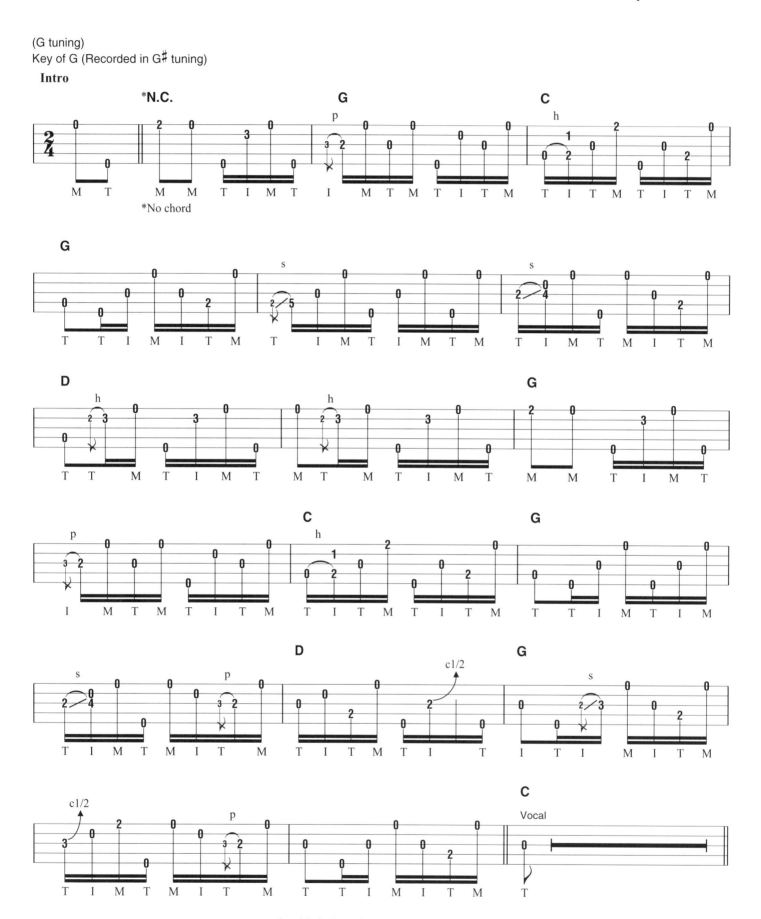

Break

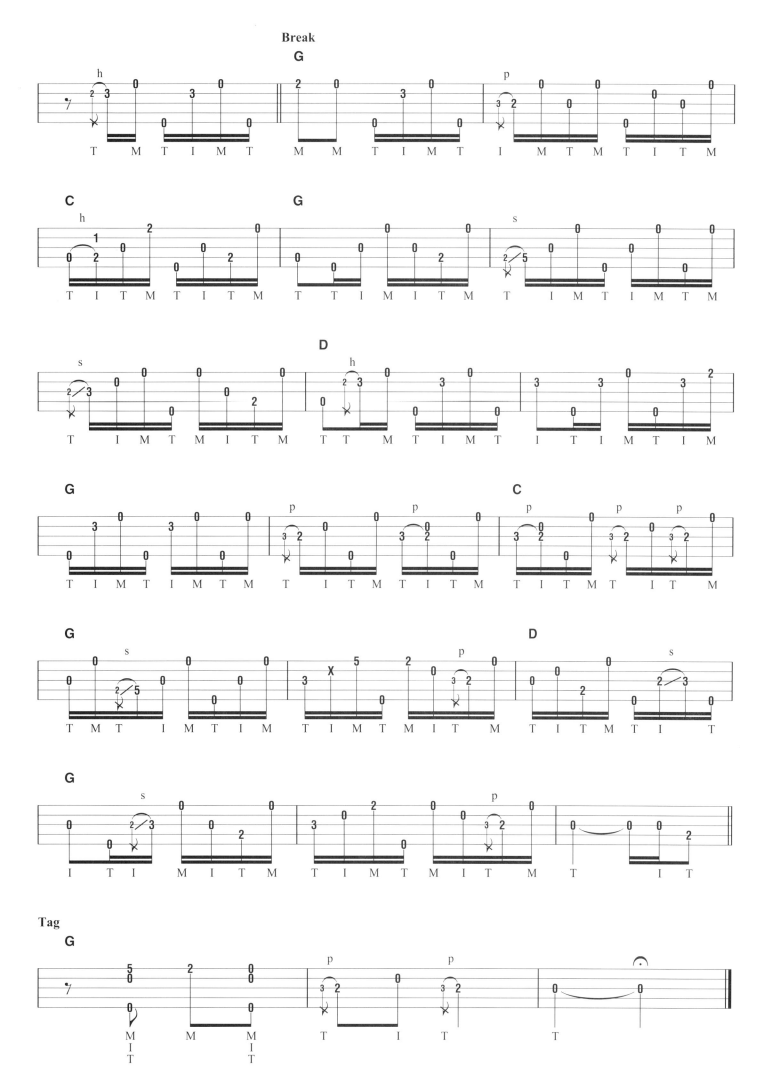

Tag

MY LONG JOURNEY HOME

Sound source—*Best of the Flatt & Scruggs TV Show, Vol. 7*

Words and Music by CHARLIE MONROE

(G tuning)
Key of A: Capo at 2nd fret and hook the 5th string

Intro

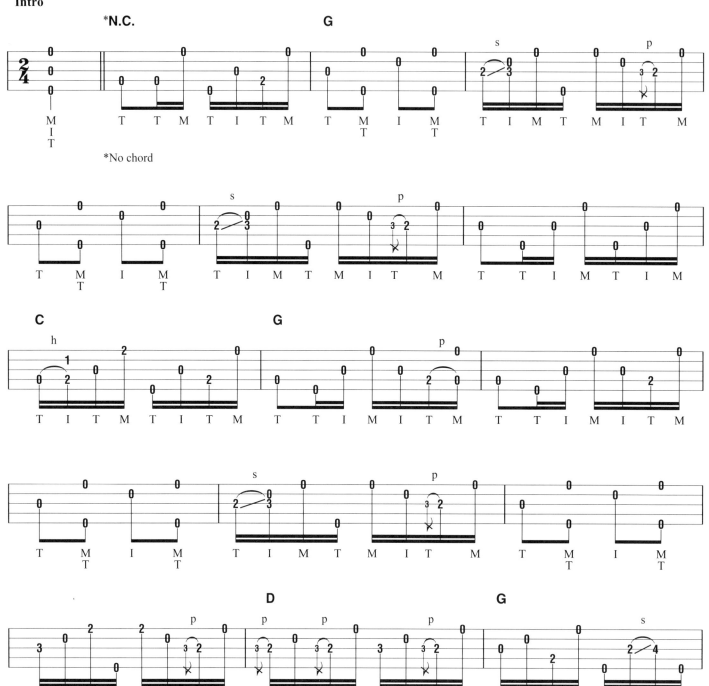

*No chord

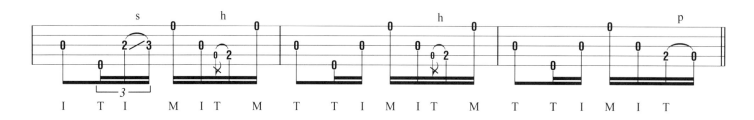

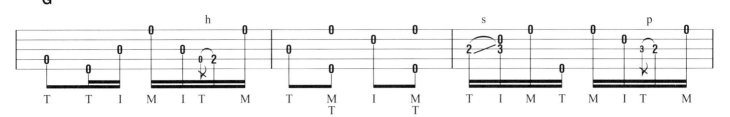

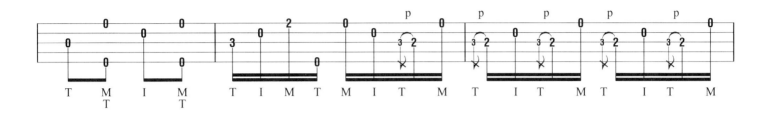

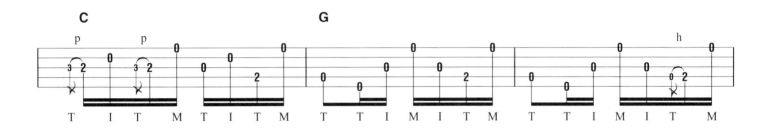

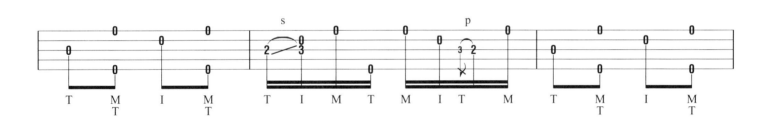

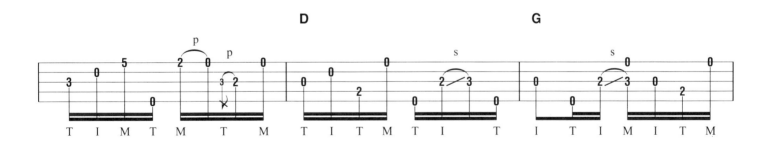

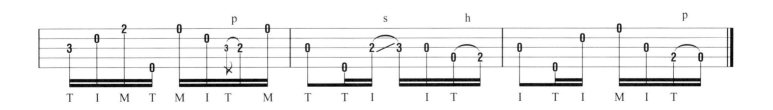

MY SARO JANE

Sound source—*The Essential Flatt & Scruggs–'Tis Sweet to Be Remembered*

Words and Music by LESTER FLATT
and EARL SCRUGGS

(G tuning)
Key of G

Intro

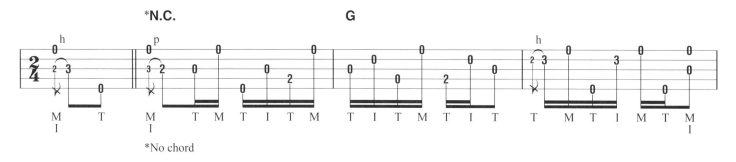

*No chord

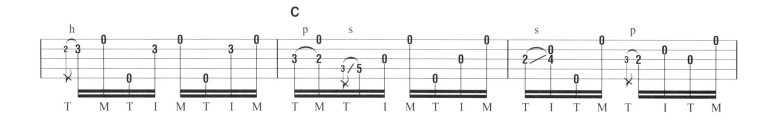

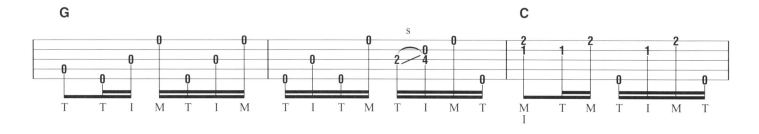

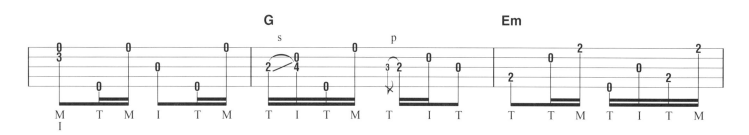

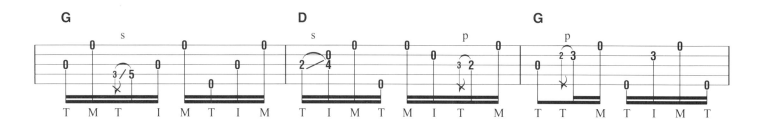

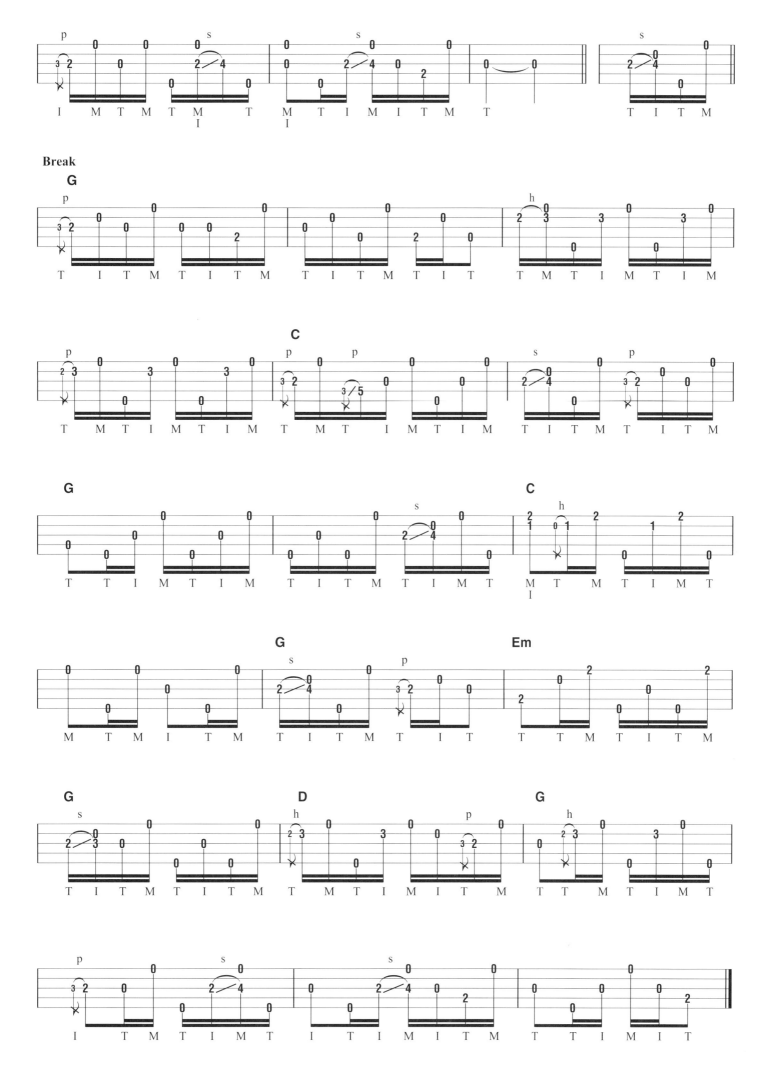

Break

125

NASHVILLE SKYLINE RAG

Sound source—*The Essential Earl Scruggs*

By BOB DYLAN

(G tuning)
Key of C

1st break

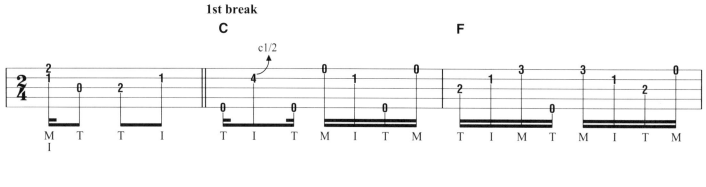

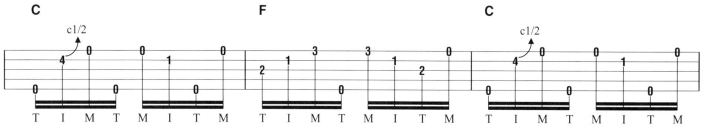

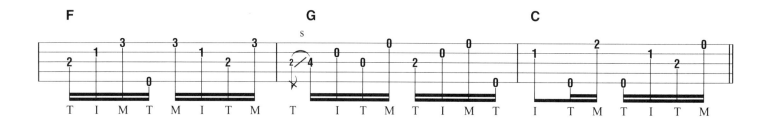

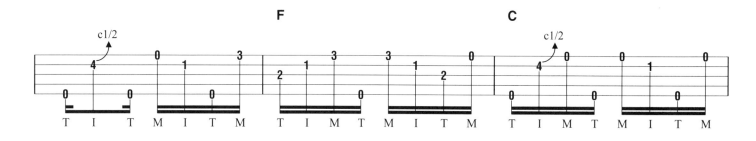

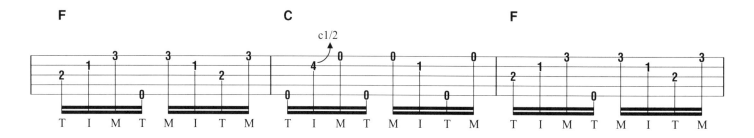

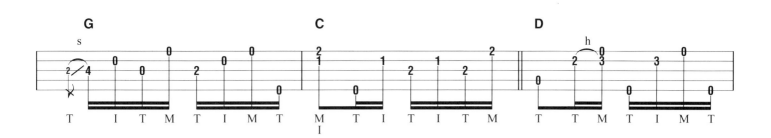

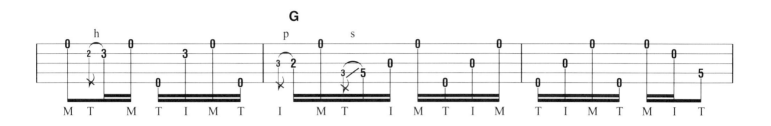

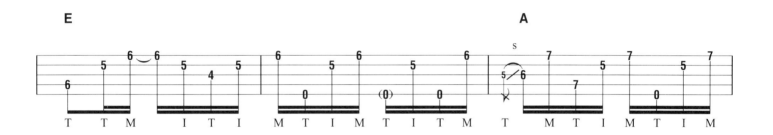

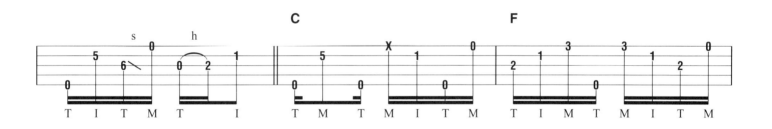

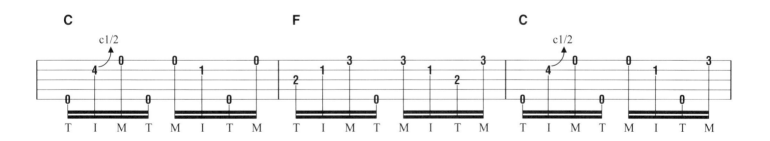

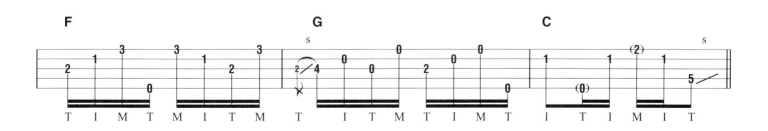

2nd break

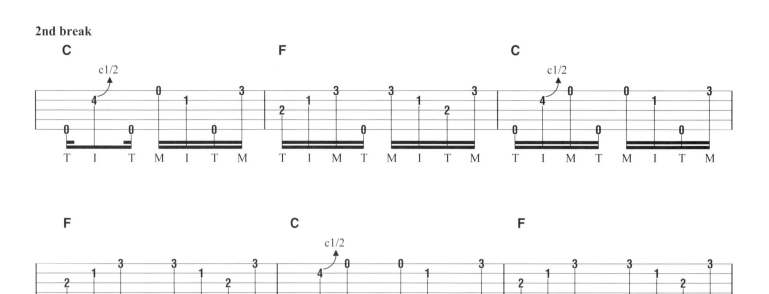

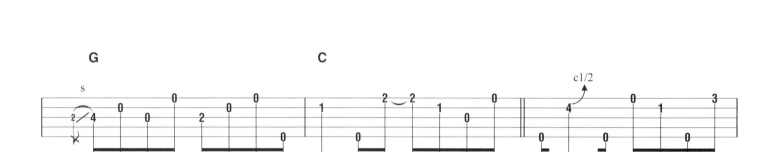

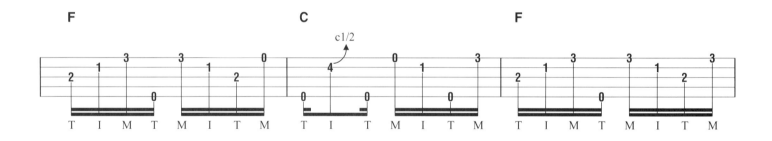

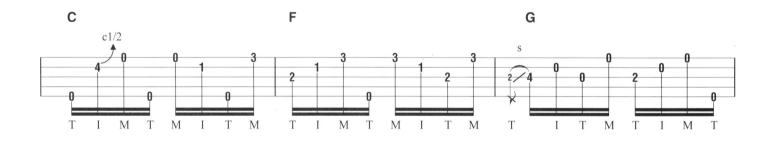

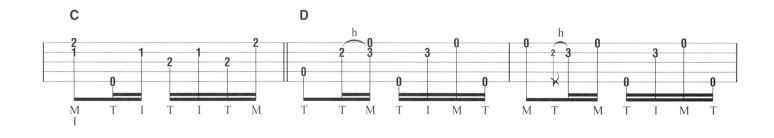

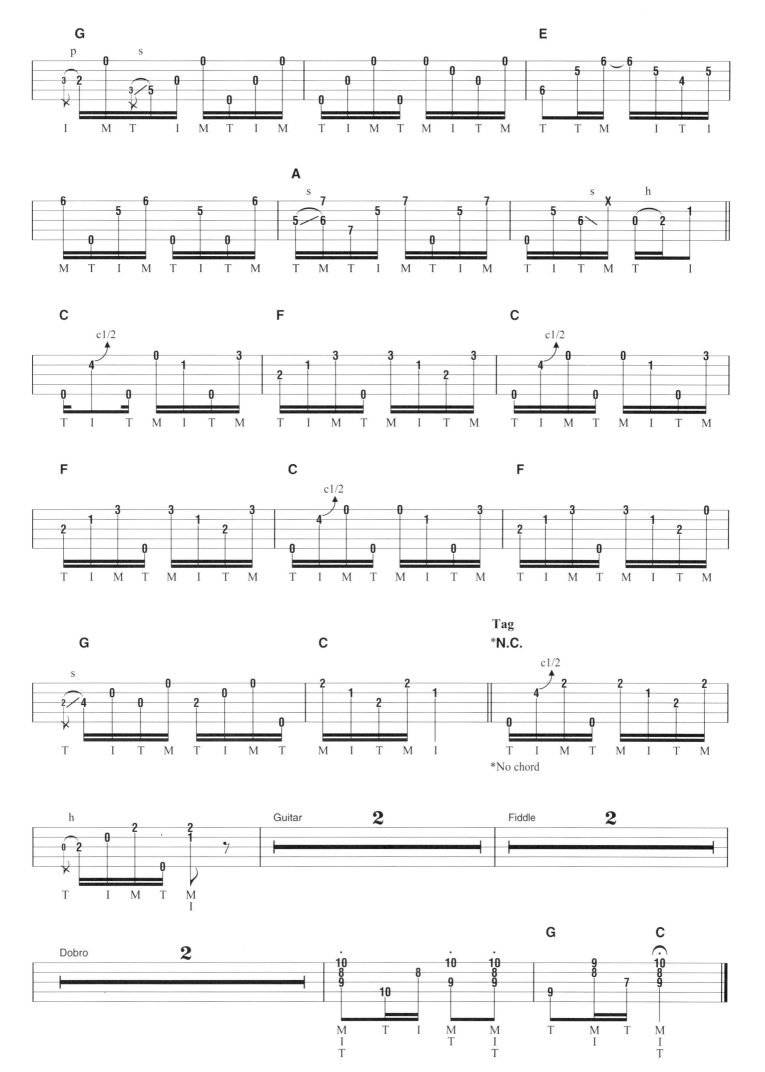

NINE POUND HAMMER

Sound source—*Folk Songs of Our Land - Flatt & Scruggs*

Words and Music by MERLE TRAVIS

(G tuning)
Key of G

Intro

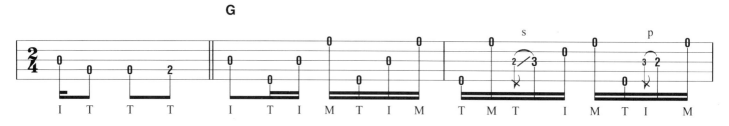

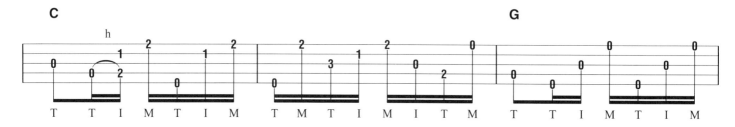

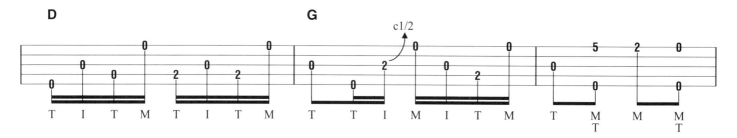

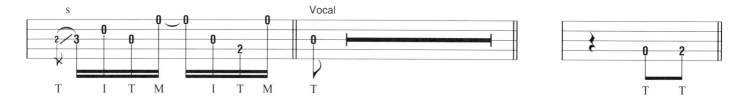

Break

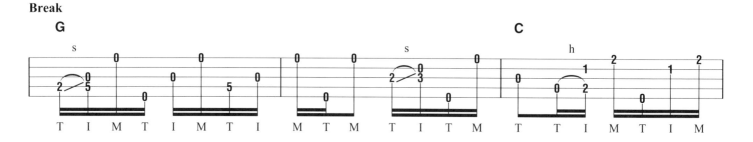

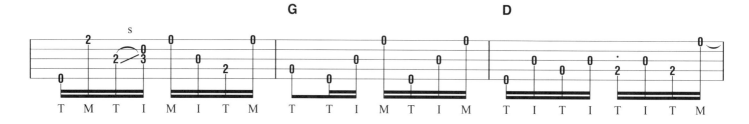

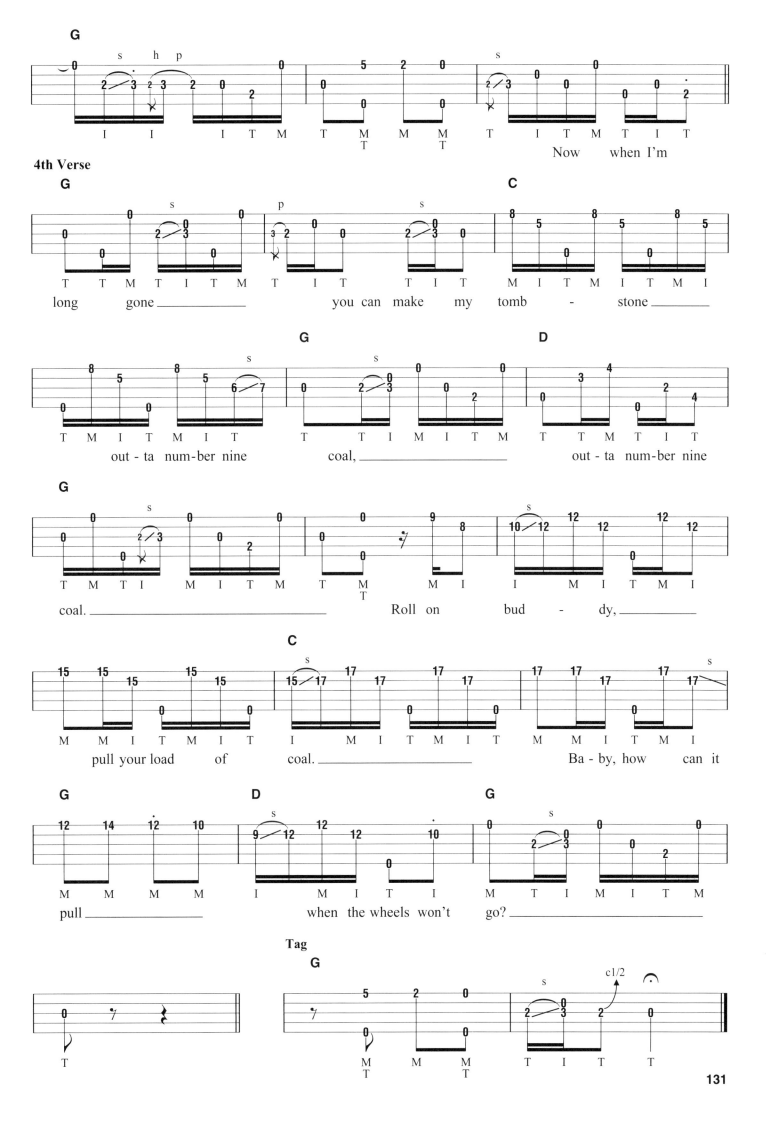

NOBODY'S BUSINESS

Sound source—*Best of the Flatt & Scruggs TV Show, Vol. 8*

TRADITIONAL

(G tuning)
Key of G

Intro

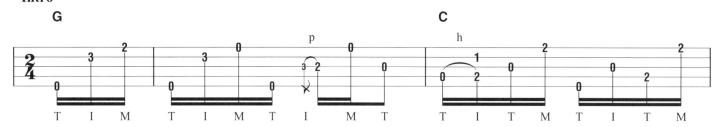

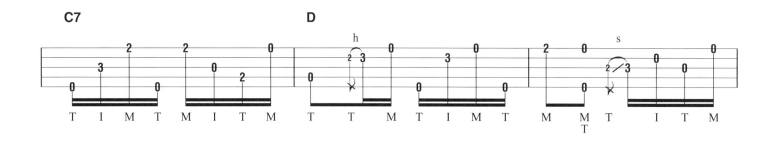

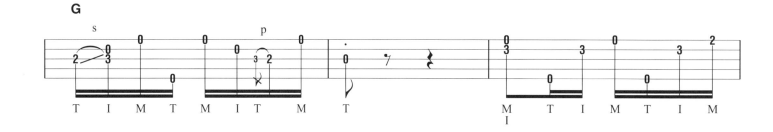

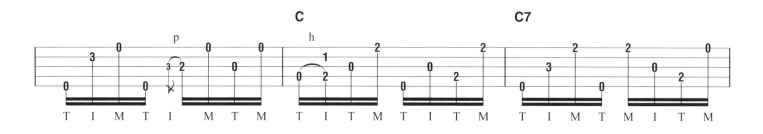

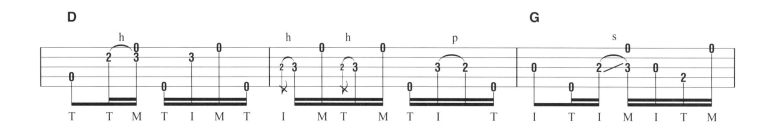

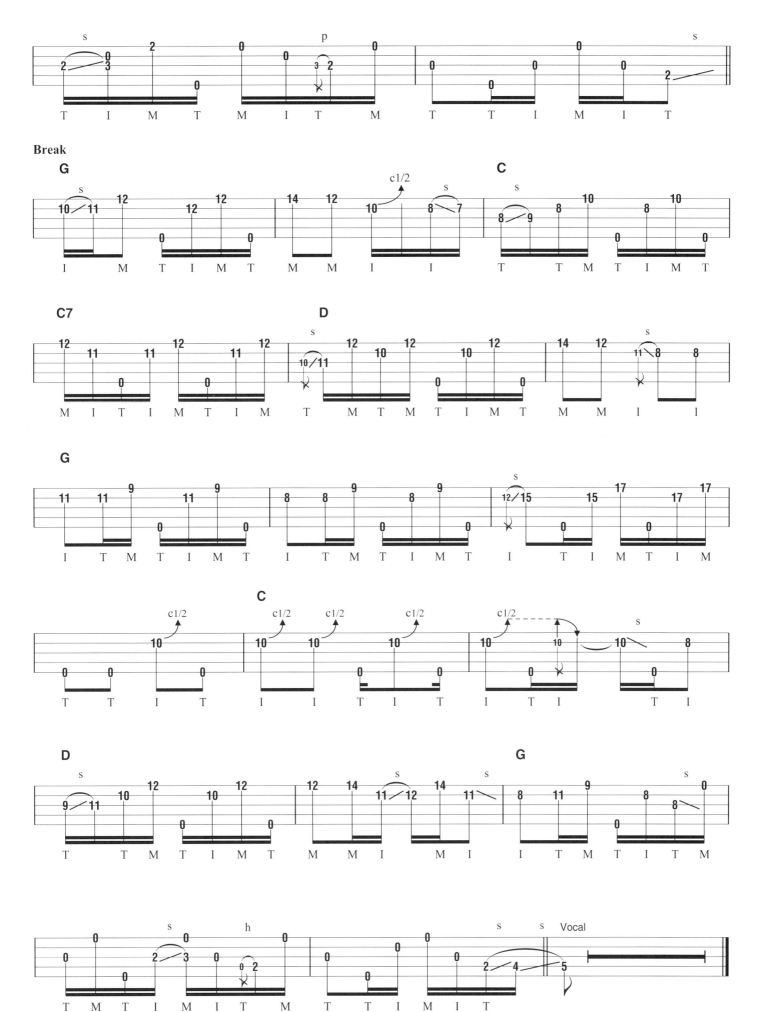

ON THE ROCK WHERE MOSES STOOD

Sound source—*Foggy Mountain Gospel - Flatt & Scruggs*

Words and Music by A.P. CARTER

(G tuning)
Key of A: Capo at 2nd fret and hook the 5th string

Intro

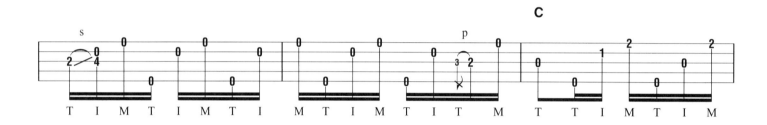

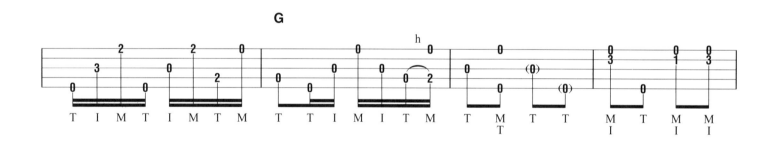

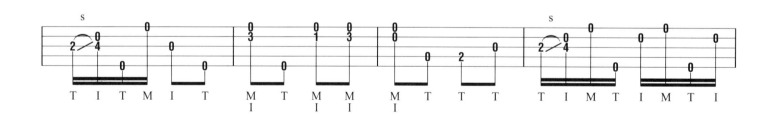

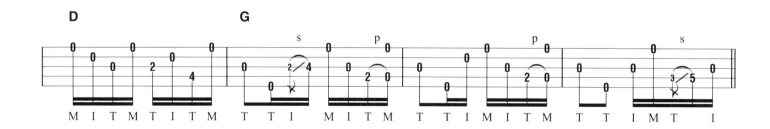

Break

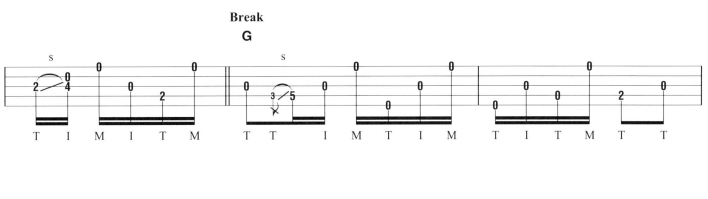

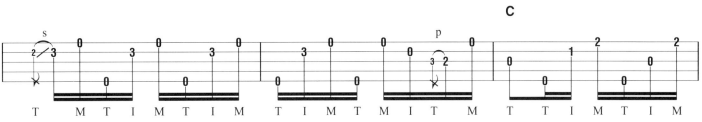

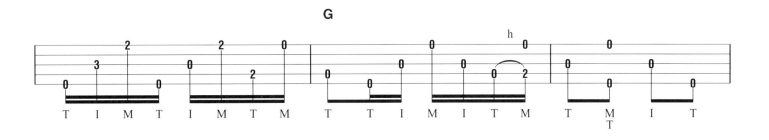

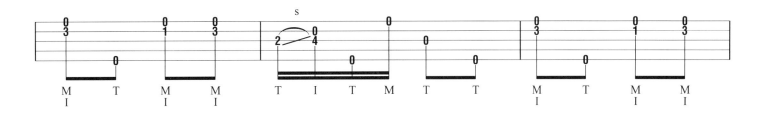

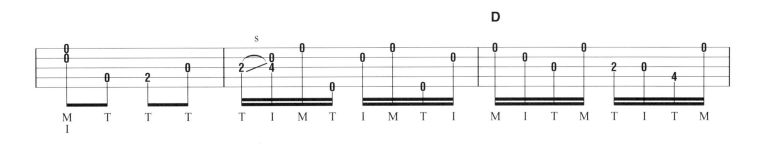

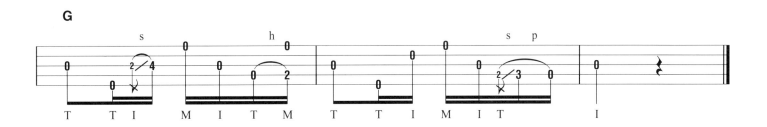

PAIN IN MY HEART

Sound source—*The Complete Mercury Sessions - Flatt & Scruggs*

Words and Music by BOB OSBORNE
and LAWRENCE RICHARDSON

(G tuning)
Key of G

Intro

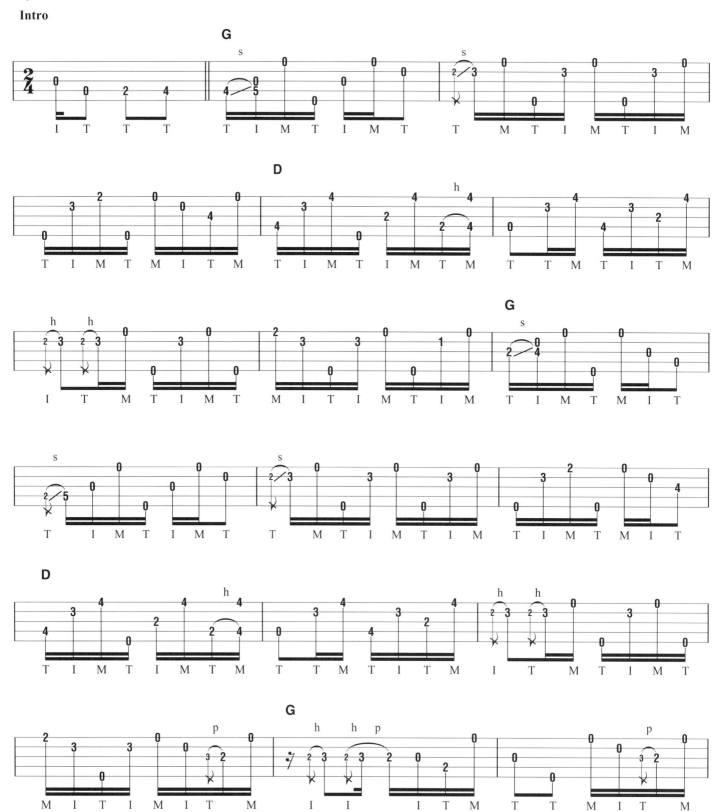

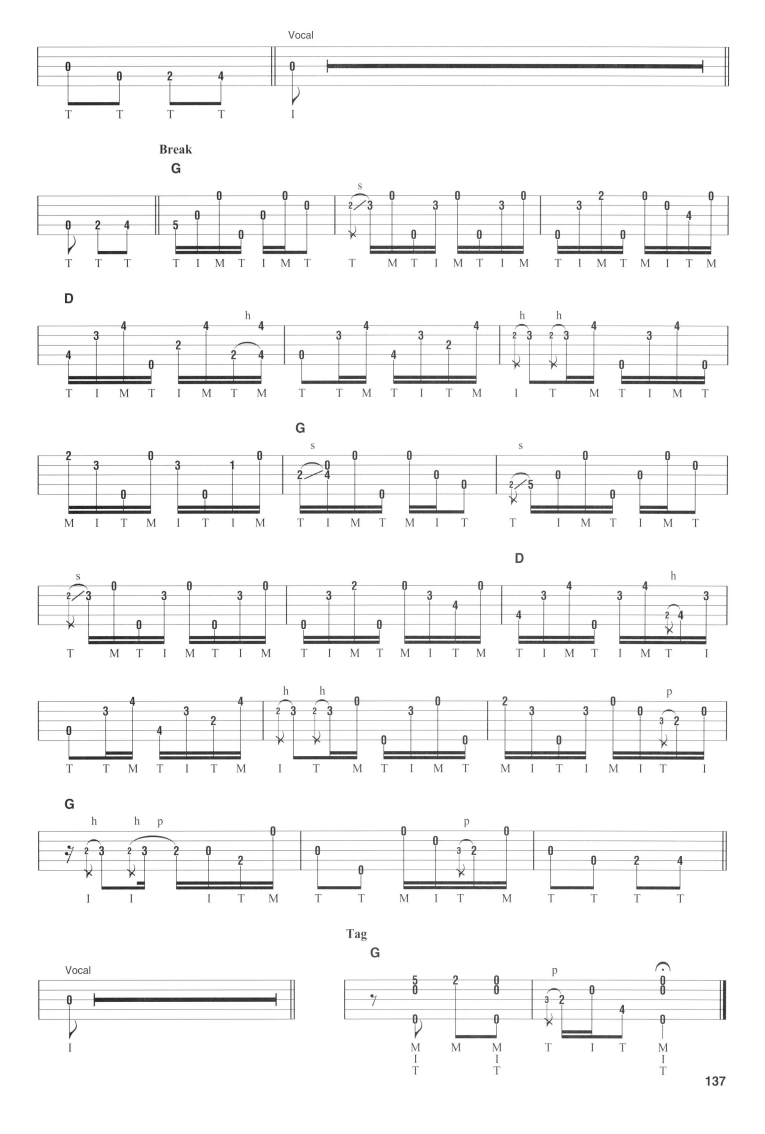

PETTICOAT JUNCTION

Theme from the Television Series
Sound source—*The Essential Flatt & Scruggs–'Tis Sweet to Be Remembered*

Lyrics by PAUL HENNING
Music by CURT MASSEY

(G tuning)
Key of G

Intro

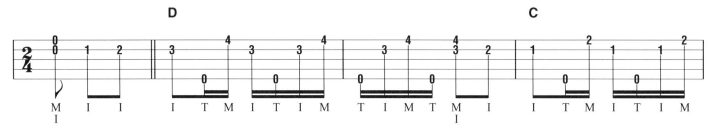

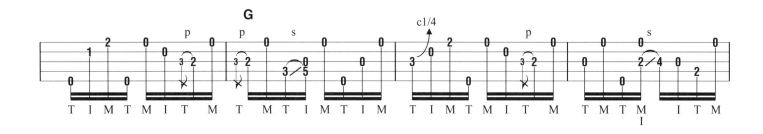

Verse

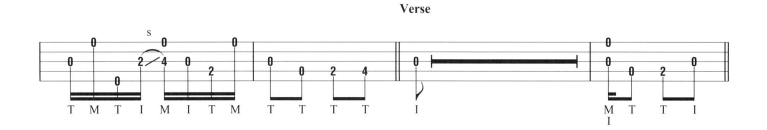

1st break

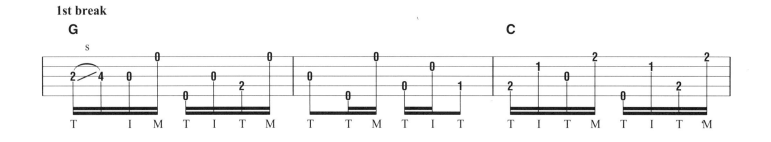

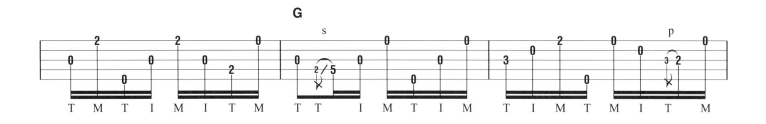

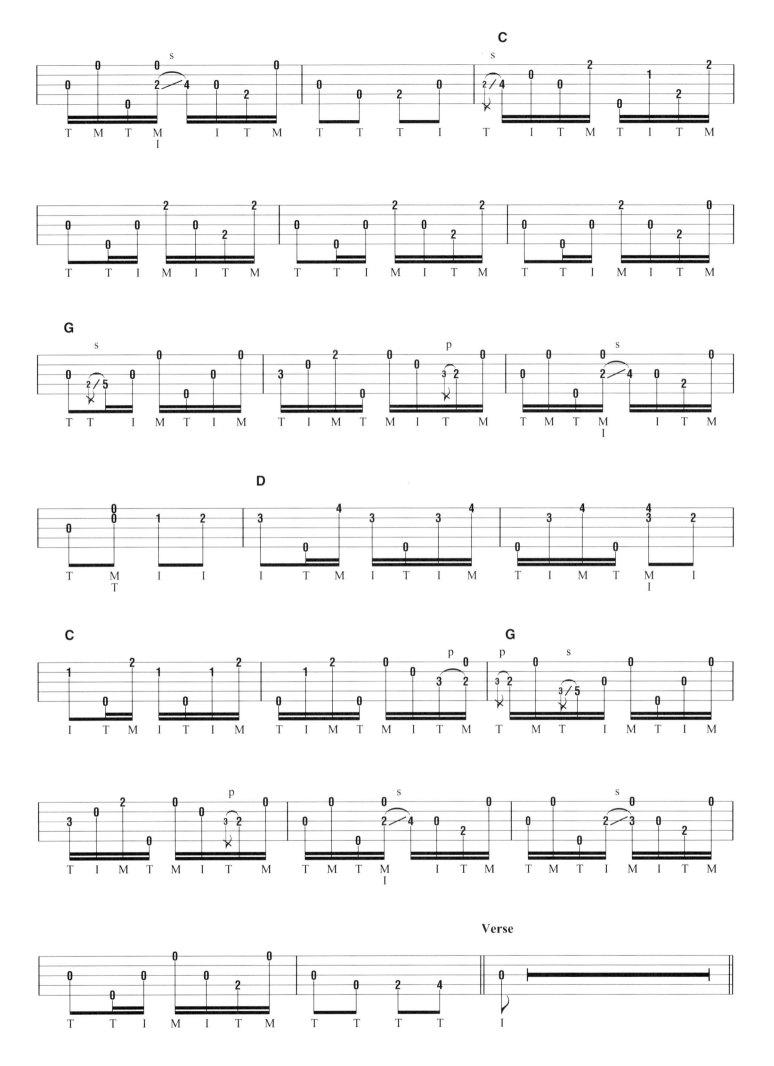

2nd break

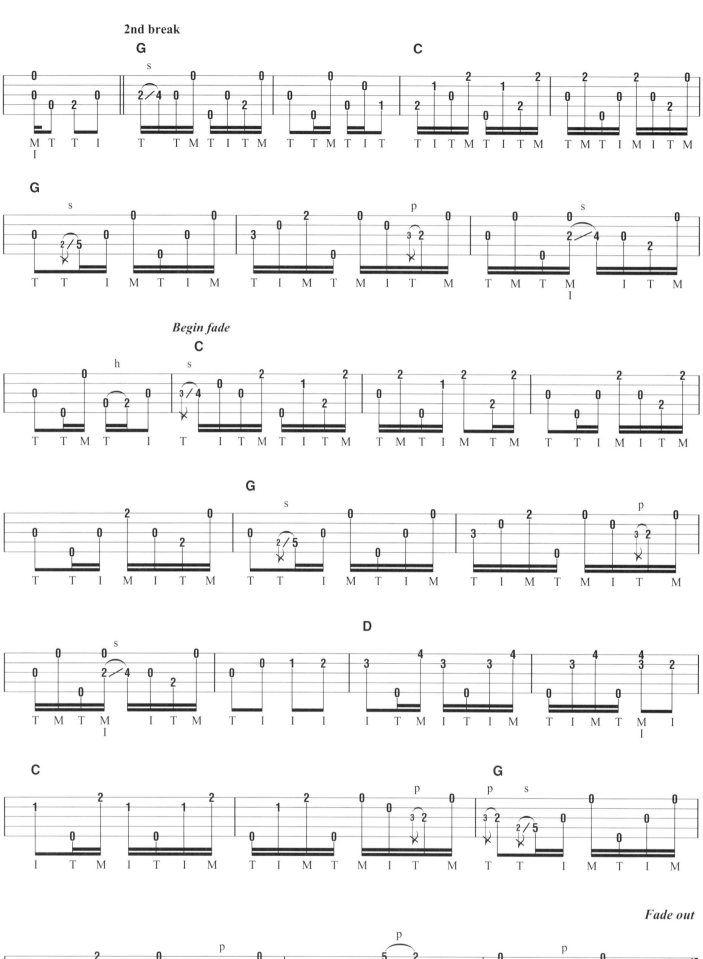

Begin fade

Fade out

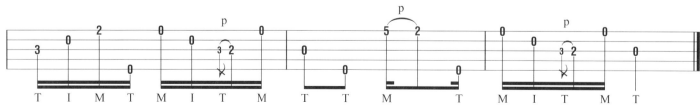

140

Nothing To It

Sound source—_Strictly Instrumental - Flatt & Scruggs with Doc Watson_

Words and Music by ARTHEL WATSON

(C tuning)
Key of C

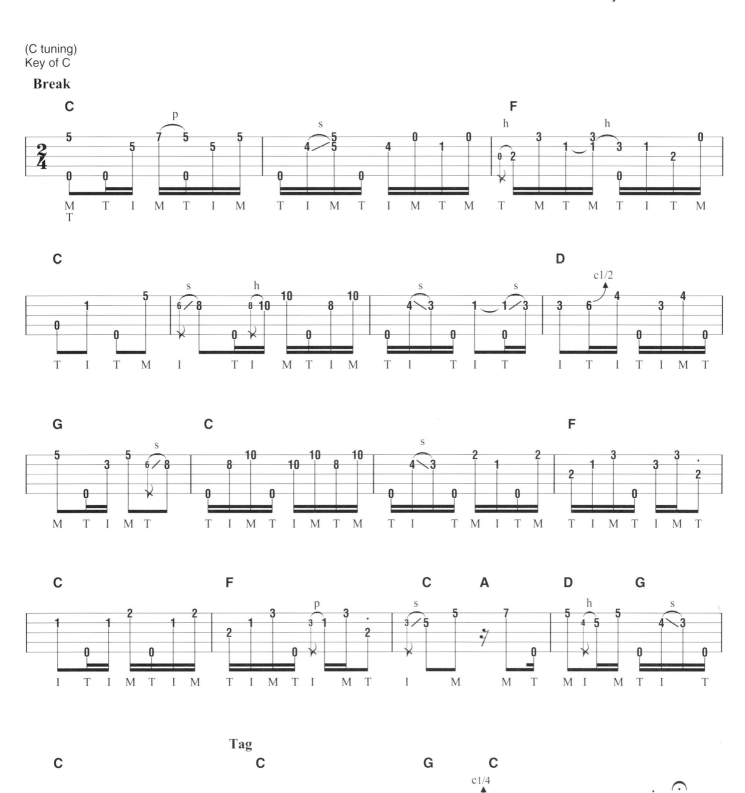

PIKE COUNTY BREAKDOWN

Sound source—*The Essential Earl Scruggs*

Words and Music by RUPERT JONES

(G tuning)
Key of A: Capo at 2nd fret and hook the 5th string.

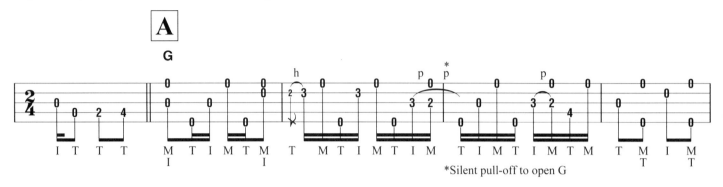

*Silent pull-off to open G

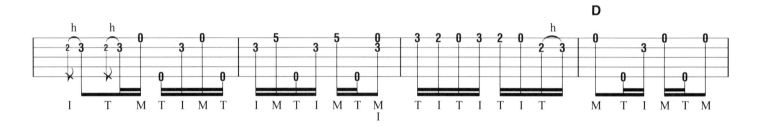

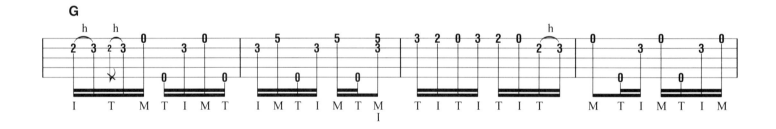

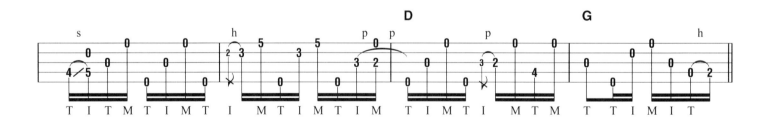

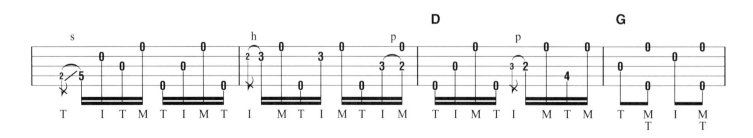

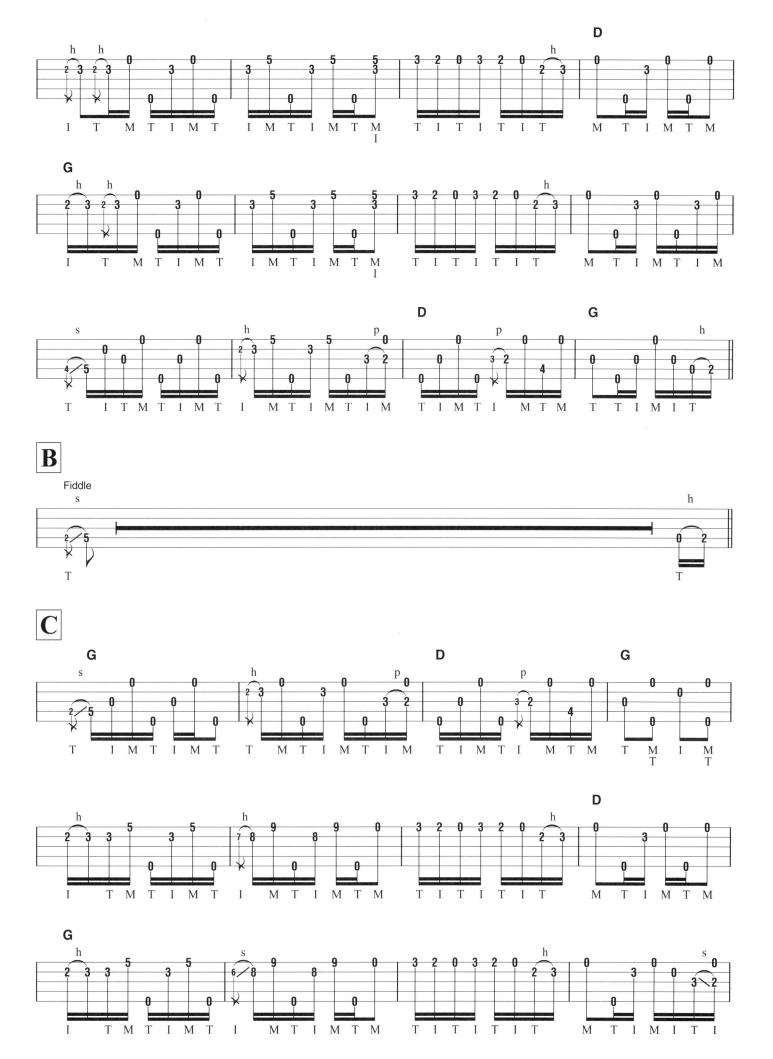

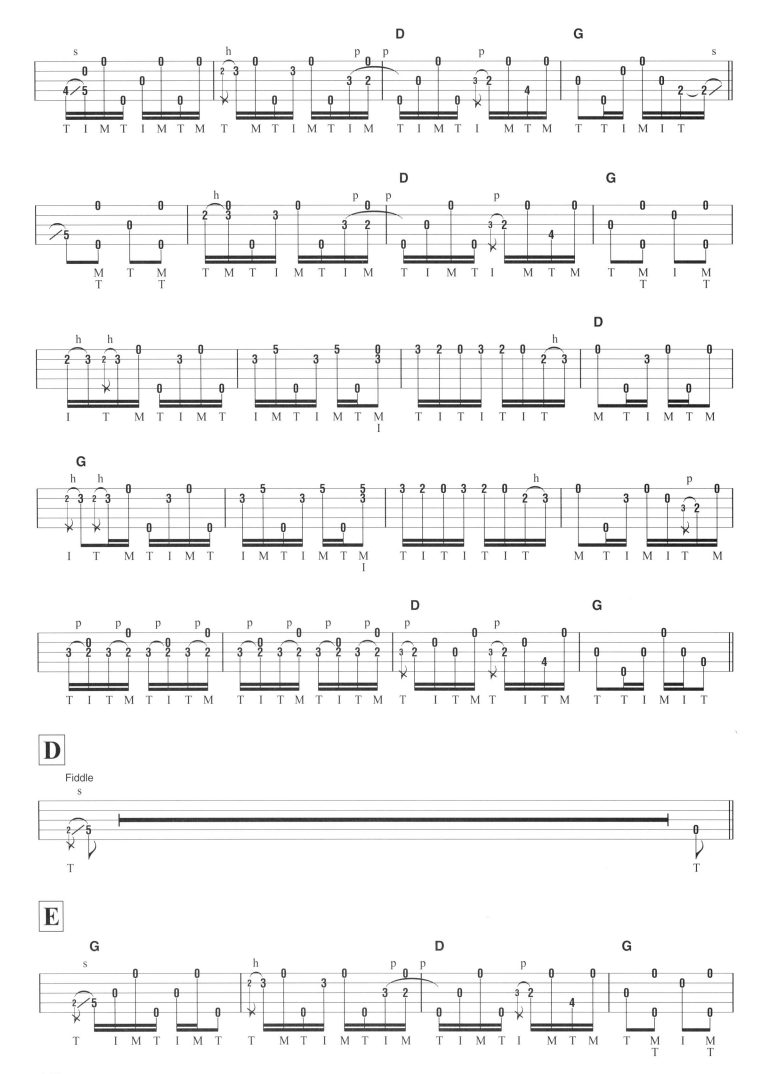

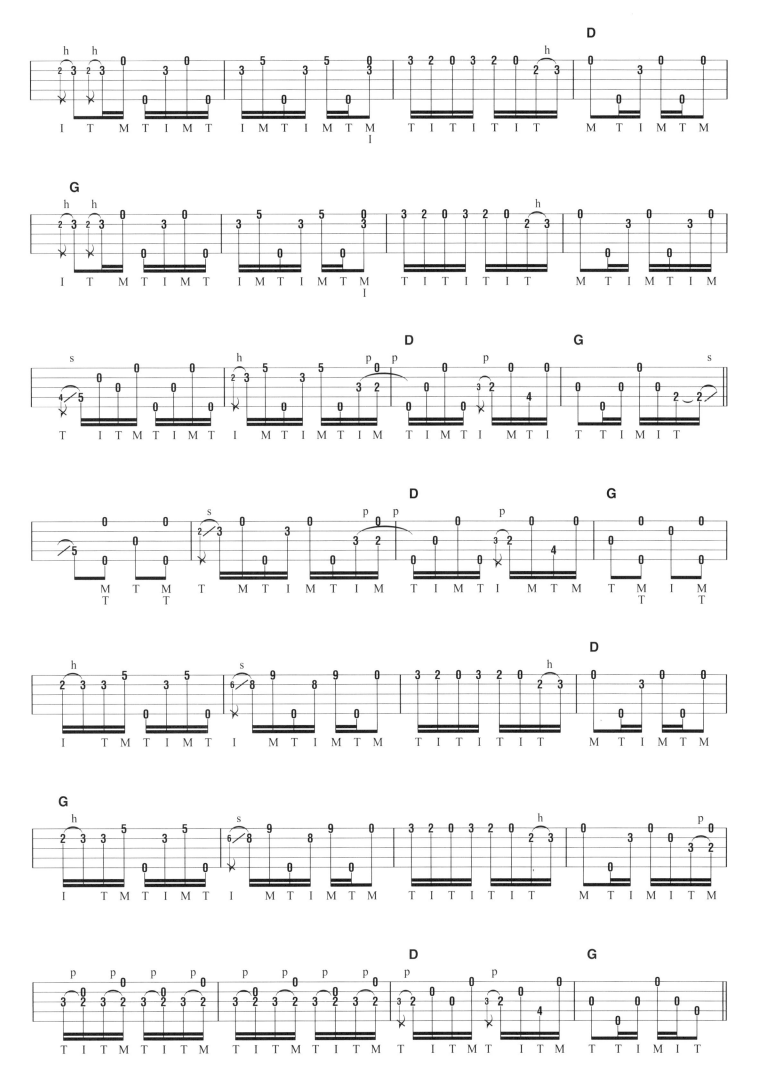

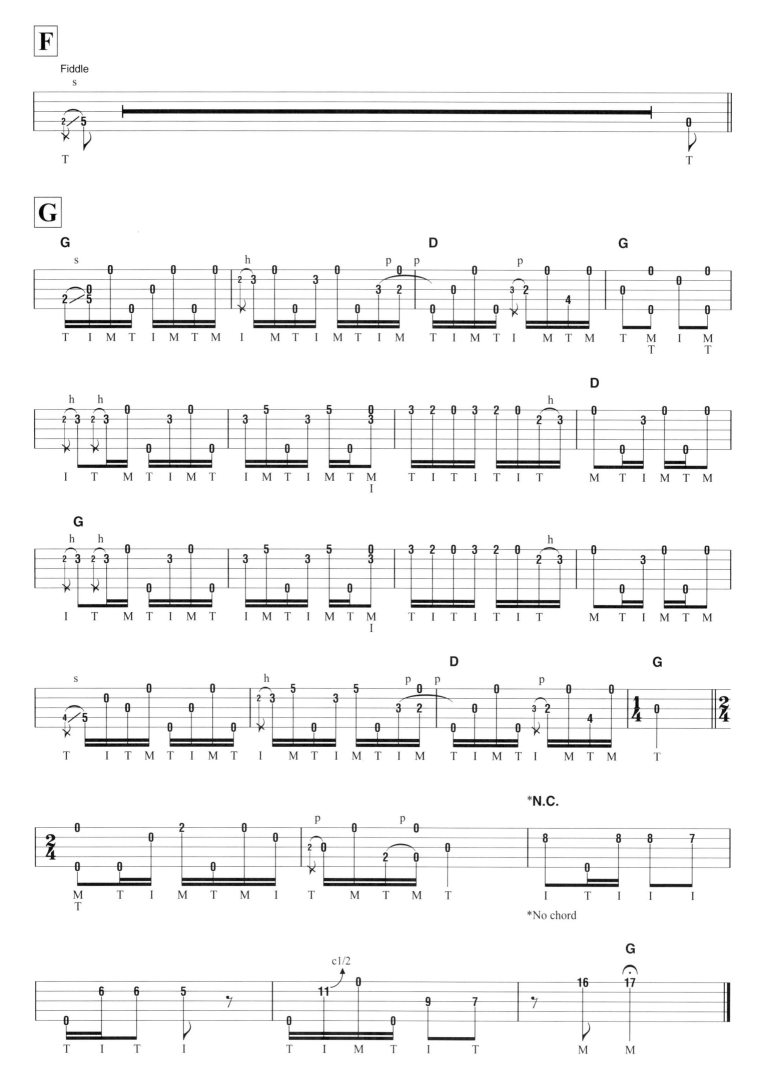

POLKA ON A BANJO

Sound source—*The Essential Flatt and Scruggs - 'Tis Sweet to Be Remembered*

Words and Music by DANIEL LUALLEN,
RICHARD TILLMAN and GEORGE WILLIAMS

(C tuning)
Keys of C and F

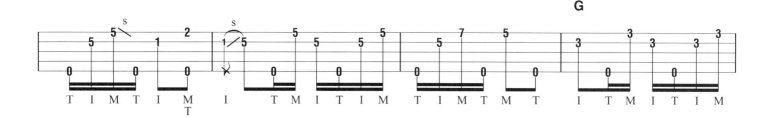

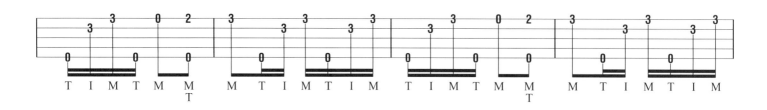

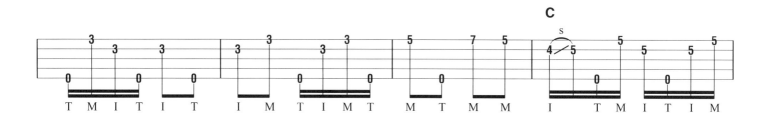

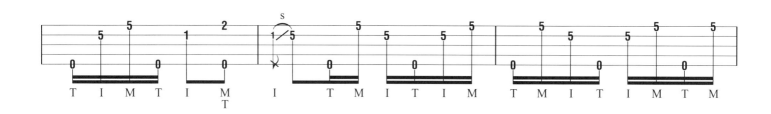

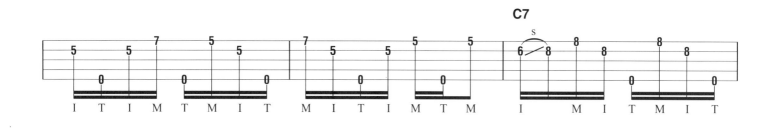

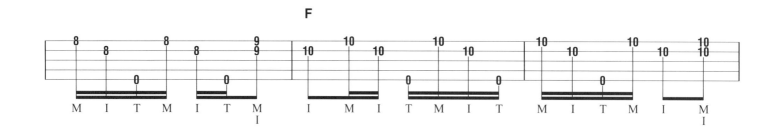

148

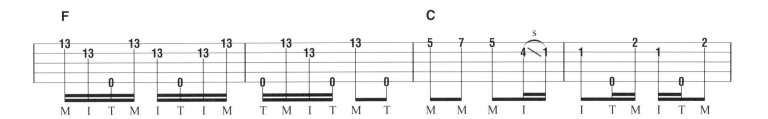

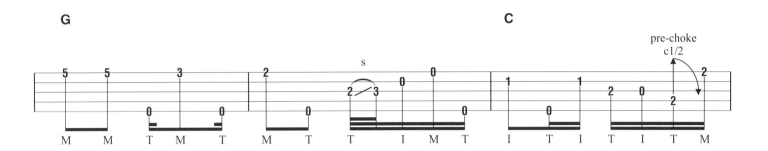

Verse

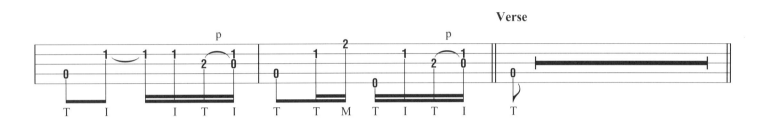

Interlude
Key of F

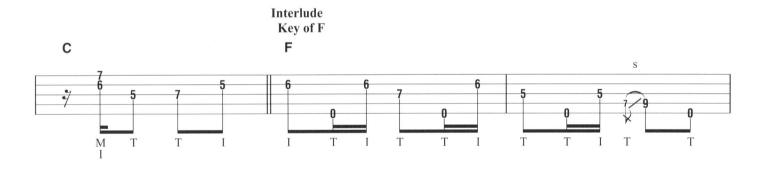

Chorus

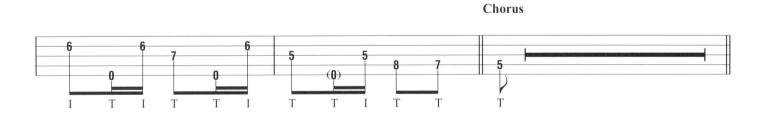

Tag

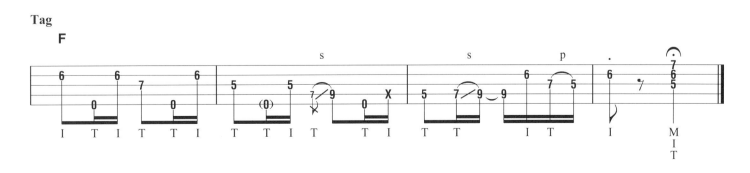

SIX WHITE HORSES

Sound source—*Breaking Out - Flatt & Scruggs*

Words and Music by CLYDE MOODY

(G tuning)
Key of G (Recorded in G# tuning)

Intro

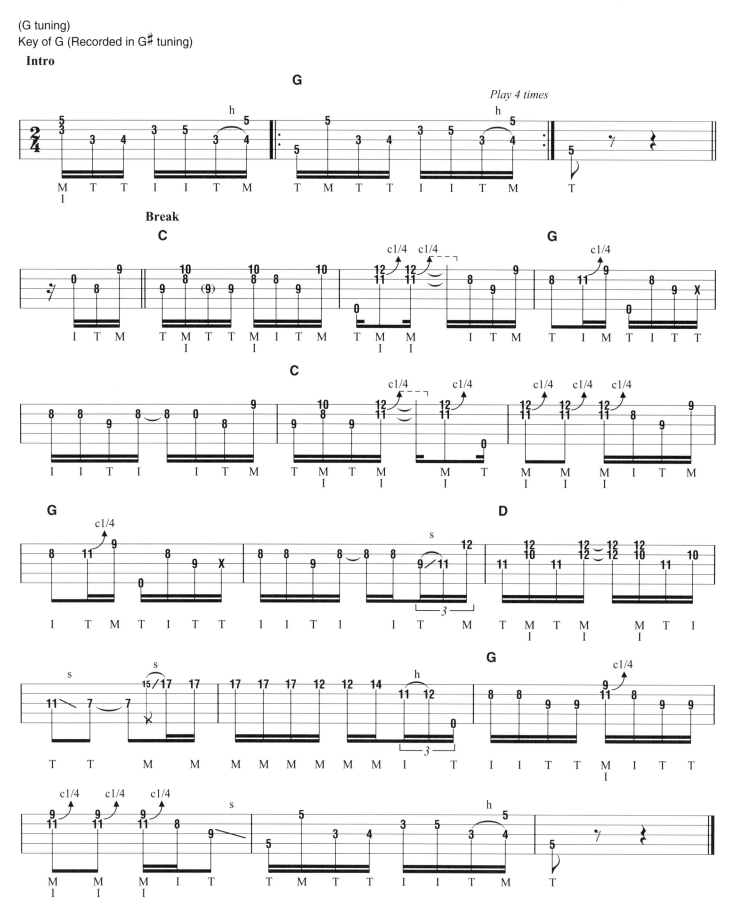

ROLL IN MY SWEET BABY'S ARMS

Sound source—*The Essential Earl Scruggs*

Words and Music by LESTER FLATT

(G tuning)
Key of Bb: Capo at 3rd fret and hook the 5th string
(Recorded in G# tuning, capoed at the 2nd fret.)

Intro

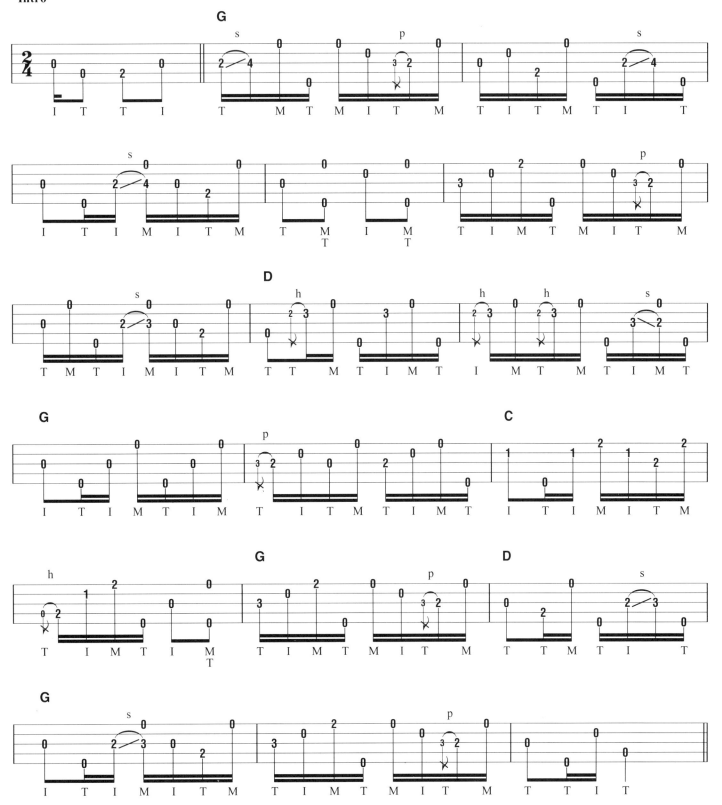

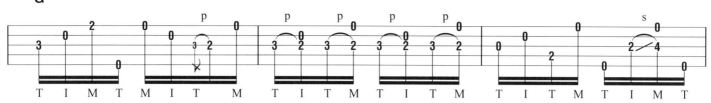

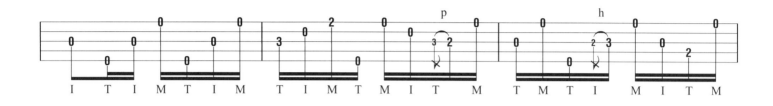

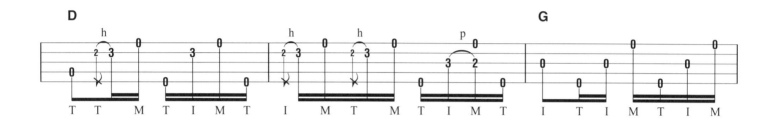

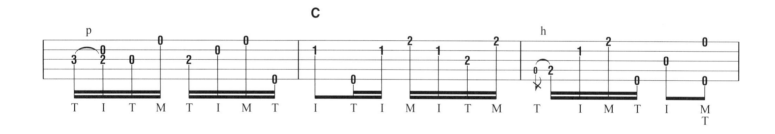

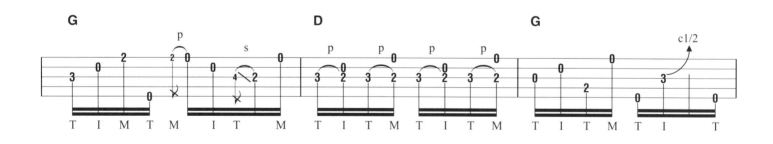

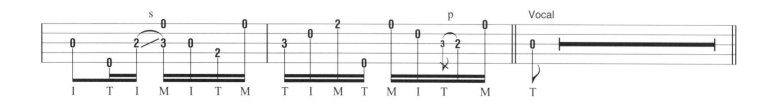

2nd break

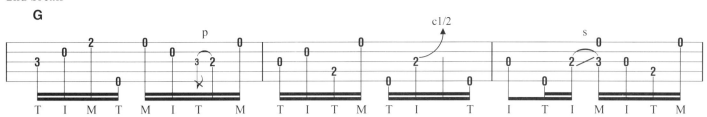

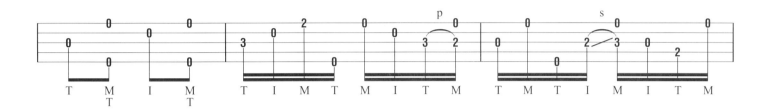

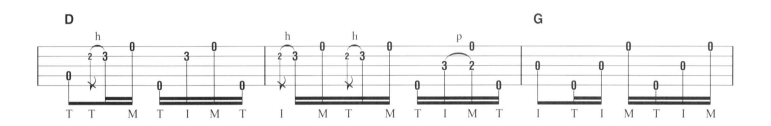

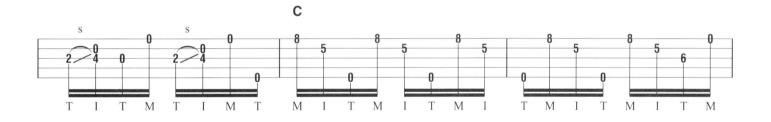

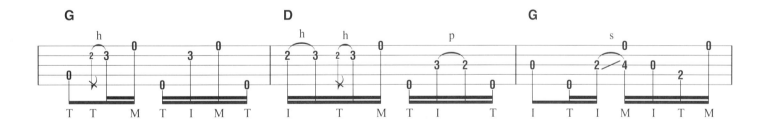

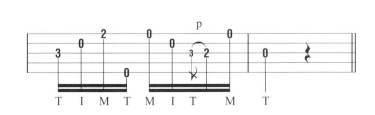

Tag

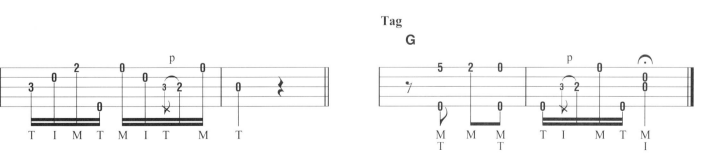

RUBY, DON'T TAKE YOUR LOVE TO TOWN

Sound source—*Final Fling–Flatt & Scruggs*

Words and Music by MEL TILLIS

(G tuning)
Key of C

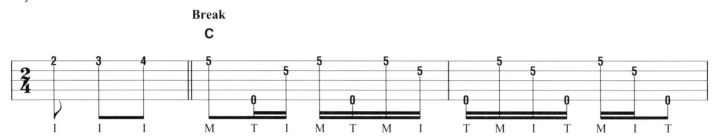

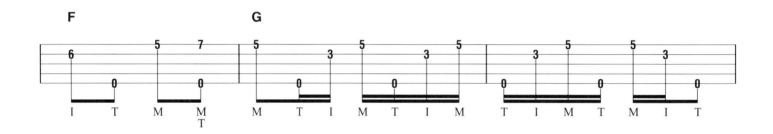

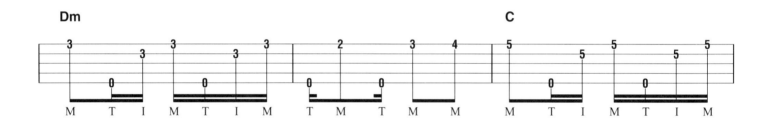

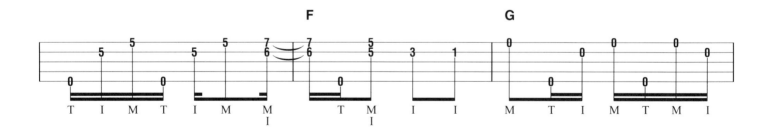

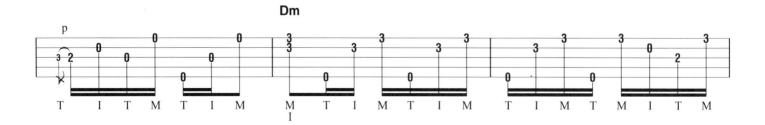

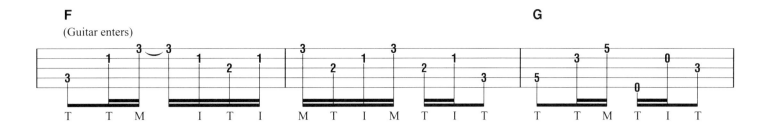

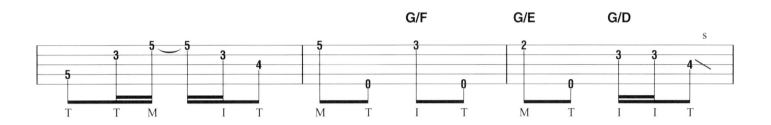

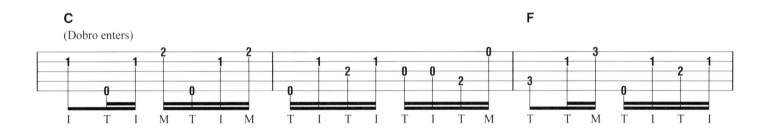

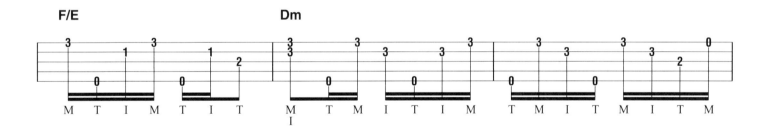

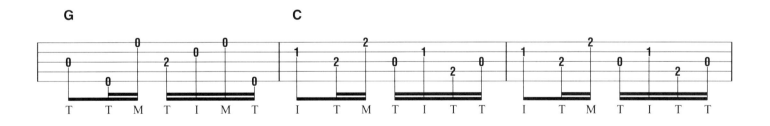

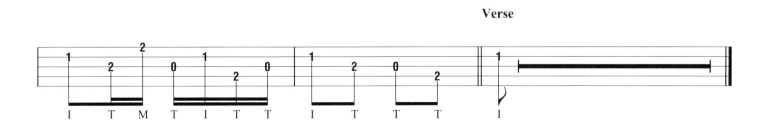

SALTY DOG BLUES

Sound source—*The Essential Earl Scruggs*

(G tuning)
Key of G (Recorded in G# tuning)

Words and Music by WILEY A. MORRIS and ZEKE MORRIS

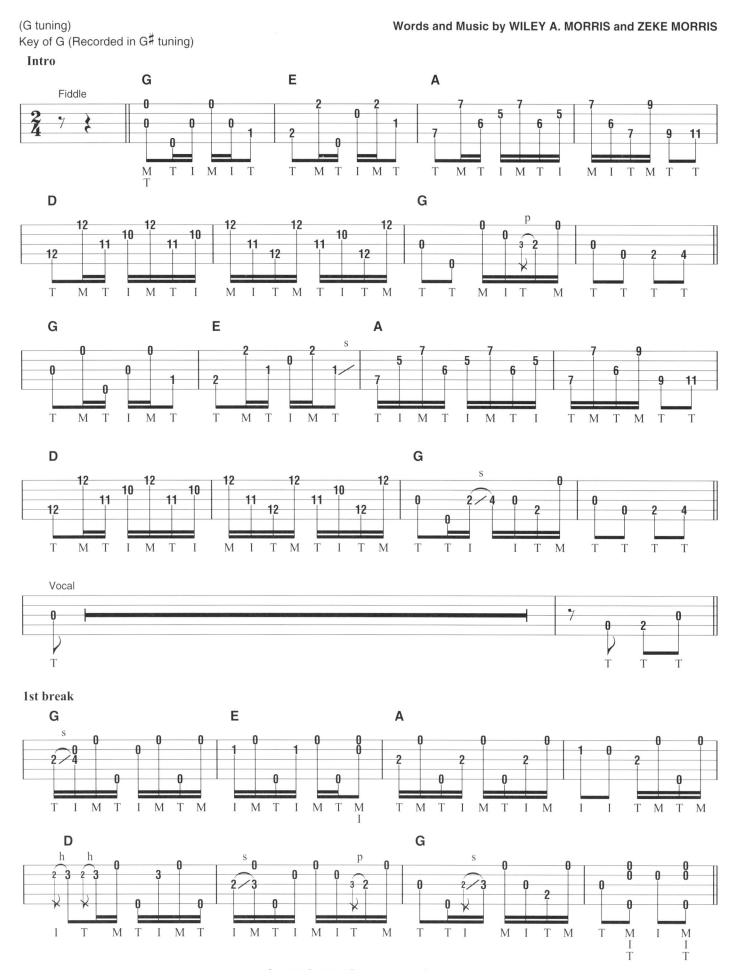

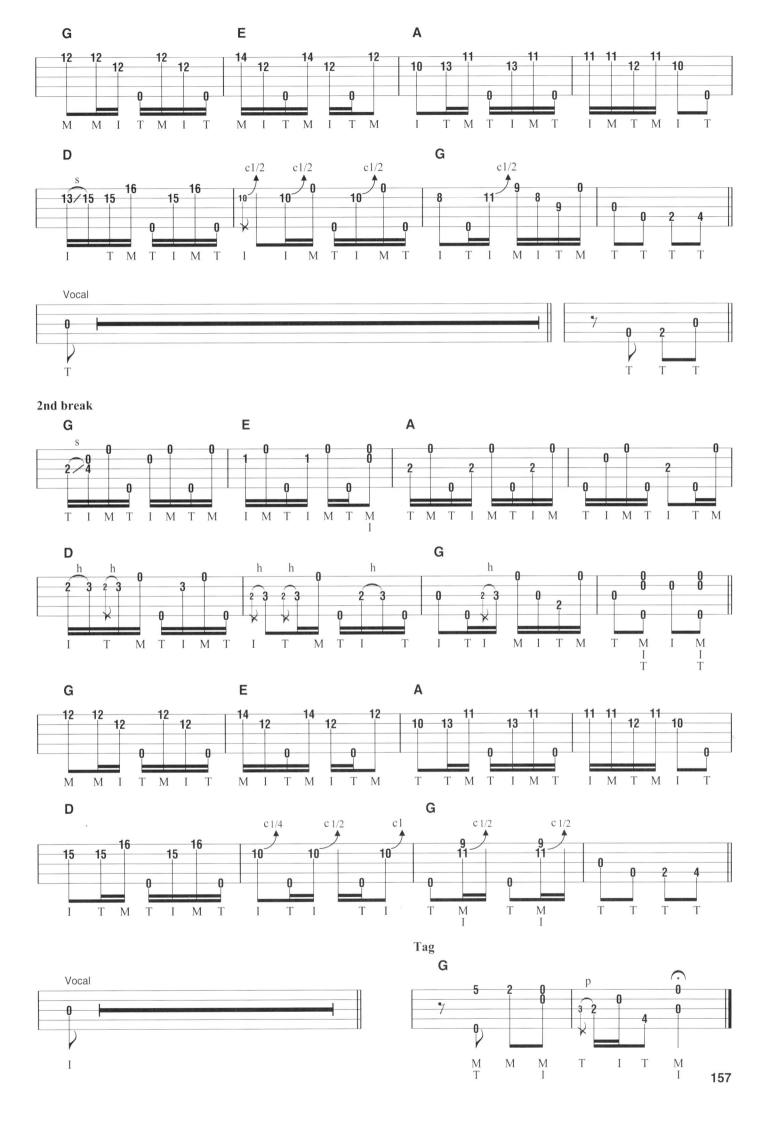

SHORTENIN' BREAD

Sound source—*Best of the Flatt & Scruggs TV Show, Vol. 1*

AFRICAN-AMERICAN FOLKSONG

(G tuning)
Key of G

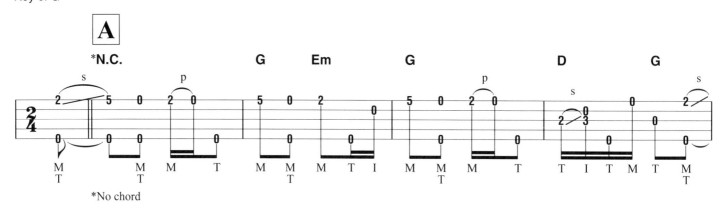

*No chord

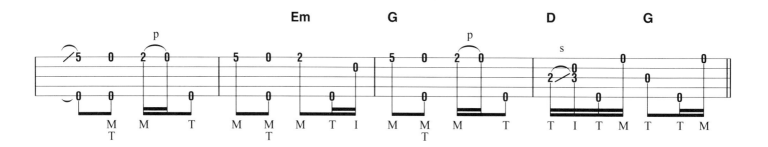

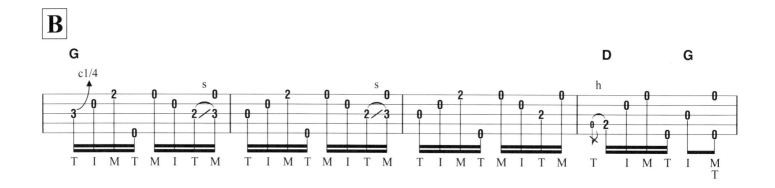

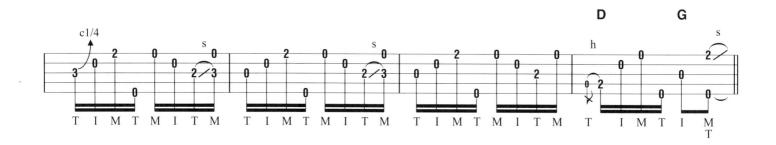

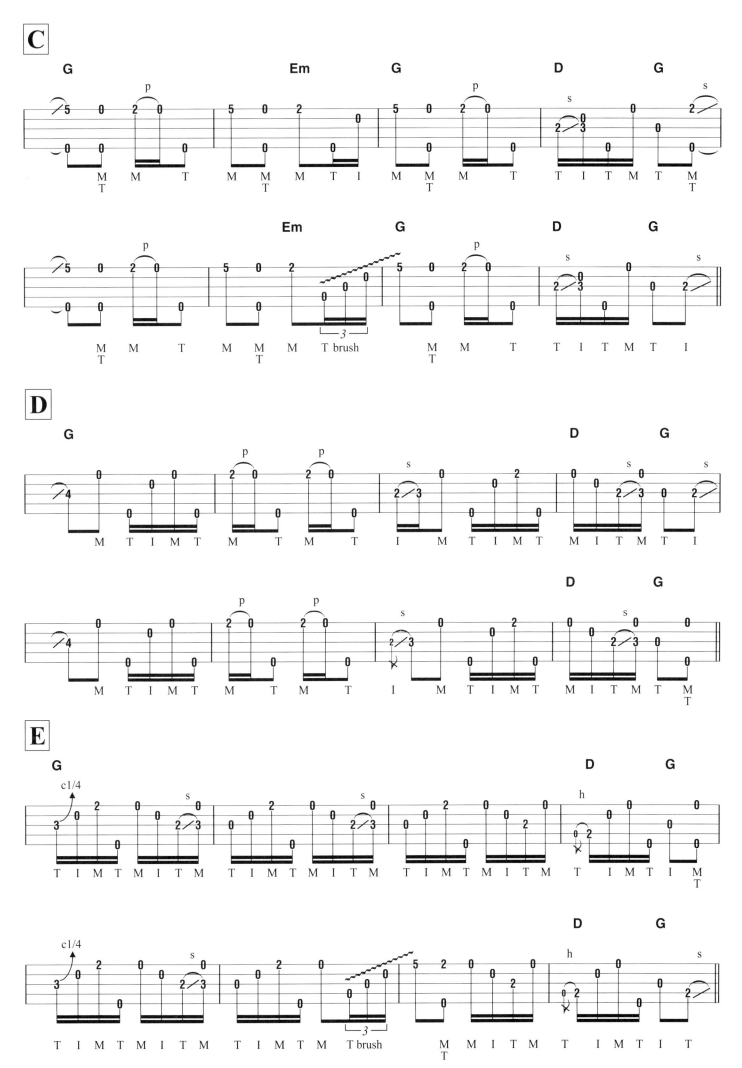

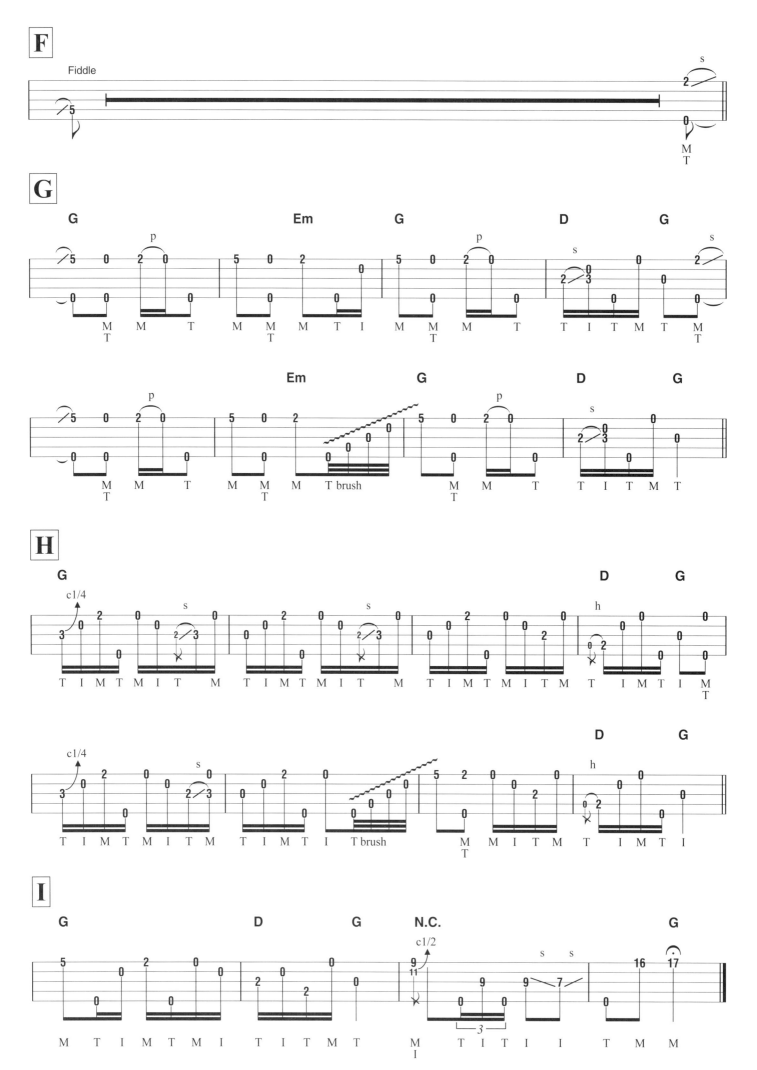

SOME OLD DAY

Sound source—*Foggy Mountain Jamboree–Flatt & Scruggs*

**Words and Music by LOUISE CERTAIN
and GLADYS STACEY**

(G tuning)
Key of F: Hook the 5th string at the 7th fret
(Recorded in G# tuning)

Intro

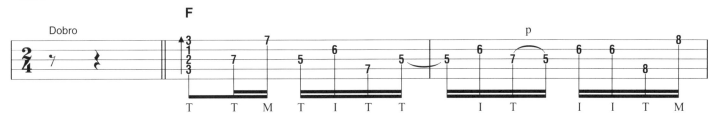

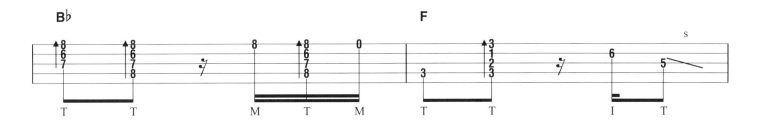

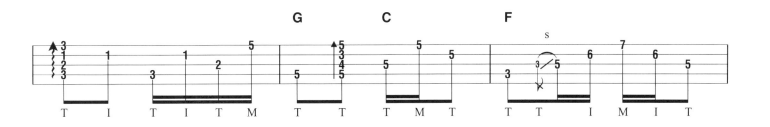

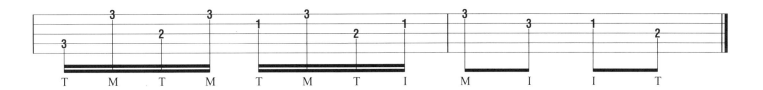

SOLDIER'S JOY

Sound source—*Earl Scruggs with Family & Friends: The Ultimate Collection - Live at the Ryman*

TRADITIONAL

(C tuning)
Key of C

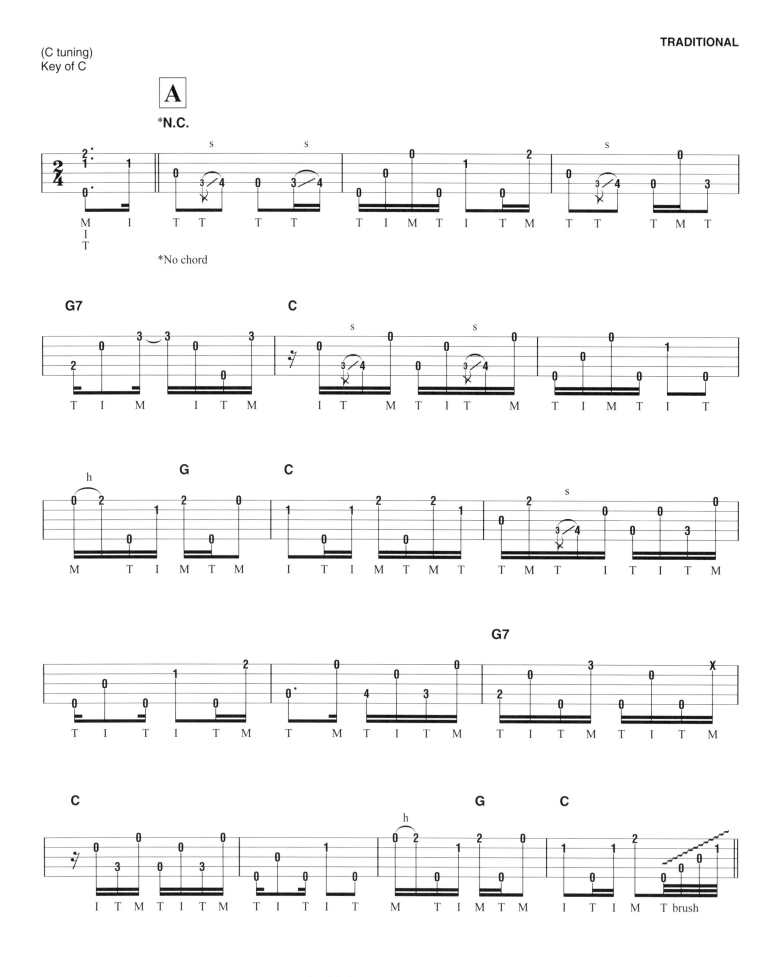

*No chord

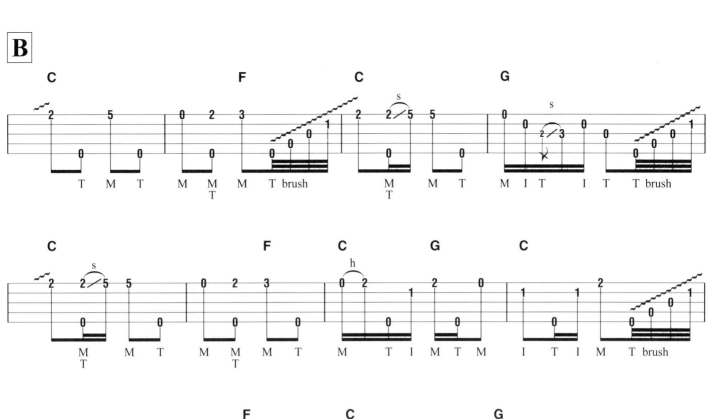

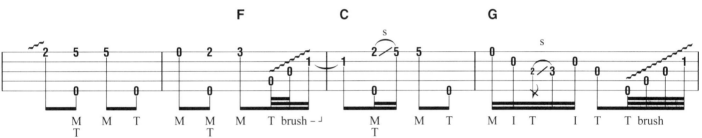

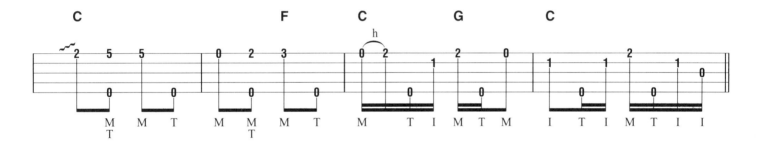

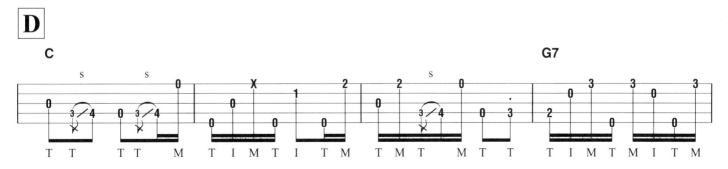

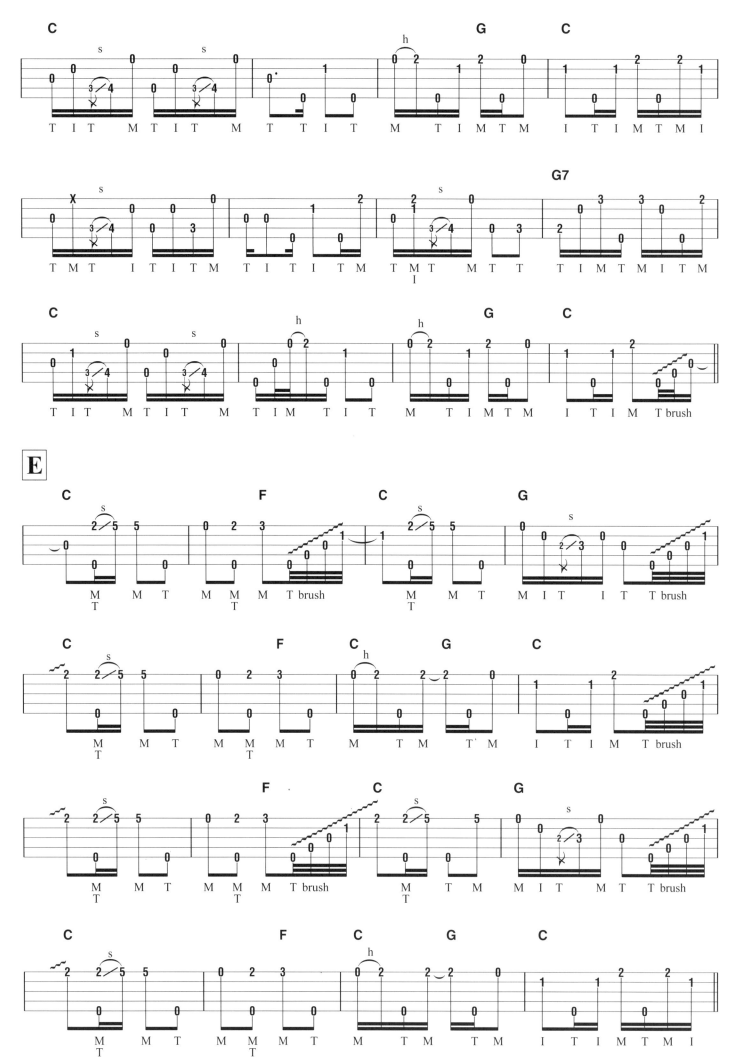

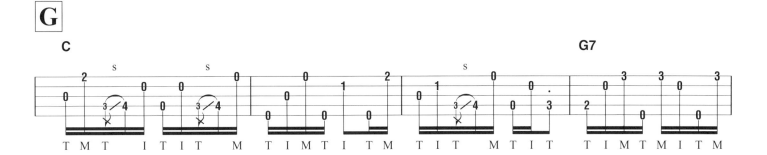

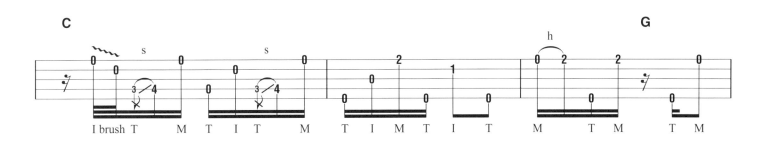

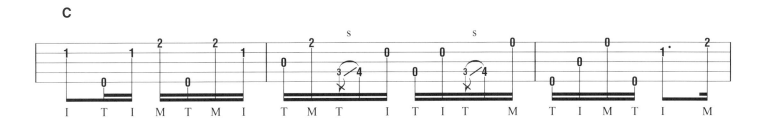

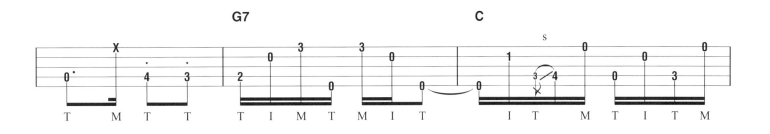

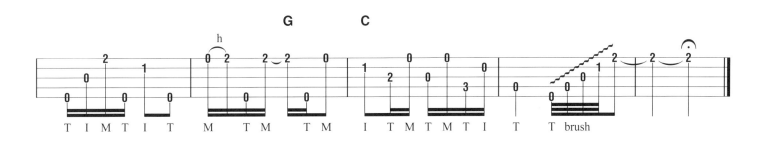

SOME OF SHELLY'S BLUES

Sound source—*The Essential Earl Scruggs*

Words and Music by MICHAEL NESMITH

(G tuning)
Key of D: Capo at 2nd fret and hook the 5th string at the 9th fret

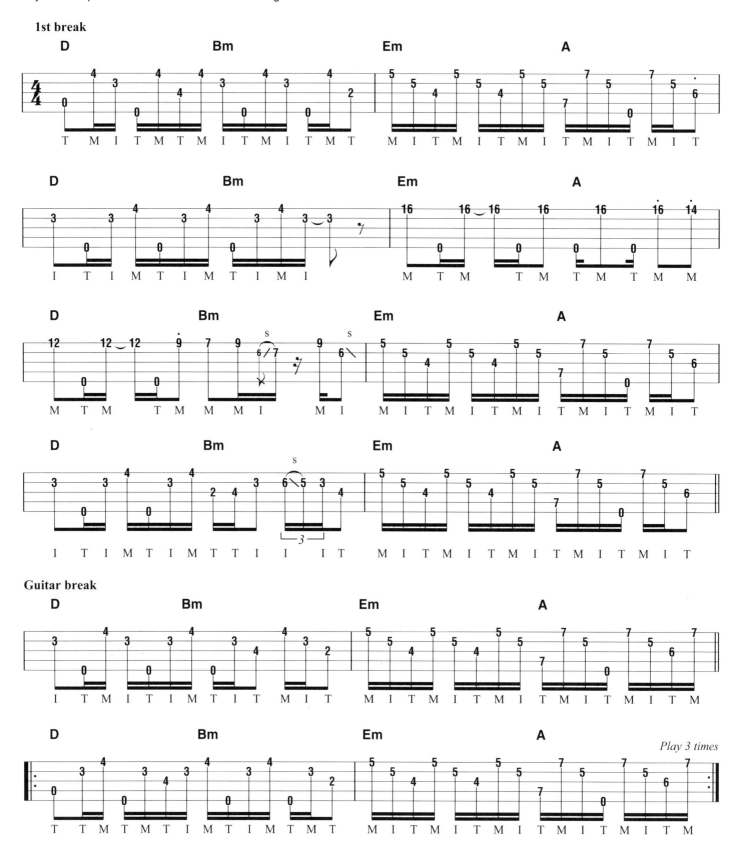

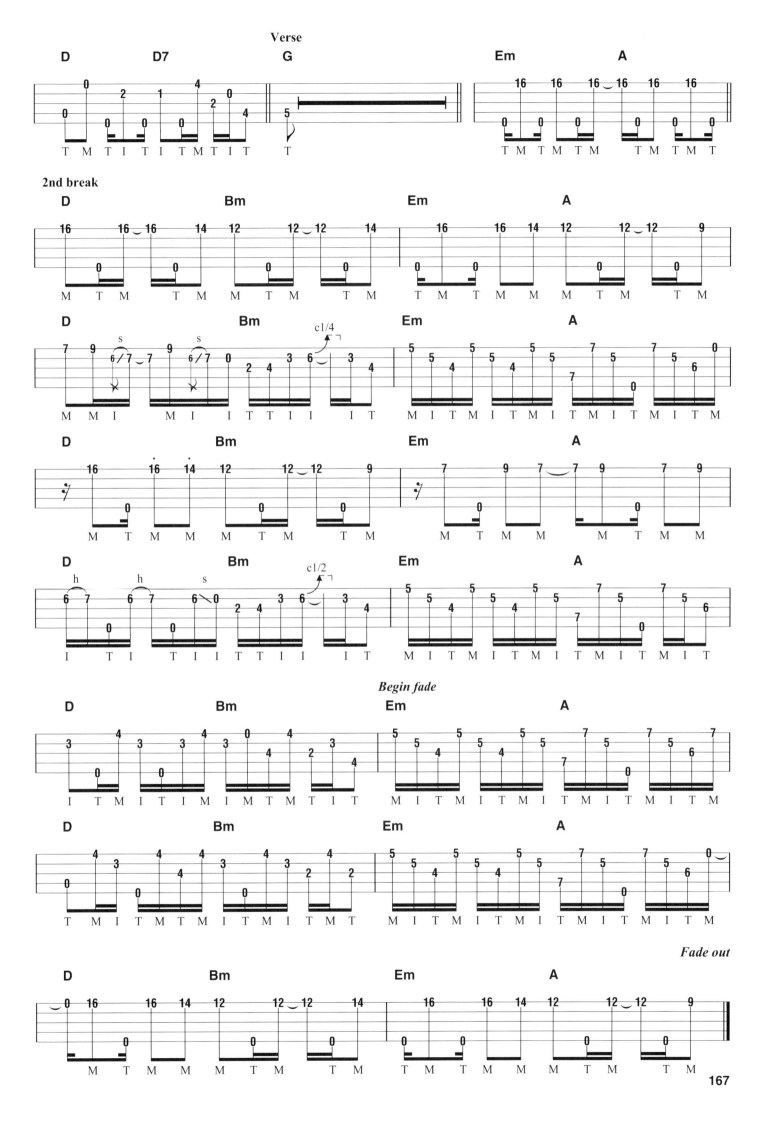

SOMEBODY TOUCHED ME

Sound source—*Best of the Flatt & Scruggs TV Show, Vol. 10*

Words and Music by JOHN REEDY

(G tuning)
Key of G

Intro

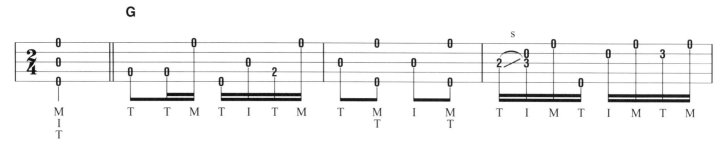

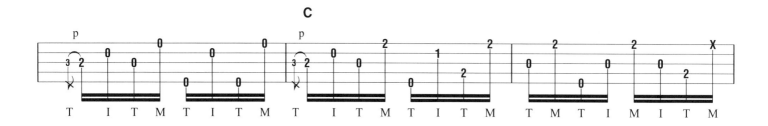

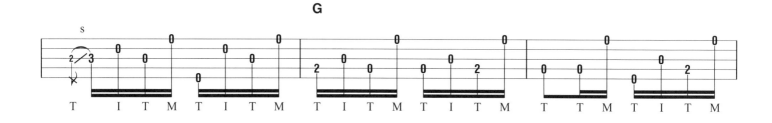

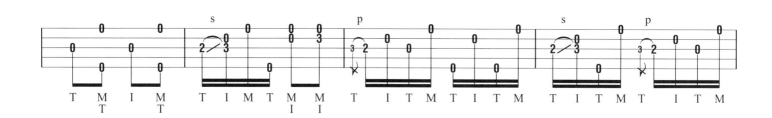

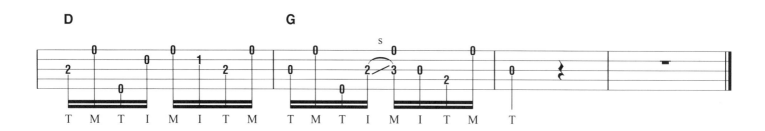

SOMEHOW TONIGHT

Sound source—*Earl Scruggs - The Ultimate Collection, 1924-2012*

Words and Music by EARL SCRUGGS

(G tuning)
Key of G

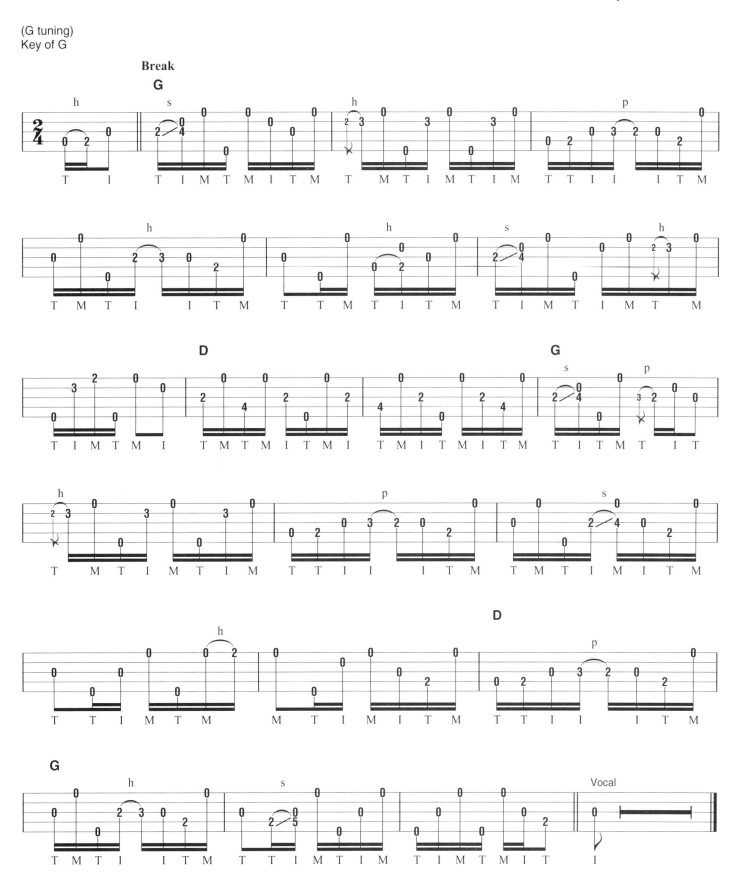

169

STANDIN' IN THE NEED OF PRAYER

Sound source—*Best of Flatt & Scruggs TV Show, Vol. 9*

TRADITIONAL SPIRITUAL

(G tuning)
Key of A: Capo at 2nd fret and hook on the 5th string

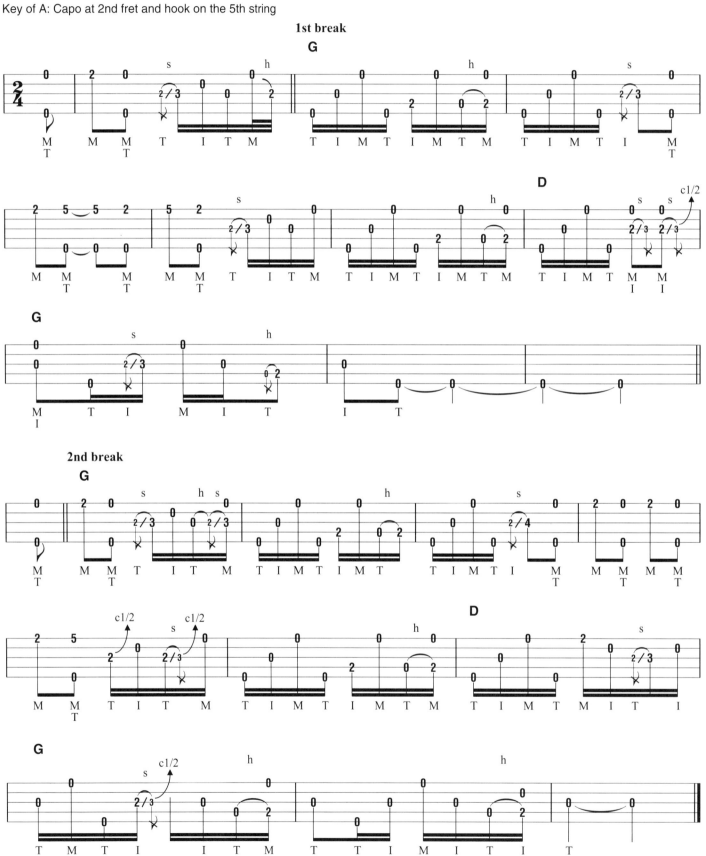

STEEL GUITAR RAG

Sound source—*Radio Gems, Martha White Biscuit Time–Flatt & Scruggs*

Words by MERLE TRAVIS and CLIFF STONE
Music by LEON McAULIFFE

(G tuning)
Key of D: Hook the 5th string at the 7th fret
(Recorded in G♯ tuning.)

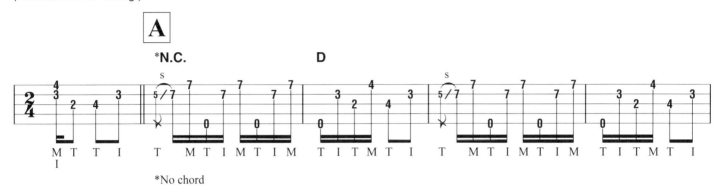

*No chord

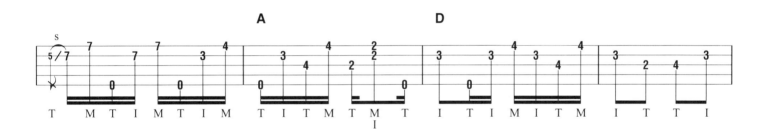

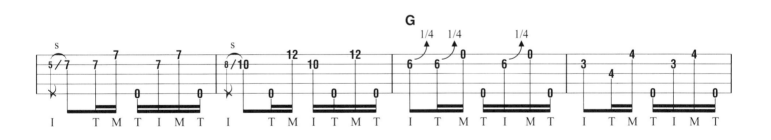

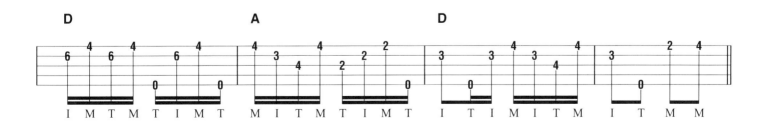

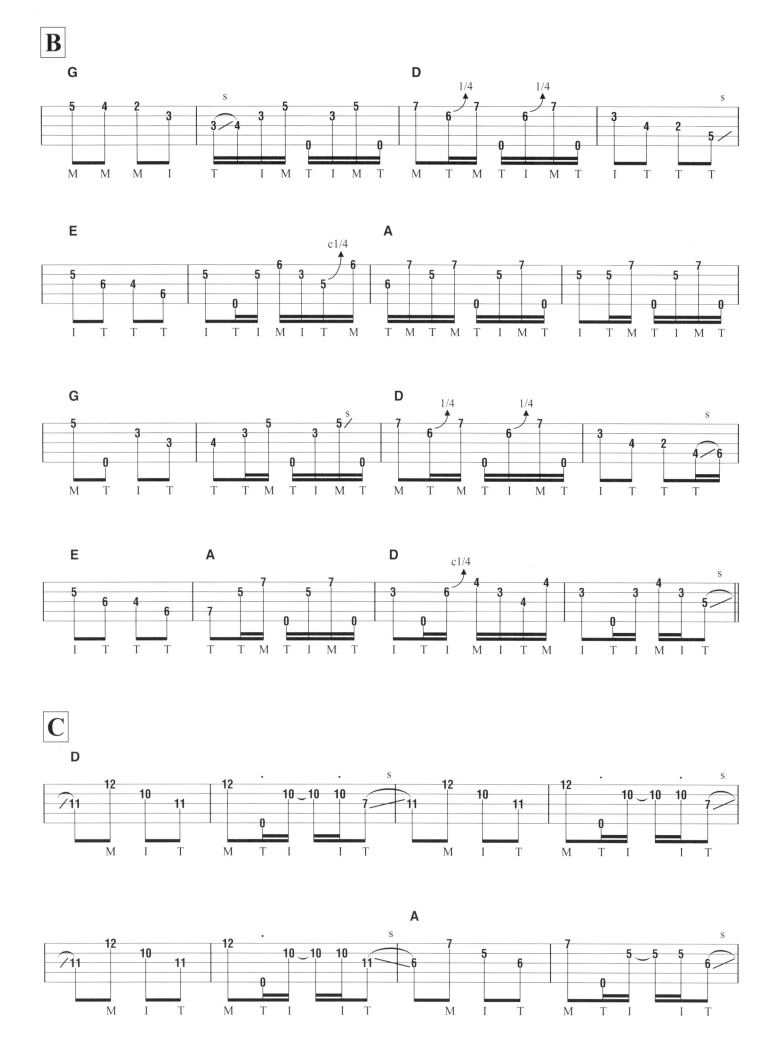

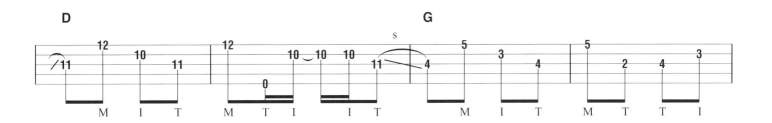

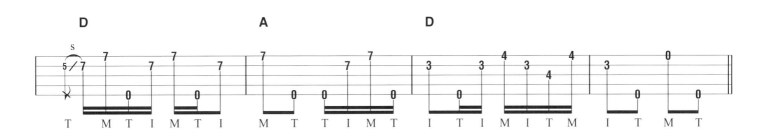

D

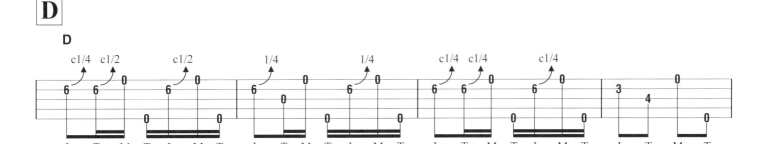

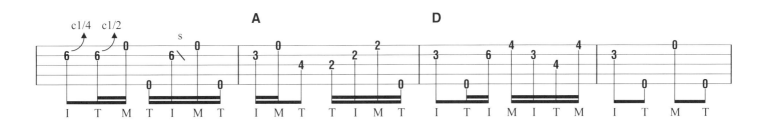

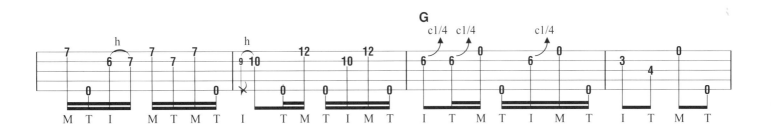

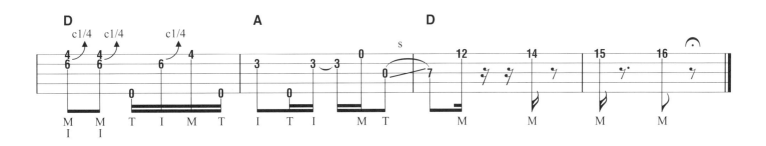

TILL THE END OF THE WORLD ROLLS AROUND

Sound source—*The Essential Earl Scruggs*

Words and Music by NEWTON THOMAS

(C tuning)
Key of C (Recorded in C# tuning)

Break

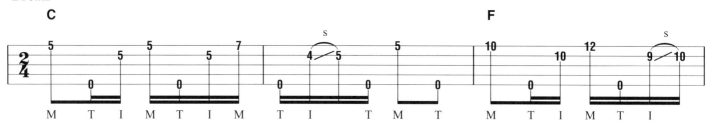

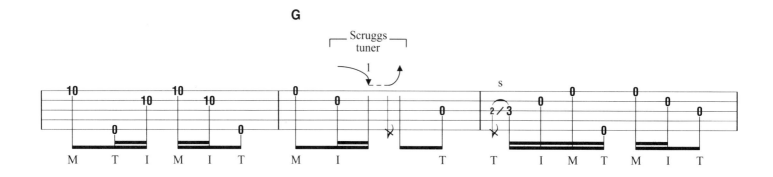

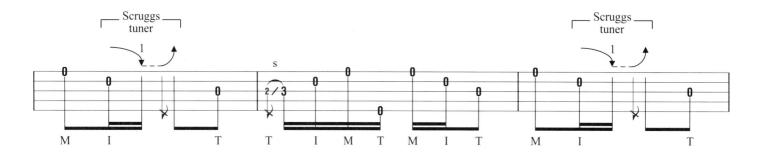

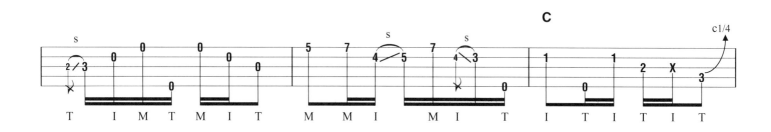

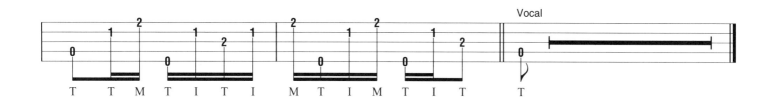

'TIS SWEET TO BE REMEMBERED

Sound source—*The Essential Flatt & Scruggs–'Tis Sweet to Be Remembered*

Words and Music by MAC WISEMAN

(G tuning)
Key of F
(Recorded in G# tuning)

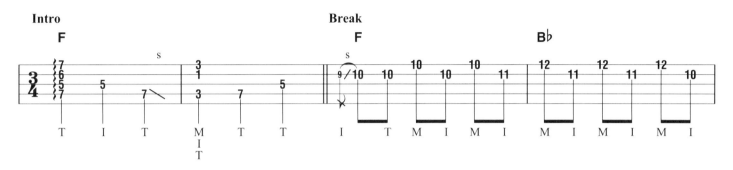

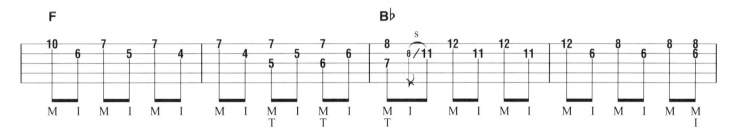

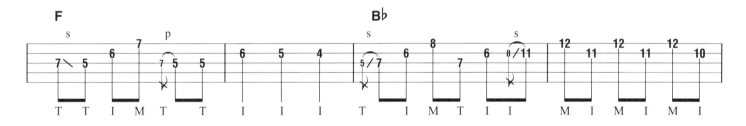

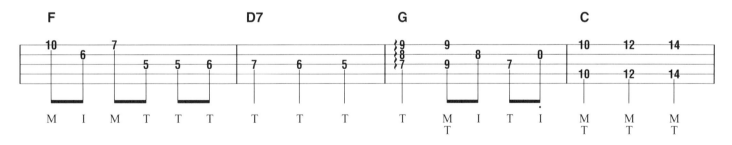

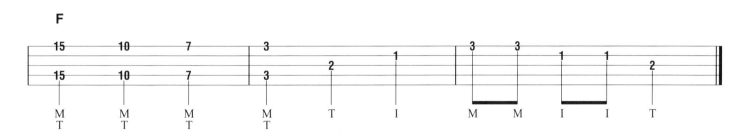

TOY HEART

Sound source—*The Essential Bill Monroe: 1945 - 1949*

Words and Music by BILL MONROE

(C tuning)
Key of C

Break

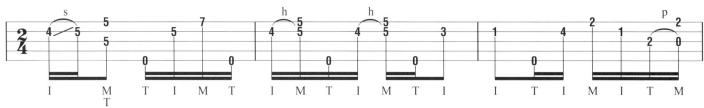

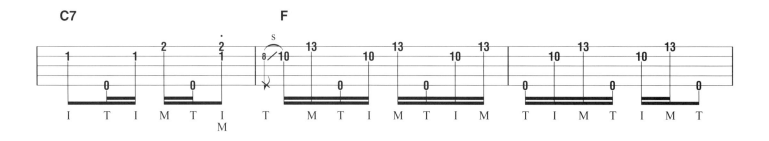

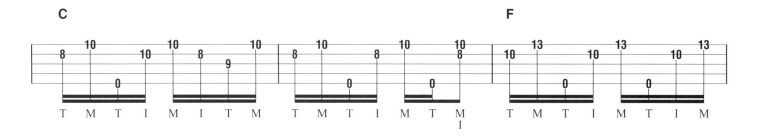

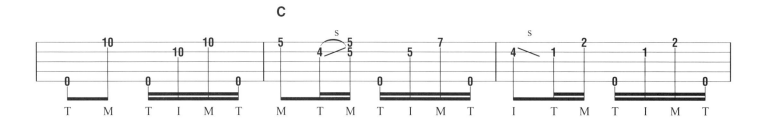

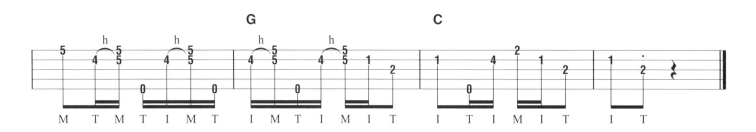

WHEN I LEFT EAST VIRGINIA

Sound source—*Hard Travelin' - Flatt & Scruggs*

By LESTER FLATT and EARL SCRUGGS

(G tuning) To match recording, tune down 1/4 step
Key of G

Intro

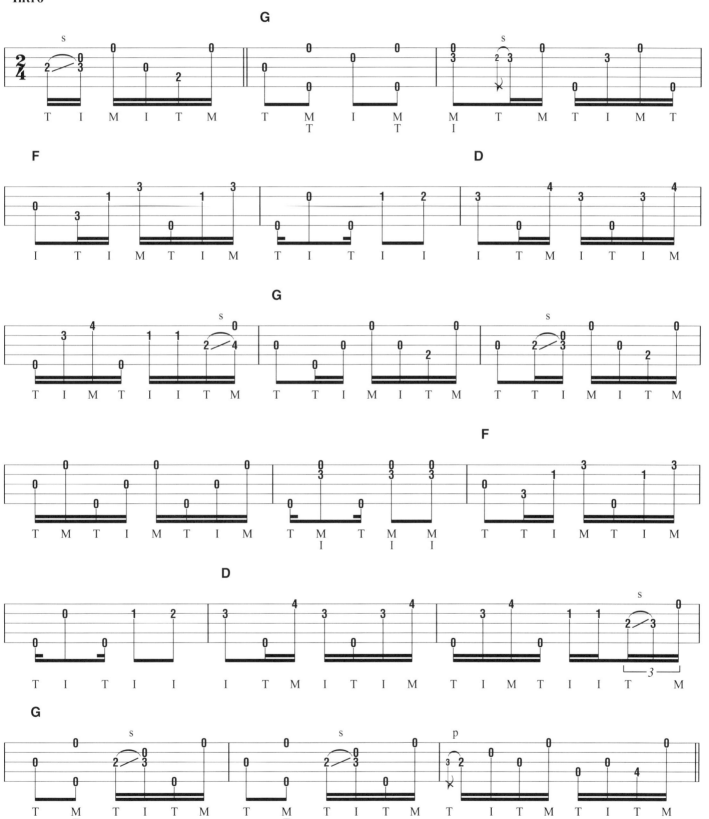

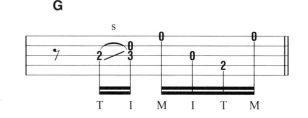

Break

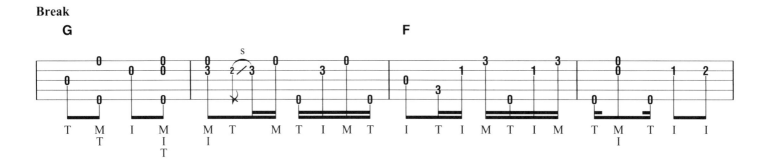

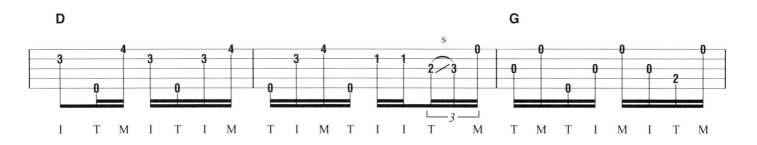

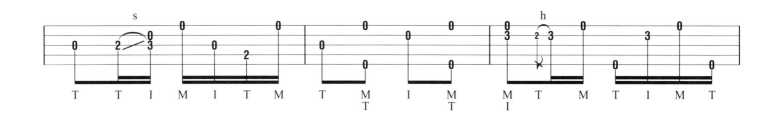

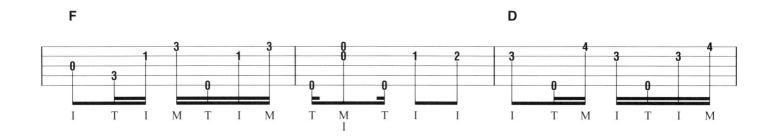

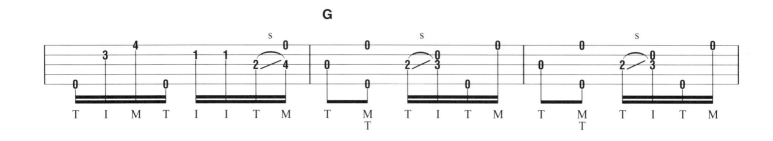

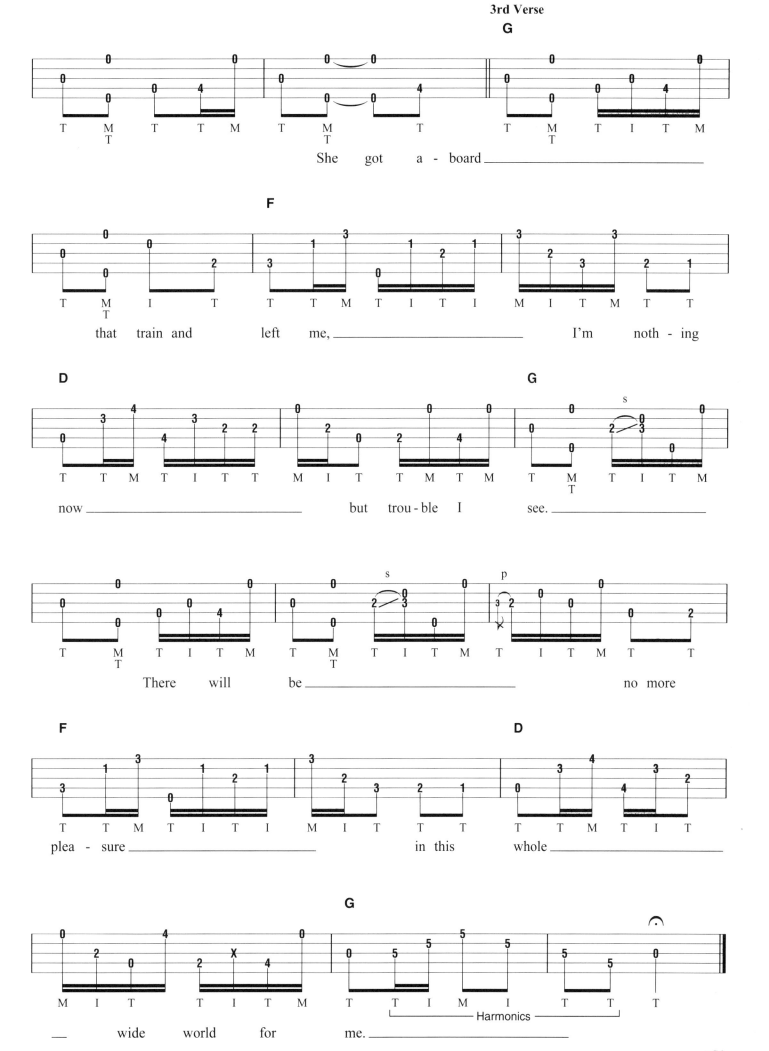

WHEN THE ANGELS CARRY ME HOME

Sound source—*Foggy Mountain Gospel - Flatt & Scruggs*

Words and Music by CHARLIE MONROE

(G tuning)
Key of B♭: Capo at 3rd fret and hook the 5th string
(Recorded in G♯ tuning, capoed at the 2nd fret)

Intro

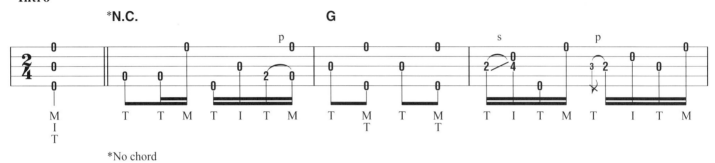

*No chord

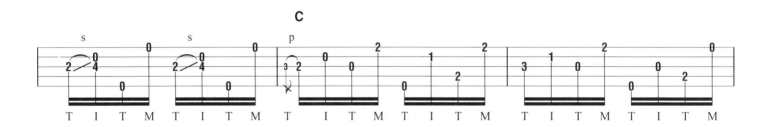

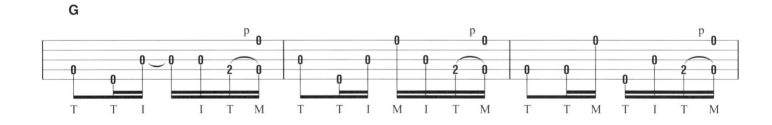

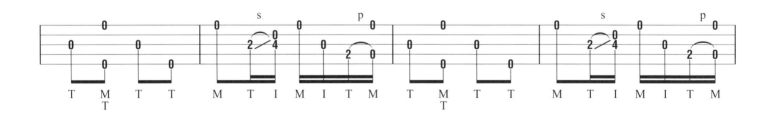

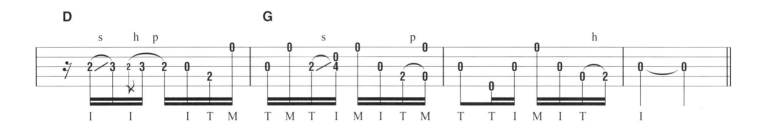

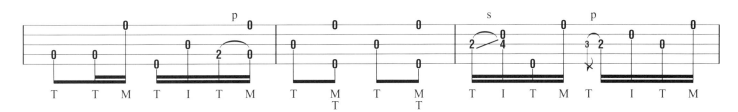

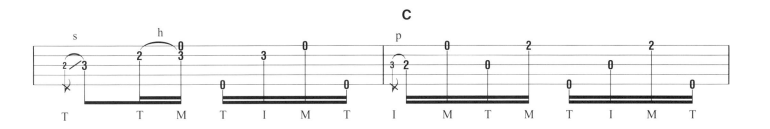

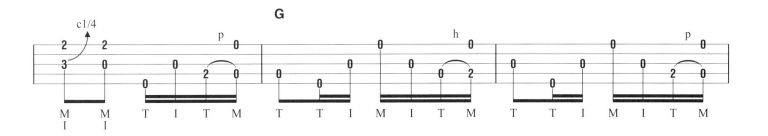

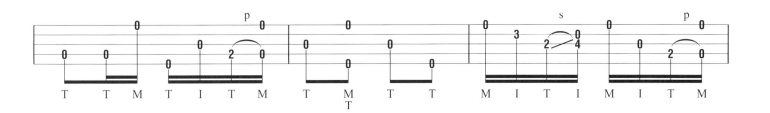

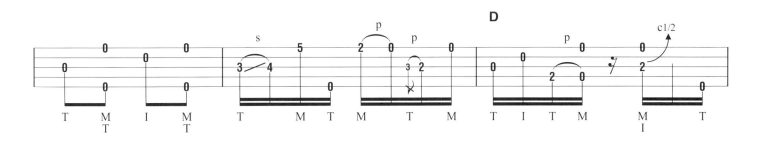

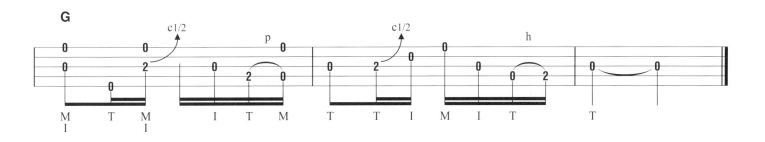

WHY DON'T YOU TELL ME SO

Sound source—*The Complete Mercury Sessions - Flatt & Scruggs*

Words and Music by LESTER FLATT

(G tuning)
Key of F: Hook the 5th string at the 7th fret
(Recorded in G# tuning)

Intro

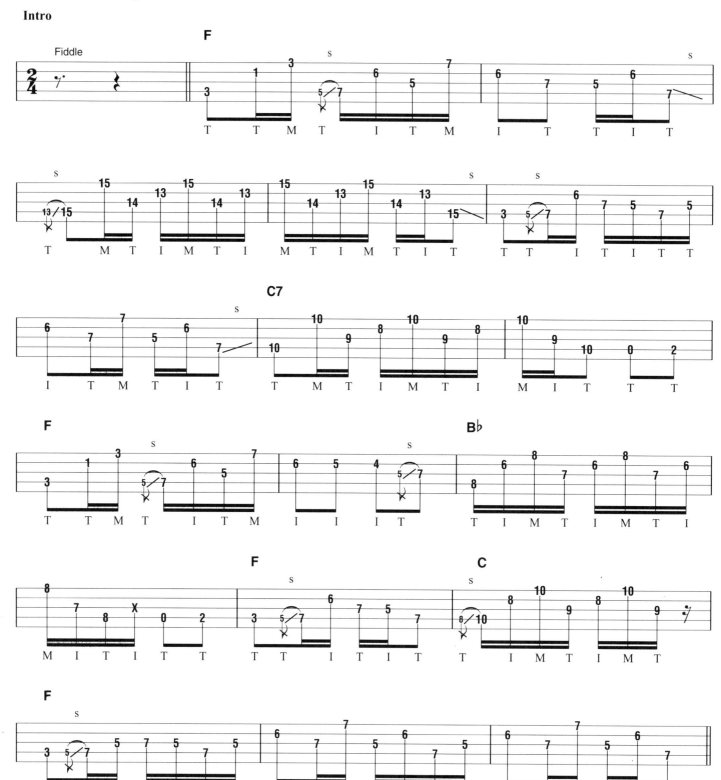

Break

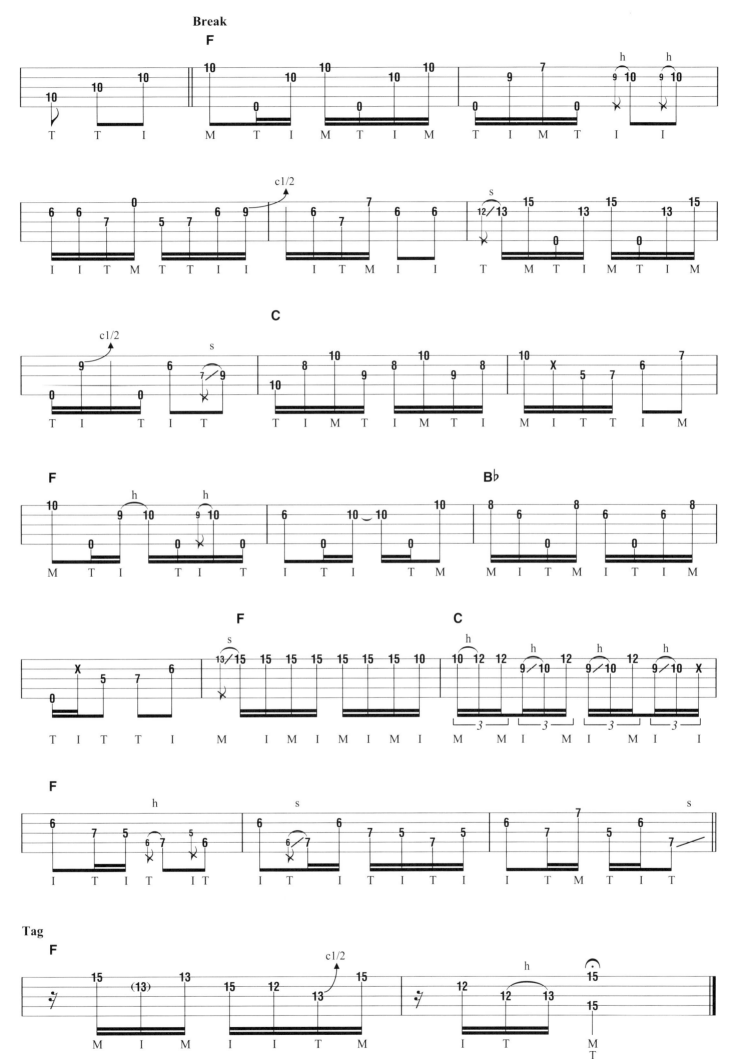

Tag

WE'LL MEET AGAIN SWEETHEART

Sound source—*Earl Scruggs, Lester Flatt & The Foggy Mountain Boys -*
The Complete Mercury Sessions - Flatt & Scruggs

Words and Music by LESTER FLATT
and EARL SCRUGGS

(G tuning)
Key of B: Capo at 4th fret and hook the 5th string

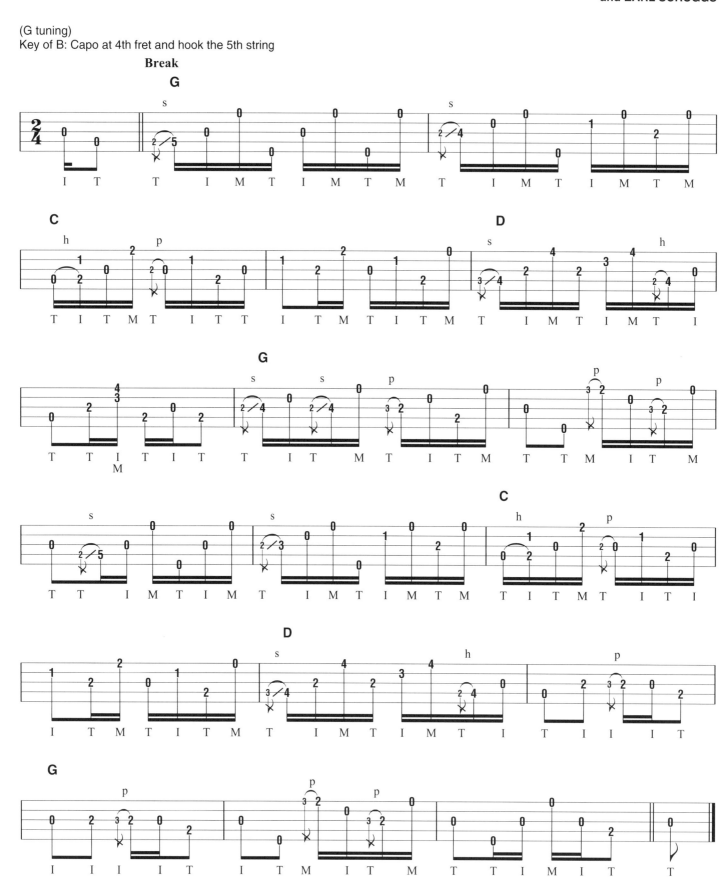

WILL YOU BE LOVING ANOTHER MAN

Sound source—*The Essential Bill Monroe: 1945 - 1949*

Words and Music by BILL MONROE
and LESTER FLATT

(G tuning)
Key of A: Capo at 2nd fret and hook the 5th string

Break

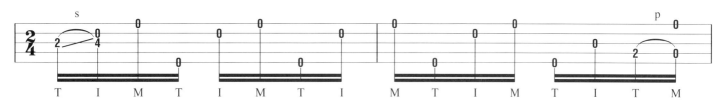

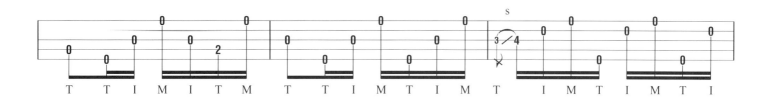

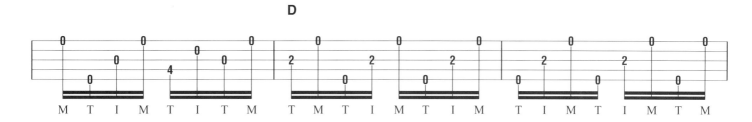

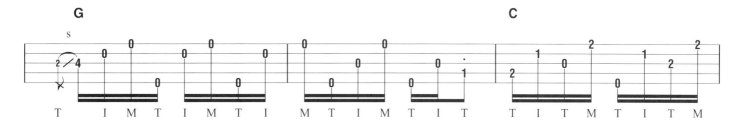

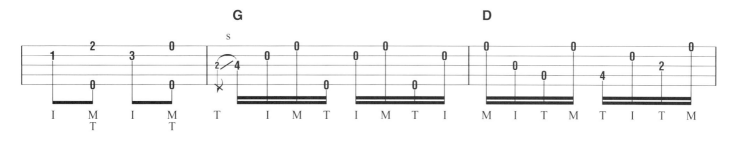

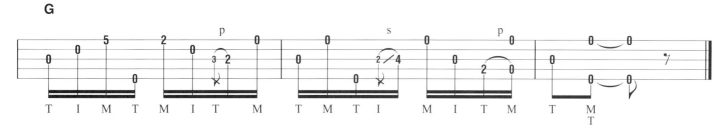

YOU CAN'T STOP ME FROM DREAMING

Sound source—*Flatt and Scruggs at Carnegie Hall! The Complete Concert*

Words and Music by DAVE FRANKLIN
and CLIFF FRIEND

(C tuning)
Key of C

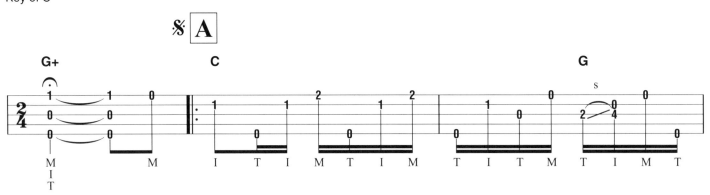

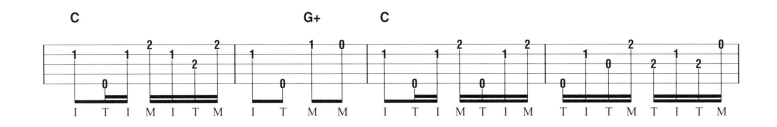

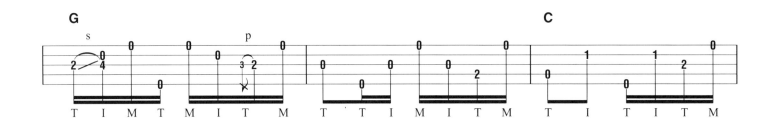

3rd time, To Coda

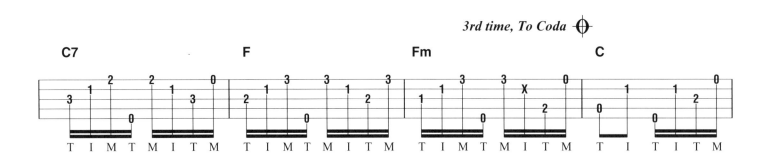

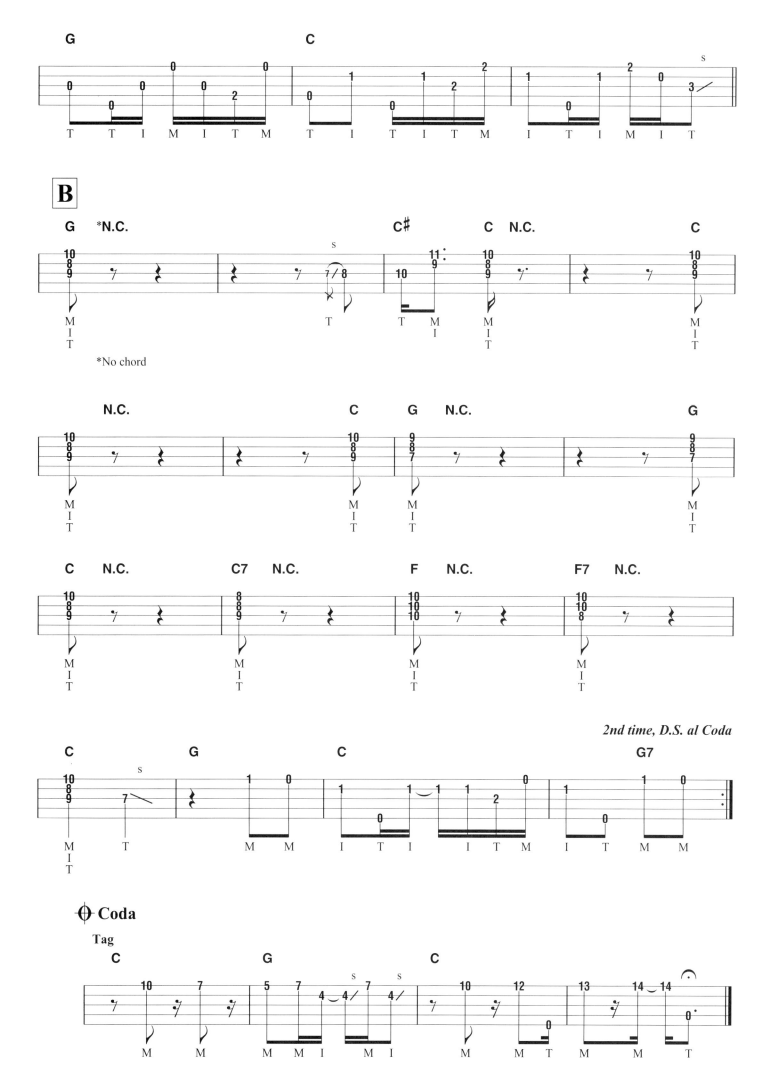

BANJO NOTATION LEGEND

TABLATURE graphically represents the banjo fingerboard. Each horizontal line represents a string, and each number represents a fret.

4th string, 2nd fret   1st & 2nd strings open, played together

TIME SIGNATURE:
The upper number indicates the number of beats per measure, the lower number indicates that a quarter note gets one beat.

CUT TIME:
Each note's time value should be cut in half. As a result, the music will be played twice as fast as it is written.

QUARTER NOTE:
time value = 1 beat

EIGHTH NOTES:
time value = 1/2 beat each

single   in series

SIXTEENTH NOTES:
time value = 1/4 beat each

single   in series

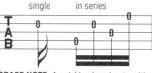

DOTTED QUARTER NOTE:
time value = 1 1/2 beat

TIE: Pick the 1st note only, then let it sustain for the combined time value.

TRIPLET: Three notes played in the same time normally occupied by two notes of the same time value.

GRACE NOTE: A quickly played note with no time value of its own. The grace note and the note following it only occupy the time value of the second note.

RITARD: A gradual slowing of the tempo or speed of the song.

rit.

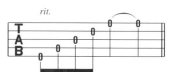

QUARTER REST:
time value = 1 beat of silence

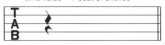

EIGHTH REST:
time value = 1/2 beat of silence

HALF REST:
time value = 2 beats of silence

WHOLE REST:
time value = 4 beats of silence

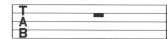

ENDINGS: When a repeated section has a first and second ending, play the first ending only the first time and play the second ending only the second time.

1.   2.

REPEAT SIGNS: Play the music between the repeat signs two times.

D.S. AL CODA:
Play through the music until you complete the measure labeled *"D.S. al Coda,"* then go back to the sign (𝄋). Then play until you complete the measure labeled *"To Coda ⊕ ,"* then skip to the section labeled *" ⊕ Coda."*

𝄋   To Coda ⊕   D.S. al Coda   ⊕ Coda

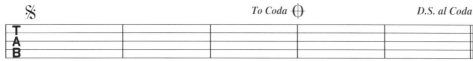

HAMMER-ON: Strike the first (lower) note with one finger, then sound the higher note (on the same string) with another finger by fretting it without picking.

h

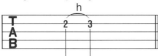

PULL-OFF: Place both fingers on the notes to be sounded. Strike the first note and without picking, pull the finger off to sound the second (lower) note.

p

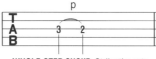

SLIDE UP: Strike the first note and then slide the same fret-hand finger up to the second note. The second note is not struck.

s

SLIDE DOWN: Strike the first note and then slide the same fret-hand finger down to the second note. The second note is not struck.

s

HALF-STEP CHOKE: Strike the note and bend the string up 1/2 step.

1/2

WHOLE-STEP CHOKE: Strike the note and bend the string up one step.

NATURAL HARMONIC: Strike the note while the fret-hand lightly touches the string directly over the fret indicated.

Harm.

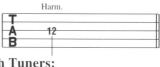

BRUSH: Play the notes of the chord indicated by quickly rolling them from bottom to top.

Scruggs/Keith Tuners:

HALF-TWIST UP: Strike the note, twist tuner up 1/2 step, and continue playing.

1/2

HALF-TWIST DOWN: Strike the note, twist tuner down 1/2 step, and continue playing.

1/2

WHOLE-TWIST UP: Strike the note, twist tuner up one step, and continue playing.

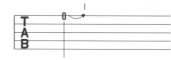

WHOLE-TWIST DOWN: Strike the note, twist tuner down one step, and continue playing.

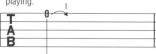

Right Hand Fingerings

t = thumb   i = index finger   m = middle finger

GREAT BANJO PUBLICATIONS

FROM HAL LEONARD

Hal Leonard Banjo Method
by Mac Robertson, Robbie Clement, Will Schmid
This innovative method teaches 5-string banjo bluegrass style using a carefully paced approach that keeps beginners playing great songs *while learning.* Book 1 covers easy chord strums, tablature, right-hand rolls, hammer-ons, slides and pull-offs, and more. Book 2 includes solos and licks, fiddle tunes, back-up, capo use, and more.

00699500 Book 1 Book Only $9.99
00695101 Book 1 Book/Online Audio $17.99
00699502 Book 2 Book Only $9.99

Banjo Chord Finder
00695741 9 x 12...$8.99
00695742 6 x 9...$7.99

Banjo Scale Finder
00695783 6 x 9...$6.99

Banjo Aerobics
A 50-Week Workout Program for Developing, Improving and Maintaining Banjo Technique
by Michael Bremer
Take your banjo playing to the next level with this fantastic daily resource, providing a year's worth of practice material with a two-week vacation. The accompanying audio includes demo tracks for all the examples in the book to reinforce how the banjo should sound.
00113734 Book/Online Audio $22.99

Earl Scruggs and the 5-String Banjo
Earl Scruggs' legendary method has helped thousands of banjo players get their start. It features everything you need to know to start playing, even how to build your own banjo! Topics covered include: Scruggs tuners • how to read music • chords • how to read tablature • anatomy of Scruggs-style picking • exercises in picking • 44 songs • biographical notes • and more! The online audio features Earl Scruggs playing and explaining over 60 examples!
00695764 Book Only...$29.99
00695765 Book/Online Audio $39.99

First 50 Songs You Should Play on Banjo
arr. Michael J. Miles & Greg Cahill
Easy-to-read banjo tab, chord symbols and lyrics for the most popular songs banjo players like to play. Explore clawhammer and three-finger-style banjo in a variety of tunings and capoings with this one-of-a-kind collection. Songs include: Angel from Montgomery • Carolina in My Mind • Cripple Creek • Danny Boy • The House of the Rising Sun • Mr. Tambourine Man • Take Me Home, Country Roads • This Land Is Your Land • Wildwood Flower • and many more.
00153311 ....$15.99

Fretboard Roadmaps
by Fred Sokolow
This handy book/with online audio will get you playing all over the banjo fretboard in any key! You'll learn to: increase your chord, scale and lick vocabulary • play chord-based licks, moveable major and blues scales, melodic scales and first-position major scales • and much more! The audio includes 51 demonstrations of the exercises.

00695358 Book/Online Audio $17.99

The Great American Banjo Songbook
70 Songs
arr. Alan Munde & Beth Mead-Sullivan
Explore the repertoire of the "Great American Songbook" with this 70-song collection, masterfully arranged by Alan Munde and Beth Mead-Sullivan for 3-finger, Scruggs-style 5-string banjo. Rhythm tab, right hand fingerings and chord diagrams are included for each of these beloved melodies. Songs include: Ain't She Sweet • Blue Skies • Cheek to Cheek • Home on the Range • Honeysuckle Rose • It Had to Be You • Little Rock Getaway • Over the Rainbow • Sweet Georgia Brown • and more.
00156862 ....$19.99

How to Play the 5-String Banjo
Third Edition
by Pete Seeger
This basic manual for banjo players includes melody line, lyrics and banjo accompaniment and solos notated in standard form and tablature. Chapters cover material such as: a basic strum, the fifth string, hammering on, pulling off, double thumbing, and much more.

14015486 ....$19.99

O Brother, Where Art Thou?
Banjo tab arrangements of 12 bluegrass/folk songs from this Grammy-winning album. Includes: The Big Rock Candy Mountain • Down to the River to Pray • I Am a Man of Constant Sorrow • I Am Weary (Let Me Rest) • I'll Fly Away • In the Jailhouse Now • Keep on the Sunny Side • You Are My Sunshine • and more, plus lyrics and a banjo notation legend.

00699528 Banjo Tablature $17.99

Clawhammer Cookbook
Tools, Techniques & Recipes for Playing Clawhammer Banjo
by Michael Bremer
The goal of this book isn't to tell you how to play tunes or how to play like anyone else. It's to teach you ways to approach, arrange, and personalize any tune – to develop your own unique style. To that end, we'll take in a healthy serving of old-time music and also expand the clawhammer palate to taste a few other musical styles. Includes audio track demos of all the songs and examples to aid in the learning process.
00118354 Book/Online Audio $22.99

The Ultimate Banjo Songbook
A great collection of banjo classics: Alabama Jubilee • Bye Bye Love • Duelin' Banjos • The Entertainer • Foggy Mountain Breakdown • Great Balls of Fire • Lady of Spain • Orange Blossom Special • (Ghost) Riders in the Sky • Rocky Top • San Antonio Rose • Tennessee Waltz • UFO-TOFU • You Are My Sunshine • and more.

00699565 Book/Online Audio $29.99

HAL•LEONARD®

Visit Hal Leonard online at **www.halleonard.com**

HAL•LEONARD BANJO PLAY-ALONG

INCLUDES TAB

The Banjo Play-Along Series will help you play your favorite songs quickly and easily with incredible backing tracks to help you sound like a bona fide pro! Just follow the banjo tab, listen to the demo audio track provided to hear how the banjo should sound, and then play along with the separate backing tracks.

Each Banjo Play-Along pack features eight cream of the crop songs.

1. BLUEGRASS
Ashland Breakdown • Deputy Dalton • Dixie Breakdown • Hickory Hollow • I Wish You Knew • I Wonder Where You Are Tonight • Love and Wealth • Salt Creek.
00102585 Book/CD Pack $16.99

6. SONGS FOR BEGINNERS
Bill Cheatham • Black Mountain Rag • Cripple Creek • Grandfather's Clock • John Hardy • Nine Pound Hammer • Old Joe Clark • Will the Circle Be Unbroken.
00139751 Book/CD Pack $14.99

2. COUNTRY
East Bound and Down • Flowers on the Wall • Gentle on My Mind • Highway 40 Blues • If You've Got the Money (I've Got the Time) • Just Because • Take It Easy • You Are My Sunshine.
00105278 Book/CD Pack $14.99

7. BLUEGRASS GOSPEL
Cryin' Holy unto the Lord • How Great Thou Art • I Saw the Light • I'll Fly Away • I'll Have a New Life • Man in the Middle • Turn Your Radio On • Wicked Path of Sin.
00147594 Book/Online Audio $14.99

3. FOLK/ROCK HITS
Ain't It Enough • The Cave • Forget the Flowers • Ho Hey • Little Lion Man • Live and Die • Switzerland • Wagon Wheel.
00119867 Book/CD Pack $14.99

8. CELTIC BLUEGRASS
Billy in the Low Ground • Cluck Old Hen • Devil's Dream • Fisher's Hornpipe • Little Maggie • Over the Waterfall • The Red Haired Boy • Soldier's Joy.
00160077 Book/Online Audio $14.99

4. OLD-TIME CHRISTMAS
Away in a Manger • Hark! the Herald Angels Sing • Jingle Bells • Joy to the World • O Holy Night • O Little Town of Bethlehem • Silent Night • We Wish You a Merry Christmas.
00119889 Book/CD Pack $14.99

9. BLUEGRASS FESTIVAL FAVORITES
Banks of the Ohio • Cotton Eyed Joe • Cumberland Gap • Eighth of January • Liberty • Man of Constant Sorrow • Roll in My Sweet Baby's Arms • Wildwood Flower.
00263129 Book/Online Audio $14.99

5. PETE SEEGER
Blue Skies • Get up and Go • If I Had a Hammer (The Hammer Song) • Kisses Sweeter Than Wine • Mbube (Wimoweh) • Sailing Down My Golden River • Turn! Turn! Turn! (To Everything There Is a Season) • We Shall Overcome.
00129699 Book/CD Pack $17.99

HAL•LEONARD®
www.halleonard.com

Prices, contents, and availability subject to change without notice.